Management
in a
Changing
World

JAKADA IMANI
MONNA WONG
BEX AHUJA

Management
in a
Changing
World

HOW TO MANAGE FOR
Equity, Sustainability, and Results

WILEY

Published by John Wiley & Sons, Inc., Hoboken, New Jersey.
Published simultaneously in Canada.

For general information on our other products and services or for technical support, please contact our Customer Care Department within the United States at (800) 762-2974, outside the United States at (317) 572-3993 or fax (317) 572-4002.

Wiley also publishes its books in a variety of electronic formats. Some content that appears in print may not be available in electronic formats. For more information about Wiley products, visit our web site at www.wiley.com.

Library of Congress Cataloging-in-Publication Data is Available:

ISBN 9781394165797 (Paperback)
ISBN 9781394165827 (ePub)
ISBN 9781394165841 (ePDF)

Cover Design: Wiley
Cover Image: © Kiely Houston

SKY10045198_033123

CONTENTS

FOREWORD

This book is a successor to *Managing to Change the World: The Nonprofit Manager's Guide to Getting Results*, which I co-wrote with Alison Green back in 2012. We received really positive feedback about that book over the years, and I reveled in. . .well, as much fame and fortune as you get from writing a popular nonprofit management book.

Why, then, am I so excited to welcome this new book—even as it pushes aside the original one (and all the glamor that came with being its author)?

Don't get me wrong: I think the previous book did many things well. As with all of our work at The Management Center (TMC), our book was focused on how leaders can deliver results that move the needle toward social change. It was deeply grounded in the reality that managers face (which Alison and I knew from experience), and it often challenged conventional wisdom. Readers told us they found it supportive, humble, real about how hard things can be—and even funny at times. Above all, people told us they appreciated that our book was deeply practical and filled with concrete ways to put our lessons into action. I still send excerpts of that book to my coaching clients to help them through tough spots. In many ways, I'm still very proud of it.

But it also badly needed an update. In one section on how to stay organized, for instance, we talked about using written lists and paper folders—a little outdated for the digital age! More substantively, TMC's coaching and training content evolved significantly over the years as we developed new insights from our work with clients. I kept a running list of things to add to a revision—like the pros/cons/mitigations chart, the "urgent vs. important" matrix, and the idea of "gold star" vs. "good enough," all of which you'll find in this book.

Most importantly, the last book had serious limitations that would have been harder to fix with a simple revision and impossible for me to do as well as this book does. Our original book was almost completely silent about race, equity, inclusion, and managing across lines of power and difference. It talked a lot about results (as this book also does), but not nearly enough about how to get them equitably and sustainably. I've always believed that management is about excellence and heart—that managers can and should be able to get great results while also being decent human beings and living their values at work. But the previous book was too easy to interpret as being all about excellence, not so much heart.

Looking back, I didn't take enough time and space to make the implicit explicit (a phrase you'll hear often in this book) about many things. I'm excited, for instance, that this book has an entire chapter on relationships and another on culture (which we talked about in the previous book, but too briefly). I love that we've turned SMART goals into SMARTIE (adding "inclusive" and "equitable"), and that every chapter has tools to help you check your biases.

The changes I've mentioned are like adding new wings to a house. In many ways, though, this book is more like building a new house from a different blueprint, and so it was important that Jakada, Monna, and Bex began fresh in writing this one. When we wrote the original book, I didn't understand nearly as much about equity and inclusion as I do now (though I still have a long way to go!)—and I learned *a lot* of what I know now from the coauthors of this book.

I can't believe how lucky I am to have worked as closely as I have with Jakada, Monna, and Bex. All three of them are not only brilliant and deeply knowledgeable practitioners of management and movement-building, but they're also some of the warmest and most genuine people I know. All three of them eventually took on bigger roles at TMC than they started with, and they all played pivotal roles in making TMC a better, more inclusive organization.

I'm forever grateful to Bex for working so closely with me during the steepest part of my learning curve around issues of equity and inclusion. We had many (often difficult) conversations about equity-related topics. Bex always had the strength and courage to keep pushing when I disagreed or didn't get it, and they did so with tremendous grace and patience. I loved every chance we got to roll up our sleeves and work directly together; we played off of each other's ideas and instincts in a way that led us to much better outcomes. As I told Bex multiple times, I don't know that I've ever worked with anyone more talented than they are. Maybe even more impressively and most tellingly, after meeting Bex, my (then-little) kids constantly asked when Bex would come over again to play marching band in the living room.

Then there's Monna, one of the funniest people I've had the privilege of working with, and one of the best at getting to the essence of an idea. Whenever I had an idea Monna had reservations about, she'd ask probing questions that helped me think about it differently and sparked awesome conversations. She thinks deeply and critically, kicking the tires and pulling all the threads until she comes up with the best possible synthesis of all your ideas, *and* the best way to phrase it (often incorporating a hilarious metaphor about food). By making ideas about management funny and palatable, Monna gets readers to do the management equivalent of eating their vegetables. Monna also helped me keep in shape during the isolating days of the COVID pandemic by taunting me through her latest planking challenge.

Finally, I couldn't be more honored that Jakada is my successor as CEO of The Management Center. From the time that Jakada first started at TMC, I was struck by his wisdom, brilliance, and commitment to doing what it takes to bring about justice in the world. Jakada embodies excellence and heart—or love and rigor, as he much more eloquently puts it. He's the perfect messenger for the things I wish I'd done a better job communicating in the first book, *and* the perfect person to take everything The Management Center does to a higher level than I ever could have. He was an incredible partner during my transition out of my role at TMC after 15 wonderful years, and he has done an *awesome* job navigating the complexities of his new role and leading the organization forward. It can be hard for founders to step away from an organization they created, but with Jakada, I was thrilled to get out of the way and watch him shine.

And now, I can't wait to get out of the way and let you read what these three have written.

—Jerry Hauser, founding CEO of The Management Center

ACKNOWLEDGMENTS

This book couldn't have happened without the labor, time, energy, love, stories, insights, and support of many people.

Thank you to Emily Crockett for wading through this with us. You asked great questions, pushed us to get clearer, found all the footnotes, and stuck it out until the words sang on the page—all with so much heart and humor and sheer determination to get the damn thing done. Thank you for wrangling our ideas until they made sense (and being honest when they didn't!). Most importantly, thank you for being a true partner in the work and caring about this book as much as we do.

Thank you to Jerry Hauser and Alison Green for your incredible work on *Managing to Change the World: The Nonprofit Manager's Guide to Getting Results,* which made it possible for *this* book to exist.

Jerry, thank you for everything from warmly inviting each of us into the TMC fold to kicking off this book with a beautiful foreword. Your consistency, integrity, and sense of responsibility for being extremely helpful and practical have been an indelible part of TMC's "secret sauce." We hope we did right by you in preserving it.

To the TMC team, thank you for sharing stories, reviewing chapters, giving pep talks, and many pomodoros (among countless other things). Thank you for the incredible care that you bring to this work and our TMC community. Thank you Addae Kwakye, Adriana Barboza, Alex McNeill, Alyssa Schuren, Amy Faulring, Amy Sonnie, Andie Corso, Andrea Stouder, Aquiles Damirón-Alcántara, Ashley Pinedo-Carlson, Avione Pichon, Breanna Wright, Carmen McClaskey, Chantá Parker, Charlie Riebeling, Cicely Horsham-Brathwaite, Cindy Kang, Cosmo Fujiyama Ghaznavi, Court Ruark, Deb Sherman, Diana Cerda, Ebony Ross, Emily Hicks-Rotella, Emma Shaver, Hanna Campbell, Jackson Darling-Palacios, Jamilyn Bailey, Janet Namkung, Jasmeet Saini, Jessica Anderson, JK Nelson, Johari Farrar, José Luis Marantes, Justine Xu, Katie Steele, Kevin Carty-Tolentino, Marissa Graciosa, Mattie Weiss, Megan Hanson, Nancy Hanks, Niamoja Morgan, Qasim Davis, Reilly Furellis, Sandra Oliver, Sarah Hodgdon, Sarah Storm, Serena Savarirayan, Stacy McAuliffe, Stephen McClain, Sumaiya Sarawat, Tamara Osivwemu, Valerie Evans, Valerie Jiggetts, Viridiana Safty, Wendy Guyton, and Yamani Yansa.

Thank you to our former colleagues who shaped our thinking about effective management through modeling, rigorous discussion, and experimentation. Special thanks to Ben Goldfarb, Delan Ellington, Elizabeth Brown Riordan, Emily Berens, Jen Chau Fontán, Jenny Griggs, Jordan Pina, Kendra Featherstone, Maria Peña, Marilyn Figueroa, Melanie Rivera, Michelle Ngwafon, Naomi Long, Peggy Flanagan, and Shawna Wells.

Thank you to TMC's original POC caucus—Iimay Ho, Isabelle Moses, Joyce Yin, Melinda Spooner, and Tasia Ahuja Smith—and Amy Faulring and Jackson Darling-Palacios, for planting, nurturing, and sowing the seeds to make equity a must-have for effective management.

Thank you to the TMC board for your vision, support, and guidance.

Thank you to Tanya O. Williams and Terry Keleher for your teachings, consultation, and influence during a crucial point in TMC's racial equity journey. Terry, thank you for choice points. Tanya, thank you for strategies for authenticity.

Thank you to our partners at Wiley—Brian Neill, Deborah Schindlar, and Kim Wimpsett—for your flexibility, support, and patience throughout this process, as well as for the opportunity to share this book with the world.

Thank you to Kiely Houston for capturing the spirit of this book with beautiful illustrations that match the nuance, vibrance, and heart of our advice.

Thank you to Chelsea Judith Wilson, Court Ruark, Jenny Griggs, Melanie Anne Conway, Melanie Rivera, and Rodrigo Heng-Lehtinen, for test-driving our manuscript and sharing honest and thoughtful feedback.

Thank you to Becca McKelvy, Benn Marine, Gabe Gonzalez, Jami Westerhold, Kelly Bates, Lily Pham, Linda Seng, Megan Mullay, Molly Griffard, and Rodrigo Heng-Lehtinen for your recollections and insight.

Thank you to everyone we each had the honor and privilege to work with, especially our teammates at the Ella Baker Center for Human Rights, Lavender Phoenix, the National LGBTQ Task Force, Rockwood Leadership Institute, and the Mainers United for Marriage campaign. Thank you for the feedback, support, advice, and grace that helped us grow as managers and leaders.

Thank you to the mentors, elders, and ancestors, who asked questions with no easy answers, gave advice (even when we didn't ask for it!), and pushed us to do better. Thank you for laying the groundwork, for being the shoulders on which we stand, and for passing the baton so we could carry the work forward.

Thank you to everyone who's conspiring and aligning, making good trouble, striving to be a more effective manager, and showing up every day to fight for freedom and justice.

And finally, a few personal acknowledgments from each of us:

- **Bex:** To my beautiful and brilliant wife, Tasia Ahuja Smith, whom I met working at TMC back in 2014, who was my teacher on equity back then, and who still is to this day. Thank you for always patiently and lovingly pointing to a deeper level of understanding and nuance in equity work. This book belongs to you. Thank you to my mother, Janet Wu, for your steadfast modeling of humility, responsibility, faith, prayer, and hard work. To my team at Rockwood, thank you for showing me what it means to set a loving table for tired and weary movement leaders, and to Darlene Nipper for scooping me up and allowing me to witness your courageous, visionary leadership every day. To my family, Anita, Randy, Zach, Max, Jim Lia,

Maya, and Jayla; and the Bloat and niblings, Juno, Mika, and Jerome, thank you for giving me home and hope whenever we gather.

- **Monna:** Thank you to all my people, my family. For the dreams and schemes, lifelong friendships, deep hangs, masterminds, snacks, childcare, commune, chats, dancing, and shenanigans. Thank you for letting me be, even as I am becoming. The Portland Potatoes and my APIENC crew: thank you for the joy, abundance, and badass work, for trusting me, for being my teachers and comrades. Thank you to the TMC content crew, for holding it down and caring for each other. Thank you, Juno, for your freedom and fearlessness. Thank you, Mandy, my ultimate co-conspirator, the one who sees how the sausage gets made. Thanks for enabling me to put my full body, brain, and heart into this project. I could not have done this without your love, labor, and most of all, our two-person psychology. Thank you for the life we've co-created, full of delighting in ridiculousness, possibility, and adventure.

- **Jakada:** Thank you to my family for supporting me to be a leader: Laura, Jael, Tehya, Nyame, Kioni, Phoenix, and Eli, you all give me hope and ground me in what is important. My crew from EBC: Ying-sun, Malakia, Sumayyah, Ian, Nicole, Diana, Zach, Van, Kristin, Glenn, the members of Families for Books Not Bars, and so many more. To all of my mentors and elders who invested in me when I was hard-headed and undisciplined: Shiree, Rev. Liza, Nell, Boots Riley, Raquel, brother Greg, and Elisha. You led by example, offered me wisdom, and reminded me to always root in values. Last, I thank all the young, uncompromising activists and organizers who refuse to settle for conventional wisdom, broken models, or stale traditions. You give me hope that the future can be better than the present. I see you, I recognize you, and I thank Spirit for you. Ashe, ashe, ashe.

INTRODUCTION

"With great power comes great responsibility."

—Proverb

"Power without love is reckless and abusive, and love without power is sentimental and anemic."

—Rev. Dr. Martin Luther King, Jr.

If you're reading this book, you're here to make a difference. You're working for immigrant rights, workers' rights, healthcare reform, and reproductive justice. You're fighting to end poverty, voter disenfranchisement, mass incarceration, and climate crisis. You're striving to improve the lives of lesbian, gay, bisexual, transgender, and queer (LGBTQ) people; disabled people; and Black, Indigenous, and people of color (BIPOC). You're pushing to make government work better for people of all identities. You're shaping the next generation's minds and lives. You have a vision of change and possibility for the communities you care about—and you feel a sacred responsibility to do all you can to make it a reality.

If you're reading this book, you also have the great responsibility—and the great power—of being a manager. Maybe you've just been promoted to a leadership role at a nonprofit or school. Maybe you were just elected or appointed into office. Maybe you've been at this for 30 years. Wherever you are in your career, you're looking for guidance on using your power and responsibility more effectively.

In today's rapidly changing world, managers need this kind of guidance more than ever. We've seen dramatically shifting expectations of what power and responsibility should look like in the workplace—especially those focused on social justice. A series of reckonings on race, inequality, and abuses of power have forced more people to grapple with questions like:

- How can we exercise power responsibly across racial, generational, gender, and other differences in identities?

- How can we balance supporting our team members through life challenges with ensuring we meet our deliverables?

- How can we achieve "work-life balance" when video calls in our living rooms and 24/7 email access on our phones have collapsed the boundaries between "work" and "life"?

- In a time of rapidly escalating climate crisis and relentless displays of injustice, how can we avoid succumbing to feelings of overwhelm, numbness, or defeat?

As managers, sometimes it feels like the weight of these questions is on our shoulders all at once. We might feel responsible not only for getting the work done, but also for our team members' well-being. We might feel unmoored and disoriented by constantly shifting circumstances and continually rising expectations.

We're not wrong to feel that way. *It's a lot to deal with.* Management is hard enough work in stable and familiar contexts. It's harder in times of upheaval when we realize that some of our familiar professional, cultural, and social norms no longer serve us—and maybe never did.

And if you've never experienced good management firsthand (as too many of us haven't), it's *exponentially* harder. After all, if your past managers were ineffective, how are you supposed to know what effective management looks and feels like, much less how to practice it?

That's where we come in. We wrote this book to offer a model of effective management. Whether you're a new or seasoned manager, an executive director, or an organizer working with volunteers, and whether you manage one person or a hundred people, this book offers insights and actionable advice for you. We'll give you the tools, strategies, and examples you need to learn the fundamentals of effective management. This book can help you lead your team with less stress, more ease, and better results.

Effective management is hard work, but it's also a privilege, an honor, and a sacred responsibility. Effective management can transform people and organizations. It can make (or break) our work and results. As managers, we are entrusted to be stewards of people's time and energy, to facilitate learning and growth, and to achieve the goals we need to create change. Effective management is hard work—but it's worth doing, and you are absolutely capable of doing it.

WHO WE ARE

We are the current CEO (Jakada Imani, he/him), the current chief content officer (Monna Wong, she/her), and the former managing partner of the training team (Bex Ahuja, they/them) of The Management Center (TMC).

TMC has been supporting managers and leaders in nonprofits, government, and schools since 2006. We have worked with thousands of teams and organizations. We've coached hundreds of senior leaders and trained tens of thousands of people. We've worked to create, curate, and refine best practices and resources about management—so you don't have to reinvent the wheel or reinterpret traditional management concepts for a social justice context.

Here's a bit more about each of us:

- **Jakada** grew up poor in Oakland, California, in the home of the Black Panther Party, mentored by former Panthers and Student Nonviolent Coordinating Committee leaders. When Jakada became executive director of the Ella Baker Center for Human Rights (EBC), he realized two things: first, his knowledge of strategy, organizing, and alliance-building didn't equip him with the management skills to help EBC deliver on its mission; and second, none of the traditional management resources he turned to could help him build and lead a Black-led, multiracial organization like EBC. So he learned by doing—forging a set of management practices rooted in love and rigor. He joined TMC as a coach and trainer in 2017 and became CEO in 2021.

- **Monna** is the daughter of refugees from Cambodia who settled in Queens, New York. She got her career start as a field organizer on LGBTQ campaigns (with Bex as her first manager!). In 2012, as a regional field director of the Mainers United for Marriage campaign, she learned to lead a team to victory without reinforcing the churn-and-burn culture of traditional campaigns. She and her team became excellent at getting people to do hard things together—usually with a healthy dose of joy and laughter. Monna joined TMC in 2018 as the vice president of special projects and has been the chief content officer since 2020.

- **Bex** was raised in a strong matriarchal Chinese immigrant family, bouncing between Long Island, New York, and Manhattan's Chinatown. Bex spent nine years at the National LGBTQ Task Force, where they had a manager who always took the time to teach, and who genuinely understood what was hard about their work. Bex came to understand management through organizing and building people power—which grounded them in the mindset of "I can't do this without you." Bex joined TMC in 2013 as a trainer and became the managing partner of our training team in 2019. Bex left TMC to join Rockwood Leadership Institute as their managing director in 2021. They returned to work on this book because of their instrumental role in evolving TMC's thinking and curriculum about racial equity in management.

The three of us don't share the same backgrounds, but we have some key experiences in common. We all have deep experience working with and for our communities to advance social justice. All three of us have a talent for getting work done with others. And earlier in our careers, we might have been overlooked by recruiters looking for "traditional candidates." None of us come with straight, white, middle-class experiences or sensibilities. Our parents never crafted résumés, wrote cover letters, or attended networking events. We come from hustlers who paid the bills through seasonal work and cleaning hotel rooms. We didn't excel academically. We learned how to operate in the working world through the grace and investment of mentors, participating in youth development programs, and organizing with queer and trans folks, poor people, and people of color.

All three of us have experienced the downsides of management in the social change sphere: having too much to do and too few resources, experiencing vicarious trauma and firsthand burnout, and putting up with too-low pay and too-long hours. We've worked with inspirational leaders whose management struggles either got in the way of realizing their grand visions or wreaked havoc for their teams in the process (or both). We know that managing can go from feeling amazing one day to feeling so horrible that you're tempted to quit. We have struggled with insecurity, loneliness, and imposter syndrome. We have been tired, overwhelmed, and unsure of how to make it through. (Bex once seriously considered quitting social justice work to become a firefighter!)

But we stuck it out—out of love for our people and commitment to our movements, and because we've also experienced the *best* of what social change work offers. We've witnessed people doing hard work to get great results while caring for each other. We know it's possible to work your butt off *and* preserve a sense of respect and camaraderie. We've seen what a diverse group of talented and committed people can achieve together. And we've seen the critical role that managers play in making this possible.

HOW TO USE THIS BOOK

This book aims to demystify effective management by offering concrete advice to help you manage in an equitable, sustainable, and results-driven way. From hiring well to giving feedback to cultivating belonging, we want to help you and your team achieve what you set out to do.

We get it if you don't have time to read the whole book from cover to cover. So here's where to turn if you're looking for help on particular topics:

- **Chapter 1: The Fundamentals of Effective Management**—Explanations of key concepts, including what *effective management* means (hint: it's in the book title!).

- **Chapter 2: Building Relationships**—How to lay the foundations for a strong working relationship, including conducting an effective check-in meeting—and why check-ins are essential.

- **Chapter 3: Delegating Effectively**—How to assign work to others and set them up for success.

- **Chapter 4: Defining Roles and Goals**—How to define people's job responsibilities and set goals like a SMARTIE.

- **Chapter 5: Making Decisions and Prioritizing**—Advice for making the big and little choices you'll face as a manager—from major strategic decisions to using your calendar to prioritize.

- **Chapter 6: Hiring and Building Your Team**—How to get great talent by running an equitable hiring process, from the job posting to the interviews to the offer.

- **Chapter 7: Giving Feedback and Evaluating Performance**—How to improve your relationship and results by giving regular, actionable feedback, and how to conduct performance reviews.

- **Chapter 8: Investing in People**—How to develop your staff to grow their competencies. Plus, a bit about retention.

- **Chapter 9: Addressing Performance Problems**—How to identify performance problems and decide what to do about them.

- **Chapter 10: Managing Up and Sideways**—How to get what you need to succeed when you don't have formal authority.

- **Chapter 11: Building a Healthy Culture**—How to create an environment that instills inclusion and belonging and gets you the results you need. Plus, how to transform an unhealthy culture.

Many of these chapters include appendix sections with sample tools and worksheets. You can find even more resources like this on our website, www.managementcenter .org.

We don't promise to have all the answers to your management challenges, but we *do* offer some fundamental tools that can help you craft solutions and meet your team's needs. As you read this book, remember that even management "experts" like us have been where you are. And even now, we are growing and figuring it out with you.

We appreciate you for every time you pushed through a tough day and did your best. Most of us have had that *one* manager, teacher, coach, or mentor whose impact transformed our lives. You could be that person to someone. Thank you for caring, thank you for picking up this book, and thank you for being on this journey with us.

CHAPTER

1

THE FUNDAMENTALS OF EFFECTIVE MANAGEMENT

Management is the art of getting things done *with* and *through* other people. The bigger our aspirations, the more we need to work with others to achieve them.

But under many traditional management approaches, people are treated more like machine parts than, well, people. And this is no accident—many modern-day management practices have roots in U.S. slavery and worker exploitation.[1] They place profit and a narrow definition of *productivity* above all else—including the well-being and dignity of employees, the greater good of society, and the health of our planet.

Following the COVID-19 pandemic and the rise of Black Lives Matter and other movements for justice, we've seen some long-overdue pushback against this model. More people are reevaluating their priorities. Many are deciding that too much of their time and energy is spent at work.

People are also expecting better from their employers—as they should! Now, more than ever, especially in social justice spaces, people want employers to practice what

---

[1] For more on this history, read Caitlin Rosenthal's *Accounting for Slavery: Masters and Management* (Harvard University Press, 2018). A good excerpt is here: www.bostonreview .net/articles/caitlin-c-rosenthal-accounting-slavery-excerpt

they preach about equity, sustainability, and justice. Staff and managers alike want to be valued as human beings, not treated like cogs in a machine. We want to do purpose-driven work—*without* sacrificing living wages, good benefits, and reasonable hours for the sake of "doing what we love." We want to build authentic connections with our colleagues. We want managers who believe in us and help us realize our potential.

At The Management Center (TMC), we believe that truly *effective* management means living up to these expectations—*and* getting important things done. This chapter covers our overall *approach* to management, the *dimensions* and *mindsets* of effective management, and some of the fundamental *tools* we use to practice it.

OUR *CONSPIRE-AND-ALIGN* APPROACH TO MANAGEMENT

If managing is about getting things done with and through other people, most traditional approaches are almost all "through" and no "with." Staff are treated like highly skilled automatons and are rarely consulted for their input.[2] This is often referred to as a *command-and-control* style of management.

The command-and-control approach is too inflexible and impersonal for those of us doing complex, human-centered work on systemic and social change. This kind of work thrives on collaboration, trial and error, and relationship-building—all of which a command-and-control approach stifles.

We take a different approach. We call it *conspire and align*. It means coming together with our team members for a collective purpose and getting on the same page about realizing that purpose. As managers, we view staff as partners—people we exercise power *with*, not over. We're not drill sergeants barking orders; we're in a team huddle, whispering plans and working out plays.

We chose the word *conspire* deliberately. For one thing, we believe folks working for justice, equity, and social change should be getting into "good trouble," as the late U.S. House Representative John Lewis put it. We're up to something—and that something usually involves trying to topple a status quo that doesn't serve us.

Conspire is also meaningful for another reason. Back in 2007, Jakada participated in a Rockwood Leadership Institute year-long program. In one of its final sessions, then-president Akaya Windwood led the group in a breathing exercise. She said, "This is the meaning of conspire—to breathe together. To be so deep in it with each other that we share the same air. This is the level of closeness—of alignment—that we aspire to as leaders and as movements."

It's true; the word *conspire* also comes from the Latin *conspirare*, which means "to breathe together," and shares a root with the words *inspire* and *aspire*. When we conspire, we *co-inspire* ourselves and our team with a shared, co-created vision of success. When we align, we get in formation—not like battle formations, but the way birds flock,

---

[2] It's worth noting that many managers don't *intend* to treat people like automatons, but when you manage with too heavy an emphasis on outputs and too little a consciousness of people, that's what happens.

dancers get in their place, and people assemble at marches and actions.[3] When we conspire and align, everyone understands where we're going *and* our role in getting there.

When we reframe management in this way—and create structures and practices to support it—a new world opens up. We're no longer limited to the brilliance of one person. When a team works well together, its members' combined powers are greater than the sum of their parts. It's still up to us to own our power and responsibility—but it's not up to us to have all the answers.

The *conspire-and-align* approach can be used in both nonhierarchical settings[4] and in places with *positional power*—the kind of power most people think of in the workplace, where an executive director has more power within the organization than a middle manager, who has more power than their direct report. *Conspire and align* is about recognizing power, being honest about it, and exercising it thoughtfully.

Many of you might already take this approach. If you've ever brainstormed a vision of success with your team, sought input before making a decision, or tapped your team's knowledge and expertise to solve a tricky problem, you've conspired and aligned.

EFFECTIVE MANAGEMENT AND WHITE SUPREMACY CULTURE[5]

Author and activist Tema Okun names 15 "White Supremacy Culture Characteristics" that white dominant culture holds up as virtues.[6] Those characteristics are perfectionism, a sense of urgency, defensiveness and/or denial, quantity over quality, worship of the written word,

(continued)

---

[3] And, yes, the way Beyoncé told us to in her 2016 masterpiece and tribute to Black feminism, "Formation."

[4] At TMC, we believe that whatever their structure, all organizations need mechanisms for accountability, support, defining success, and decision-making (all of which come with effective management). We've seen our tools and advice work in all kinds of hierarchical configurations, including in flat structures.

[5] As the National Education Association points out, "white supremacy culture" isn't just about overt, violent racism like the Klu Klux Klan (KKK); it's a culture that generally perpetuates the social, economic, and political dominance of white people over people of other racial backgrounds. "Characteristics of white supremacy manifest in organizational culture, and are used as norms and standards without being named or chosen by the full group. The characteristics elevate the values, preferences, and experiences of white people above all other racial groups, to the detriment of everybody (including white people). Organizations that are led by people of color or have a majority of people of color can also demonstrate characteristics of "White Supremacy Culture Resources" (National Education Association, 2020). More at: https://www.nea.org/resource-library/white-supremacy-culture-resources

[6] See whitesupremacyculture.info for an updated version of Okun's original 1999 article on the subject.

(continued)

the belief in one "right" way, paternalism, either/or binary thinking, power hoarding, fear of open conflict, individualism, progress defined as more, the right to profit, objectivity, and the right to comfort.

Packaged together and left unchecked, these are some of the worst habits of ineffective management and toxic workplaces. They promote a narrow definition of success, keep power in the hands of a few, demand productivity at all costs, and stifle diversity and difference. The antidotes to white supremacy culture are a social justice–oriented management approach, centering equity, inclusion, and belonging.

We want to be clear: effective management isn't just about saying "no" to everything on Okun's list and doing the opposite. After all, we *do* feel a sense of urgency about social injustices, and sometimes progress *is* more—white supremacy culture didn't invent goals, y'all! Effective management isn't just about being *against* racism and other systems of oppression. It's about being staunchly *for* racial equity and social justice, which leads us to question the status quo and seek different approaches. Instead of believing in only one "right" way, we work to apply multiple ways of knowing,[7] and draw on the wisdom of marginalized communities—whether they be BIPOC, queer, trans, disabled, immigrant, or many others.

THE THREE DIMENSIONS OF EFFECTIVE MANAGEMENT

A command-and-control view of management treats people like robots and the natural world like something to be tamed and conquered. It takes a stance of domination, extraction, and exploitation—classic examples of white supremacy culture in action.

Conspire and align, on the other hand, approaches management the way we'd ideally tend a garden: by engaging in reciprocal acts of care. By gardens, we're not talking about manicured green lawns in desert climates and prize-winning roses behind fences. Instead, we're talking about healthy, sprawling ecosystems that sustain life for generations through thoughtful, active stewardship.

This is why, under the *conspire-and-align* approach, we believe management can only be "effective" if it has three dimensions: *equitable, sustainable*, and *results-driven*.

Equity, sustainability, and results are like three strands of a braided rope. The braid weakens if you try to separate the strands. They reinforce each other and depend on each other. And effective managers don't play favorites—they don't routinely focus on one dimension at the expense of the others.

---

[7] Elissa Sloane Perry and Aja Couchois Duncan describe four interdependent ways of knowing: practical, artistic, generalized, and foundational. Practical and generalized ways of knowing tend to dominate in Western culture. Read more at "Multiple Ways of Knowing: Expanding How We Know," *Nonprofit Quarterly*, 2017, https://nonprofitquarterly.org/multiple-ways-knowing-expanding-know/

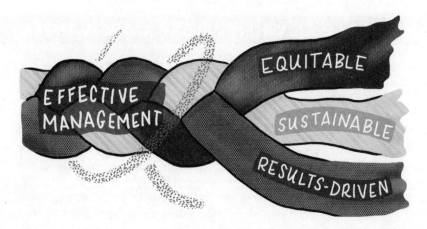

Equitable

Ever tried to grow a tomato in a desert? In the same way that specific environments favor some plants while creating barriers for others, some workplaces are easier for some people to succeed in than others. Most people aren't consciously trying to oppress others, but we can't help being steeped in white supremacy and other systems of oppression. Equity is about disrupting these systems and creating new practices so that more people—especially those with marginalized identities—can thrive.

Note that *equity* and *equality* are different. Equality means treating everyone the same—but equal treatment doesn't always lead to equal outcomes. Equity calls for managers to account for unconscious bias and systemic barriers in supporting people to succeed. For example, let's say you work at a majority-white organization. You have a Black staff person who just joined the team and a white staff person who's been on your team for four years. Who might benefit from more of your time, energy, and support in the coming months?[8]

A manager's job is to spot where these different experiences and identities might disproportionately impact people and work to remove barriers and support their staff to succeed.

Sustainable

Social change work, while often purpose-driven and joyful, can be grueling. In the worst-case scenarios, people start out feeling hopeful and energized, only to burn out and leave their organizations, schools, or even movements. In the introduction to this book, we named some of the downsides that lead to people leaving—lack of resources, long hours, and low salaries.

---

[8] Of course, it's usually more complex and nuanced when you layer in other aspects of identity and life experience. Class, ability, age, sexual orientation, and gender identity, among many other things, all impact our experiences of marginalization and privilege.

WHAT WE MEAN WHEN WE SAY *MARGINALIZED*

When we say *marginalized*, we're not using it as a euphemism for "people of color." We believe in making the implicit explicit, *especially* when it comes to race and other social identities. If we don't see color, we can't address racism. If we don't discuss gender, we can't address sexism and cissexism. And so on and so forth. As writer James Baldwin said, "Not everything that is faced can be changed, but nothing can be changed until it is faced."

So, let's face it: because these oppressive systems are the water we swim in, margins and mainstreams show up at every level in society and in organizations. "Mainstreams" are the groups that set the underlying norms and culture (often unconsciously). "Margins" are the groups whose behaviors and practices are pushed to the edges. While people often think of margins and mainstreams along racial lines, we know from experience that it's not that simple—especially in organizations that are led by and for BIPOC.[9]

For example, when Jakada was at the Ella Baker Center for Human Rights, cisgender Black folks were the mainstream. They were hired, retained, and promoted at a higher rate than anyone else. At EBC, marginalized staff included Latin,[10] trans, and gender nonconforming folks. When Monna was at Lavender Phoenix, an organization for Asians and Pacific Islanders (APIs), differences in class, education, and ethnicity created margins and mainstreams.

In this book, when we intend to refer to a specific identity or cluster of identities, we name them explicitly. When we want to be inclusive of a wider variety of identities, we use broader language—such as *marginalized*. (In those cases, feel free to fill in the blank with the margins and mainstreams in your context.)

In the best cases, though, people stick around long enough to recruit, train, and mentor a new generation of leaders. Sustainability is about the longevity and durability of results, organizations, people, and movements. It means getting the results we need and doing the hard work—but not at the expense of our individual or collective well-being.

---

[9] The concepts of mainstreams and mainstreams originated from the Process Work Institute and were further developed by Training for Change.

[10] At the time of this writing, there's debate about what terms to use for people who trace their roots to Latin America and/or Spain—some options include Hispanic, Latino, Latinx, Latine, and Latin. Language is always evolving and no community is a monolith. In this case—and throughout the book—we chose the term that represents what the folks in the story would use to self-identify.

YAMANI'S STORY

For managers, part of sustainability is doing what you can to keep people around in a sector or movement. Here's a story about a make-it-or-break-it moment early in a TMC coach's career:

Yamani was a 22-year-old Black parent of a one-year-old who worked at a small feminist foundation, running a grantmaking program for young women. Yamani was often late to work or had to leave unexpectedly because of unforeseen childcare challenges. She didn't have alternative childcare, so if an incident happened at the daycare, she or her partner would have to leave work to resolve it. She was good at her job, but unreliable childcare made Yamani an unreliable staff person. One day, Yamani showed up to pick up her baby to find that he wasn't there. When she eventually found him (safe!), she learned that the caregiver had taken him and the other children on an errand without informing the parents. She took him out of the daycare and called out of work for the rest of that week.

When she returned to work the following week, Yamani's manager Alicia, the head of the foundation, pulled her aside and asked, "Hey, what's going on? I don't want to lose you, but I need you to be here to do your job." Yamani told her what was happening—that she didn't have childcare and wasn't sure when she'd get off the waitlist for a center. She couldn't afford a nanny. After discussing Yamani's situation and options, her manager said, "Bring your baby to work."

To Alicia, this decision was part of living up to her—and the organization's—feminist values. She was committed to supporting Yamani. She saw Yamani's inconsistent performance not as a failure on Yamani's part, but as a result of challenges exacerbated by multiple systemic barriers—challenges they could get through together. So, until a spot opened up at another childcare center, Yamani set up a playpen in her office and brought her baby to work. Her colleagues and the young women in her grantmaking program happily spent breaks playing with the baby.

This was a game-changing moment for Yamani, not just because she kept a job she was good at (and needed to support her family), but also because it showed her what was possible. When she moved on to other jobs—including serving as executive director at two reproductive justice organizations—she brought the same compassion, grace, and support she'd experienced to her management.

Results-Driven

The "results-driven" part of management means grounding our work in what our team is trying to accomplish, whether it's registering enough voters to build local power or increasing math scores for fourth graders. Being results-driven helps us understand the impact we can make if we succeed—and what's at stake if we fail. This drive for results motivates us to strive for excellence, innovate, take calculated risks, and stretch beyond our comfort zones. And, when bolstered by our commitments to equity and sustainability, we set guardrails to avoid the dangers of prioritizing results over people.

Being results-driven has led us to do things like:

- Share difficult feedback with a staff member whose lack of awareness about race and gender negatively impacted our team of mostly women, trans people, and people of color.

- Let someone go (with a generous severance package) because they consistently couldn't deliver on expectations, even though they had been at the organization for a long time.

- Intervene when a critical project was off-track, including by rolling up our sleeves to work alongside the team member to help reprioritize and develop a new timeline.

- Try an entirely different—and rather unorthodox—approach because the traditional methods weren't getting the results we needed.

An often-overlooked part of management is supporting *others* to get results, which makes it possible to go beyond the results you would have gotten on your own. After all, if you could do it yourself, you wouldn't need to work with and through others! We bet you've been pretty successful at getting results on your own. Many managers we know ended up in their roles not because they were great managers, but because they'd gained issue area expertise or were highly skilled at an area of work (like communications or legal advocacy). As they progressed in their career, they took on increasing responsibility, including managing others. Unfortunately, being an excellent writer doesn't mean you're excellent at supporting others to write well.

EXCELLENCE VERSUS PERFECTION

In our quest for excellence, we sometimes fall into the trap of perfectionism (a tenet of white supremacy culture!). Where excellence is about doing our best to get great results, "perfection" is a narrow target that defines "one right way." In perfectionistic cultures, people are afraid to fail, go off-script, or be wrong. The relentless demands of perfectionism can cause burnout. It leads us to spend months wordsmithing goals before sharing them, even when the work has already started. It causes us to hold back useful feedback or ideas until we've figured out the "best" way to share them. On the other hand, when we commit to excellence, we exercise discernment. We differentiate between "gold star" and "good enough," knowing that our efforts should be proportionate to our intended impact (more on this in Chapter 3).

One colleague told us about attending a yoga retreat where the facilitator welcomed participants by saying, "Some of you have as much experience practicing yoga as I do. Here, we've agreed that I'll hold the space so you can practice." As managers, we take up the power and responsibility of *holding space* for others to do the work (even as we're also doing some of the work ourselves) to get the results we're after. We help everyone stay focused on what we're there to deliver and why.

MINDSETS OF EFFECTIVE MANAGEMENT

When we use a *conspire-and-align* approach that centers equity, sustainability, and results, we adopt new mindsets about management.

To us, three essential mindsets about management are:

- Management is a **practice**.

- Management is a **duty**.

- Management is a **balance**.

Management Is a Practice

Management is like jazz, dance, or basketball. These disciplines (and many others) require fundamentals, freestyle, and flow. The fundamentals are the building blocks—the skills you learn, practice, and develop muscle memory for, like scales for pianists or toprocking for breakdancers. With any skill, you gain proficiency in the fundamentals before you add your flavor and freestyle. Eventually, it might become so second nature that you find yourself *in flow* with your work or *flowing with* the people around you, like in a dance cypher or jam session.

But, before you get to that place of being easy, free, and in flow, you must take the time to learn the fundamentals. Getting good at management requires consistent and rigorous practice (and the occasional failure). In this book, we're covering the fundamentals.

Management Is a Duty

It's more than performing the "duties" of your job. Yes, we are responsible for daily tasks and outcomes. But we must also *be responsible,* in the sense of being ethical and acting with care and conscience.

We have a duty to be good stewards of our team members' time and energy—and that of our own. After all, people spend a lot of their lives at work, and how we manage people influences whether they feel a sense of purpose or dread coming back the next day.

We have a duty to our team members, organizations, communities, and movements to manage toward strong, equitable results—without burning people out. We are responsible for our team's impact on those we aim to serve.

Management Is a Balance

When managers struggle, it's often because they can't figure out how to balance competing priorities, values, or approaches. For example, they might feel trapped between resource constraints on one hand and staff capacity on the other—with no free hands for long-term planning or self-care.

The art of management will always involve the act of balance. It's the balance between power and love, as Dr. King put it, between holding others accountable and being accountable, between supporting and giving space, between rigor and flexibility, between focus and play.

Crucially, we don't have to—and shouldn't—choose only one option when two (or more!) necessary things are in tension with one another. Just like breathing requires inhaling and exhaling, we often need something from both elements.[11]

Balance can mean:

- Flowing between two opposite approaches, like putting in extra hours for a sprint, then taking a week off after the end-of-quarter crunch.

- Finding a happy medium between two undesirable extremes—like not micromanaging and not neglecting your team completely.

- Holding two (or more) things as equally important so they keep you stable—such as your care for people and your commitment to results.

THE EFFECTIVE MANAGEMENT TOOLKIT

Now that we've gone over the philosophy behind our approach, let's look at some foundational tools that will help you manage. We'll reference these frequently, so consider this your starter kit. Each tool can help you make more equitable, sustainable management decisions to get strong results.

In particular, some of these tools can help you spot and avoid biases. Bias is like dental plaque—we all have it, it's hard to see (at first), and it's a big problem when it builds up. Regular maintenance with various tools is the only way to keep it in check.

Sphere of Control

Our colleague Jessica compares *sphere of control* to playing spades—the card game of strategy, teamwork, and luck. With spades, like most card games (and life in

---

[11] This type of leveraging is also known as a "polarity," a concept developed by Barry Johnson in his book *And: Volume One Foundations* (Human Resource Development Press, 2020) and expanded on in *And: Volume Two Applications* (Human Resource Development Press, 2021). "Polarity mapping" is a great exercise to help you think through the positives and negatives of two contrasting "poles," like activity and rest or structure and flexibility.

general), you can't choose your hand. The skill is recognizing what you have and then strategizing, communicating, and keeping your cool—so that you can win, even with a terrible hand.

Sphere of control helps us focus our precious time and energy on the things we can control so we can claim our power and agency. As managers, we have control over many things that can impact our staff and others. Sphere of control lets us identify those things so we can make strategic choices.

Knowing your sphere of control helps you see what you can do to get (closer) to the outcome you want, turning your "possibles" into wins.

Some things that are usually within our sphere of control:

- The relationships we build.

- How we spend our time.

- Solutions we propose.

- Feedback we share.

- The choice points we consider (more on this later).

SELF-REFLECTION QUESTIONS

What's within my sphere of control? What's outside of it? Where do I have influence? What choices can I make to promote equity, sustainability, and results?

Choice Points

"When people come together to solve problems, they do not automatically become immune to the ways society and the economy are organized. We bring the things that shape us, consciously and unconsciously, everywhere we go. Unless we are intentional about interrupting what we've learned, we will perpetuate it, even as we are working hard for a better world."

—*Alicia Garza, author of "The Purpose of Power: How We Come Together When We Fall Apart" and co-founder of Black Lives Matter*

Our friends at Race Forward taught us the term *choice point* to describe forks in the road. Some paths replicate the status quo—they are well trod, paved by history and tradition. Others (usually less familiar or might not even exist yet) open opportunities for more equity, inclusion, and belonging.

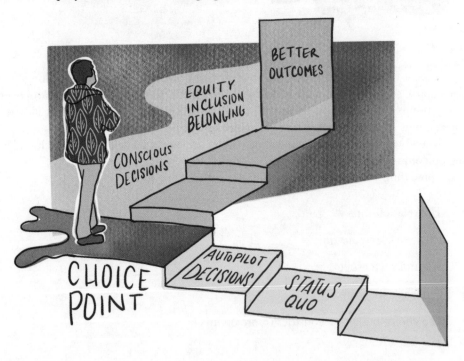

When we consider our choice points, we take ourselves off autopilot and pause to consider the impacts of our decisions. We take a moment to reflect, generate options, and choose the ones that advance equity and inclusion.

In Yamani's story (see the "Yamani's Story" box), her manager Alicia encountered several choice points. A major one was what to do when she learned of Yamani's child-care challenge. In that situation, Alicia had a few options:

- She could've let Yamani exhaust her paid time off (if she had any) and hoped for the best.

- She could've treated the most recent absences as proof of Yamani's poor performance and written her up—or worse, fired her.

- She could've approved time off for Yamani to take care of her baby for as long as she needed.

In this scenario, the "status quo" would have been something like: let Yamani use up her PTO and once it ran out, let Yamani work it out on her own. However, when Alicia paused to consider, she saw the systemic barriers Yamani faced and knew that the status quo option would only perpetuate them. Unfortunately, given the uncertainty of Yamani's situation, Alicia couldn't give Yamani unlimited time off. So, Alicia did the next best thing she could think of: make it possible for Yamani to care for her kid and show up to work.

When you arrive at a choice point, pause to:

- **Spot bias and barriers.** What underlying or implicit assumptions inform your current approach?

- **Look at unintended consequences.** Who benefits? Who's burdened or disadvantaged?

- **Generate options.** What alternatives might create more equity, inclusion, accessibility, and belonging, especially for those on the margins? What can you do to get more equitable results?

Preferences, Traditions, and Requirements (PTR)

PTR helps you distinguish between your biases or habits and the things that *really* matter.[12] Notice the difference, as illustrated in Figure 1.1.

- **Preferences:** "I like to share updates in writing"

- **Traditions:** "We always communicate organizational updates via email"

- **Requirements:** "We need everyone to know that we've changed the dates and location for our upcoming staff retreat"

---

[12] The concept of PTR comes from Ernst & Young's diversity and inclusion programs.

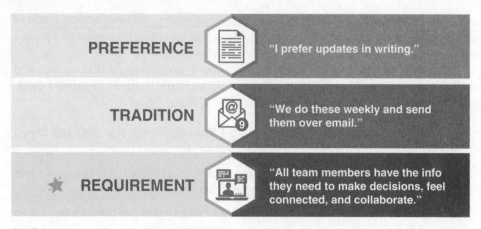

FIGURE 1.1 *Examples of PTR.*

We all have preferences and traditions—there's nothing wrong with that! But Ps and Ts don't exist in a vacuum; they're shaped and reinforced by identity, culture, and experience. As managers, we can't let our preferences and traditions become default requirements—that's how bias takes over. Instead, use PTR to make more equitable decisions, communicate clearly when delegating, and stay open to new approaches.

SELF-REFLECTION QUESTIONS

Did I check my PTR? How are my preferences and traditions showing up? What are the requirements, and why?

Make the Implicit Explicit

The premise is simple: don't expect other people to read your mind. Instead, share what's in your head directly, clearly, and specifically. When managers don't make the implicit explicit, they create conditions for misunderstanding, which costs time, energy, and trust.

Making the implicit explicit is about embracing the idea that people are different. We each come to the table with worldviews, assumptions, and values shaped by our identities, backgrounds, and life experiences. The more lines of difference between us and those we manage, the more likely we will make different meanings of the same information.

SELF-REFLECTION QUESTIONS

What's in my head that I haven't said aloud? What do I assume this person already knows that they might not? Is there anything I'm worried about that I haven't shared explicitly?

Seek Perspective

"It's hubris to think that the way we see things is everything there is."
—*Lisa Randall, American theoretical physicist*

Making the implicit explicit is about sharing what's in your head; *seeking perspective* is asking people what's in theirs. After all, two (or more) heads are usually better than one! Our experiences impact our perspectives, and because our experiences are limited, we must seek perspective to mitigate our biases and expand our thinking.

It's crucial to seek perspective from people who will be most impacted by your decisions. For instance, you should seek your staff's perspective on things like:

- A policy that will impact the whole team.

- What success looks like for a project they're responsible for.

- Next year's goals.

If these tools seem like a lot to keep track of, don't worry. We refer to these ideas often throughout the book, with stories and examples to help you apply them to your work. And if you need even more templates, tools, or support on any given topic, check out our website at www.managementcenter.org.

SELF-REFLECTION QUESTIONS

Did I seek perspective? Did I hear from the people who might be most impacted?

KEY POINTS OF EFFECTIVE MANAGEMENT FUNDAMENTALS

Here are the takeaways from this chapter:

- We use a *conspire-and-align* approach to management. This means treating staff as partners, coming together with team members for a collective purpose, and getting on the same page about realizing that purpose.

- **Effective management** has three dimensions, which reinforce each other:

  - **Equitable:** accounting for unconscious bias and systemic barriers in how we support people to succeed.

  - **Sustainable:** ensuring the longevity and durability of results, organizations, people, and movements.

  - **Results-driven:** knowing what we're striving to accomplish; and being willing to stretch beyond our comfort zones and make hard decisions to get great results.

- Three key **mindsets** about management are:

  - Management is **a practice.** Like any craft or discipline, we must practice consistently and rigorously.

  - Management is **a duty.** We must exercise our power responsibly and get the best results we can for our movements and communities.

  - Management is **a balance.** Balance can mean flowing between two poles, finding a happy medium, or holding two or more things of equal importance to stay stable.

- The five most important **tools** we use daily in management are:

  - **Sphere of control:** identifying what you can control.

  - **Choice points:** turning off autopilot and pausing to consider equity implications and alternative options.

  - **PTR:** identifying preferences, traditions, and requirements (and focusing on requirements!).

  - **Make the implicit explicit:** saying what's in your head.

  - **Seek perspective:** getting input from others, especially those most impacted.

CHAPTER

2

BUILDING RELATIONSHIPS

"Movements are born of critical connections rather than critical mass."
—*Grace Lee Boggs, American author and activist*

Bex once worked with people who embraced the command-and-control management approach. One time, someone observed Bex with their team and asked, "Why do you take so much time to explain things? Can't you just yell at them?" Baffled by these questions, Bex responded, "No one has won same-sex marriage before. The way we've always run campaigns hasn't worked. To win, we need people at their most engaged, and yelling isn't going to help."

Years later, Monna had Bex as a manager at her first post-college job. When they went to small-town Ohio to protect an LGBTQ nondiscrimination ordinance, Monna went to her first canvass. She *struggled*. As a New Yorker, Monna hated talking to strangers. As a small Asian American woman, she felt ridiculous knocking on random people's doors, not knowing if the people behind them would be homophobic, racist, or just plain creepy. On the plane ride back, she confided in Bex. "Canvassing is *weird!* It goes against everything I know about staying safe in this world." Bex took that in and replied, "Yeah, it's hard." Then they said, "It's not just you. I've been there too. Let's figure out how to make it easier next time."

For Monna, that conversation was pivotal. Her manager related to her concerns and was willing to help her overcome them. This was enough to get her to stick it out and try canvassing again.

If Monna had worked with the people on Bex's other campaign and confided in them, they might have told her to quit whining and get over it. Feeling invalidated, she might have written off campaigns entirely. She wouldn't have gone on to organize and train hundreds of people to work through their own discomfort to fight for social justice. Instead, with Bex, Monna learned not only to talk to complete strangers, but also to change their hearts and minds. She learned to mobilize them. After that campaign ended (they won!), they continued working together in other contexts—on campaigns, nonprofit boards, and at TMC.

Effective management is built on relationships. The stronger our relationships, the more we endure together. And there's a *lot* to endure in social justice work. We deal with families being separated, kids not getting enough food, and people suffering when the change we fight for doesn't come soon enough. We put our bodies on the line by leading marches, knocking on strangers' doors, or standing in front of a classroom. A solid sense of connection and community makes it easier to show up, persevere through ups and downs, and avoid burnout. Stronger relationships make stronger teams, organizations, movements, and results.

To be clear, a management relationship is not a friendship. However, it *is* usually one of the most significant relationships in a working person's daily life. People sometimes spend more time with their managers than their families; we work, mourn, and celebrate together. As managers, we influence our staff's livelihood, how they spend their time, and how they feel about their work. And our relationships with staff also have a profound impact on how we managers feel about our work.

Relationships are a two-way street, but it's the manager's job to ensure the road is smooth and work to keep the relationship on a good course. In this chapter, we cover the following:

- The use of one-on-one check-in meetings to build a strong relationship.

- The four elements of relationship-building.

- Advice for navigating skip-level relationships with the people your direct reports manage.

- Tips for resolving conflict and repairing relationships.

BUILDING RELATIONSHIPS THROUGH CHECK-INS

One of the best relationship-building tools for management is regular one-on-one check-in meetings. If our clients don't already do check-ins, we always insist they start. Check-ins are the soil where a *conspire-and-align* management relationship takes root, grows, and thrives. They're the basic hygiene of management—the good habits that can catch problems early and prevent them from growing.

If you're very busy, your check-in might be the only time your staff gets your undivided attention each week. If you manage multiple people, consistent check-in practices promote equity by ensuring that each person gets what they need to succeed (not just the ones you enjoy talking to or find easy to work with). Especially in times of uncertainty, check-ins are critical tools for helping your staff feel supported.

The goals of check-ins are to:

- **Get what you need from each other.** Does your staff person need approval on something? Is there a challenge that they need your help resolving? Do you need their input to make a decision? Whether it's information, feedback, trouble-shooting support, or approval, check-ins allow each of you to get what you need to do your jobs well.

- **Align on priorities and stay engaged.** Check-ins help you stay updated on your staff person's projects and priorities. They give you time for debriefing, feedback, and other things that might not happen in the rush of day-to-day work. And when circumstances change, check-ins help you reprioritize (see Chapter 5 for more on prioritization).

- **Build connection.** Check-ins help you get to know each other's likes, dislikes, habits, and preferences. They let you better understand what's happening in each other's lives, especially things that may impact your work and how you show up.

- **Troubleshoot.** "Do they ask you for help?" is a question that one TMC coach asks her clients to gauge the strength of their relationships with staff. If you regularly anticipate problems and support your staff to solve them, they're more likely to come to you with challenges (rather than hiding them until they grow).

- **Provide and invite feedback.** Feedback is relationship maintenance. When it's a routine and expected part of your check-ins, it's much easier to talk about issues when they arise. (See Chapter 7 for more on feedback.)

Tips for Successful Check-Ins

Here are some tips for making the best use of check-ins:

- **Set a regular time and stick to it.** Start with weekly 60-minute check-ins and adjust as needed.

- **Be prepared and present.** Don't just wing it! Use an agenda with items for updates and discussion. Some things should be standing items, like your staff person's biggest projects for the year. Remember that preparation isn't just about listing your agenda items. It also means being fully present so you can use your time wisely.

THE GREEN LENS

We recommend the Green Lens[1] as a practice to ground yourself in your relationships and check-ins. Think of a time when someone saw your inherent value and humanity and treated you with dignity and respect (even when you messed up!). How did it feel? When you believe the best about someone, you approach them with a presence that empowers them to see the best version of themselves.

The following five statements make up the Green Lens. Try reading these to yourself before your next check-in, and notice if you feel a difference in how you communicate:

- This person is a hero, whole and complete.
- This person has goals and dreams and a desire to make a difference.
- This person has their own answers.
- This person is contributing to me right here and now.
- This person deserves to be treated with dignity and respect.

- **Have the staff person drive it.** Check-ins reinforce a person's sense of ownership in their role when they have the power to drive them. Don't just bring a laundry list of items that leaves no time or room for them to get what *they* need.

- **Check in personally.** Build rapport and connection by asking how they're doing—and share how you're doing too.

- **Tailor your approach.** The staff person's role, responsibilities, and communication styles will all affect how you approach check-ins. For instance, some folks take 15 minutes for personal updates; others like to keep it brief.

- **Be a coach.** When your staff person shares a problem or challenge, help them problem-solve without swooping in and taking over. Ask questions like, "What do you think?" or "If you were the decider, what would you do?" to help them get unstuck by tapping into their knowledge and experience.

- **Capture next steps.** Keep track of action items, even if it's just, "Think this over and discuss next week."

See Tool 2.1 at the end of this chapter for a sample filled-in version of our template for a check-in meeting agenda. (Fun fact: many people have told us that this tool was the most helpful resource they took away from our trainings!)

---

[1] The Green Lens is a concept developed by Maria Nemeth, the director of the Academy for Coaching Excellence.

One last note on check-ins: They're *one* forum for communication and management, but they aren't the *only*. Save conversations about strategy and problem-solving for your check-ins, but don't let check-ins be the only time you two communicate. You don't want their work to be stalled while they wait for your check-in if a quick exchange would allow them to move forward. On the flip side, don't forgo check-ins just because you two regularly communicate through email, chats, or team meetings.

THE FOUR ELEMENTS OF RELATIONSHIP-BUILDING

Check-ins are a space for your management relationship to grow, but you and your staff must decide how to cultivate it. To guide those decisions, consider the four elements of relationship-building: cultivating trust, practicing authenticity, navigating power and difference, and aligning on a shared purpose.

Think of these elements not as discrete building blocks but as ingredients. When you make a cake, the eggs, sugar, butter, and flour don't just sit on each other—they bind and react, yielding new flavors, textures, and shapes. The quality of the final product depends on the ingredients, execution, and of course, time.

And, of course, relationships are never finished "baking" like a cake is. The relationship between two people is like another living thing, constantly growing and evolving. Many Pacific Islander cultures have a concept called "Vā," which literally translates to "the space in between." It refers to the sacred relational space between people. *Teu le Vā*[2] ("nurture the relationship") is a common Samoan expression that influences how we think about relationship-building. Considering these four elements helps us nurture our relationships and be thoughtful stewards of that space in between.

Cultivating Trust

Relationships are built on reciprocal trust. As managers, it's our job to earn, build, and communicate it. We want our staff to believe they can count on us to act with care, integrity, and competence (and vice versa!). These qualities are like three legs of a stool; if you lose one, people's trust in you gets wobbly. Build a sturdy foundation of trust by paying attention to the following:

Care

The root of most interpersonal conflict comes down to one person feeling that the other person doesn't care about them. Here are a few ways to demonstrate care:

- Check in personally before getting down to business.

- Show interest in who they are. This includes the seemingly trivial (their pet's names, whether they like crunchy bread on sandwiches[3]) and the things that are core to who they are (who they consider family, what they're passionate about).

- Pay attention to the big moments in their lives, even if they're not work-related.

- Seek their perspective when making decisions.

- Appreciate them for their ideas and hard work.

- Invest in their growth by creating meaningful development opportunities. (See Chapter 8 for more on investing in your people.)

- Offer support and encouragement if they're going through a hard time.

---

[2] *Vā* also refers to the space between people and their environment, their ancestors, and the heavens. Dr. Melanie Anae at the University of Auckland has written extensively on *Teu le Vā*, especially in an education context.

[3] Jakada does not!

On that last point, one staff person recounted a time when she received a "Jerry-gram" (a lengthy voice memo) from our former CEO: "I was struggling with something, and Jerry sent me a Jerrygram telling me he believed in me. I felt so cared for and appreciated. I left it at the top of my inbox for almost a year and replayed it whenever I had a bad day."

Integrity

Jakada learned a lesson about trust and integrity the hard way: early in his time at EBC, he got feedback that he was pretty bad at follow-through. His staff told him that if he agreed to do something, there was a 50/50 chance he'd actually do it. Essentially, he was teaching them that they couldn't trust him. He fixed this by making sure to track and keep his commitments.[4]

Build trust by being true to your word. Say what you mean and mean what you say. When you can't live up to your commitments, own up to it and do better next time. Note, too, that trust is built in and out of other people's presence. It's not just how you act in front of your staff; what you do behind the scenes and how they observe you treating others matters too. (Integrity is also key to a healthy culture—more on this in Chapter 11.)

Competence

Let's be real—when you're not good at your job, the people who feel it most are those you supervise. Hold yourself to a standard of excellence and continually seek feedback on how well you meet the competencies for your role.

Of course, being competent doesn't mean having all the answers. In fact, one day, you'll probably manage people whose roles you don't have experience or expertise in. When that happens, be honest and lean into collaboration and coaching. Defer to their expertise, add yours where you can, and try to be a helpful sounding board and support system.

DEALING WITH DISTRUST

It can be challenging to build trust immediately. If you've ever been burned at a previous job, you know those wounds don't go away just because you're at a new job with a new manager. After all, we carry our baggage with us. If we manage someone who has had a bad experience with a former manager, building trust will be harder—and much more important. It's not our job (or within our *sphere of control*) to resolve someone else's baggage, but don't pretend it's not there. Instead, talk about it honestly and dig deeper. "Can you tell me about your previous experiences with managers? What were positive things you experienced that you'd like to replicate here? What would you like to avoid?" It can also help to acknowledge the distrust directly and get curious about it. Try saying, "It seems like you've had some bad experiences with managers. What do you think it'd take for us to build trust?"

---

[4] Monna can confirm that Jakada still successfully tracks and keeps his commitments!

Practicing Authenticity

Authenticity is the foundation of inclusion and belonging. If inclusion is being invited to a potluck, then belonging is having people swoon over your kimchi tacos (even if it's totally new to them and they'd never make it themselves). It's feeling seen and valued for the things that make us who we are. It's feeling safe and secure in being part of a community, despite our imperfections.

We get these kinds of responses when we ask training participants about their most supportive relationships:

- "They saw me as a person, not just a co-worker."

- "They're honest and vulnerable with me, so I know I can do the same."

- "I can be myself around them."

Bex and Monna's conversation on the plane was a moment of authenticity. Bex validated Monna's feelings about canvassing and shared that they'd had similar experiences. And the authenticity went both ways: Bex appreciated Monna's willingness to learn and be vulnerable when she confessed, "I don't want to suck at this." To Bex, that attitude invited mentorship. And as a trans person of color who often experienced bias and skepticism from the people they managed, Bex found Monna's attitude especially meaningful.

We can't push an "authenticity" button to make someone reveal themselves to us. But we *can* invite people—especially those on the margins—to be more of themselves with us. We do this by showing that we respect and value how they wish to be seen through basic but essential practices like:

- Using their correct pronouns.

- Asking about their access needs (more on this in Chapter 6).

- Checking in about their preferences.

- Respecting their boundaries.

Setting Healthy Boundaries

Being authentic is not about sharing all your unfiltered thoughts. Every relationship—especially professional ones—is contained by boundaries—the limits we set to keep ourselves safe and secure. Knowing and respecting boundaries helps us be responsible stewards of vā so that we can mindfully nurture that space in between. Prentis Hemphill, therapist, writer, and somatics teacher, describes boundaries as "the distance at which I can love you and me simultaneously."[5]

---

[5] Instagram post from https://www.instagram.com/p/CNSzFO1A21C/?hl=en

In a world where the divide between "work" and "life" is regularly redrawn, the boundaries of our working relationships can get blurry, leading to misunderstanding. In the worst cases, a lack of boundaries can lead to harmful dynamics and abuses of power.

Here are four ways managers can set and navigate boundaries:

- **Understand your sphere of control.** Managers have more positional power than staff—but that power has limits. As a manager, you're (likely) not a therapist, social worker, or mediator. Even if you are, you don't have the power or responsibility to solve your staffer's personal problems or trauma. Know what you can offer—like flexible work arrangements and information about benefits to support employee well-being—and what you can't.

- **Watch out for emotional dumping, gossiping, and oversharing.** Watch out for these behaviors that might make your staff uncomfortable. You're not immune to life's stressors, and you get to be human, too. But because you have positional power, it's generally not fair or appropriate to turn to staff for emotional support without their explicit and enthusiastic consent.

- **Invite, don't demand.** Set the table, but don't force people to sit at it. Everyone has different preferences about how they relate to their manager and colleagues, so don't assume intimacy or demand vulnerability. Some people want to chat about weekend plans with their manager; others prefer to focus on the work.

- **Talk about it.** *Make the implicit explicit* by asking about and sharing your relationship-building *PTR*. In your first check-in, try asking: "What do you think success would look like in our relationship?" or "What are some elements of a staff/manager relationship that haven't worked for you in the past?" Remember to share your limits, too (maybe *you* don't want to chat about your weekend plans!).

On the last point, here's a reflection from one of our colleagues about using PTR to have that conversation:

"When Tamara became my manager, we discussed how we wanted to relate as manager and staff. She asked about my preferences, and we discussed organizational traditions that would work for us, like sharing stories about our families. We also talked about what success would look like for our relationship.

"I've had managers who assumed that I wanted to be friends with them. I've also had managers who kept our relationship strictly professional. In most cases, I felt like I had to follow the manager's lead to match what they wanted because they had positional power. As an immigrant, these experiences reinforced a belief I held as a child: to belong, I had to 'follow the lead' of the people around me and not challenge authority. This conversation affirmed that I could bring my needs and interests in how I related to my supervisor."

If you're a newly promoted manager, take note! You'll need to redraw boundaries if you manage people who were your peers (and friends!). You can start that conversation by saying, "Now that I'm your manager, let's talk about what might need to change about our working relationship."

Navigating Power and Difference

A TMC trainer once shared this story about a former manager: "As a Black man working in education, I haven't always had the best experiences working with white women. But in my first check-in with Libby, she said, 'I know there's a power dynamic because of our positions and identities. I want you to know that we're partners. We're doing this together. I'll learn from you, and you'll learn from me. Let me know how you communicate best, and I'll do the same.' She said this before we talked about anything else. Because she started by naming the elephant in the room—power—we connected authentically. I trusted her."

Working with others means navigating differences in power and privilege. It can be uncomfortable to acknowledge these things, but unless you talk about them, you won't be able to show up authentically.

Take a page from Libby's book and be upfront. For example, you might say, "I care about us working well together. I want us both to feel respected and valued. I also know that relationships get tricky when there's power involved. Here's where I think I hold power, and here's where I feel like I have less. What about you?" This works best at the beginning of a relationship, but even if you've been working with someone for a while, you can say, "I know we haven't discussed this explicitly before, but I want to talk about how power shows up for us. I think this will help us understand each other and work better together."

Navigating Power

Managers can fall between two extremes when dealing with their power. On one end are managers who cling too tightly to their power. These managers tend to:

- Claim to have all the answers.

- Hide or minimize their shortcomings.

- React defensively to feedback while being critical of others.

- Impose their preferences and traditions and reject new ideas.

- Make unilateral decisions without consulting others.

- Be overly rigid and act as gatekeepers.

On the other end of the spectrum are managers who shy away from asserting authority. The reasons vary: some people feel guilty about it, some struggle with imposter syndrome, and some fear the conflicts that can come from exercising authority. These managers tend to:

- Minimize or withhold their ideas and expertise.

- Avoid holding others accountable, or take all the responsibility when something goes wrong.

- Avoid sharing constructive feedback.

- Frame expectations and requirements as suggestions or "offers."

- Over-rely on consensus-building and avoid making tough calls.

- Struggle with setting and maintaining boundaries.

The behaviors of managers who cling too tightly to power often lead staff to disengage—whether out of fear, resentment, or hopelessness—and leave the managers with too much responsibility. Conversely, when managers *never* assert power and authority, there's usually a lack of clarity, honesty, and alignment, which allows standards to wane, problems to persist, and bad feelings to fester. In both cases, the ultimate consequence is that relationships and results suffer.

Most of us fall somewhere in the middle. Many oscillate between the two poles depending on our context, relationships, and moods. The most effective managers maintain a balance by owning our authority and power, and using it as a tool to *conspire and align* (not as a weapon to command and control). This leads us to:

- Own our ideas, experience, and expertise.

- Be honest about being the decision-maker or approver *and* seek and value others' perspectives.

- Share and receive feedback thoughtfully, especially if performance issues arise.

- Own our shortcomings and mistakes while supporting others to be accountable.

- Be clear, direct, and firm about expectations and requirements, *and* treat people with empathy and flexibility.

- Use our power to advocate, remove barriers, and support others.

Navigating Difference

"Without community, there is no liberation, but community must not mean a shedding of our differences, nor the pathetic pretense that these differences do not exist."

—*Audre Lorde, American writer, radical feminist, and activist*

An essential part of relationship-building is expecting, facing, and celebrating differences, whether they're rooted in race, gender, or other identities. Unfortunately, as humans, we sometimes tend to minimize differences because there's security in sameness—it's why we gravitate toward people who look and talk like us.[6] And for those of us in a mainstream group, it can feel like opening ourselves up to conflict by acknowledging differences. But when we don't, we miss out on the learning and growth that comes from being influenced by others' perspectives. On the other side, when we're in a marginalized group, having our differences minimized can make us feel invisible. Minimization squashes growth, trust, and authentic connection.[7] As managers, being curious about difference is a way to say, "I see you. I value you. I have something to learn from you."

Aligning on a Shared Purpose

Whether you work at a school, nonprofit, or government agency, we bet you're working toward *something* you can't achieve alone. Shared purpose distinguishes our working relationships from most of our other relationships. It makes us feel like part of a collective whole—not just a random collection of individuals.

Remember the image of the team huddle for our *conspire-and-align* approach? We're *conspiring* toward a shared purpose—a common mission and vision—and *aligning* by clarifying what we're after (goals) and how we'll get there as a team (values, strategy, and roles). We're the birds in formation flocking to our destination.

Having a shared purpose also helps us have each other's backs. Jessica, one of TMC's managing partners of our training team, once had a co-worker at a youth advocacy organization who literally stood in front of a bus for her. One time, Jessica was responsible for getting a group of teenagers to offer testimony at a legislative hearing. The plan was for the teens to meet at the office first so everyone could go together. Unfortunately, as anybody who works with youth knows, someone was bound to be late—and by the time they got to the bus stop, the bus had already arrived. With two youths straggling behind, Jessica's co-worker, understanding how important this meeting was, stood in front of the bus so that it wouldn't leave until everyone arrived. They made it to the meeting that day, and all of the teens shared their testimonies with the committee.

Now, we're not telling you to stand in front of a bus. We *are* saying that having shared purpose helps us take decisive action to get the results we need—and it also lets

---

[6] Referred to as "like me" bias, "similar-to-me" effect, or "affinity bias," this is a bias for people who look or think like us. See "The Similar-To-Me Effect," The Decision Lab (n.d.), https://thedecisionlab.com/reference-guide/psychology/the-similar-to-me-effect

[7] The Intercultural Development Continuum, a concept developed by Dr. Mitchell Hammer, rates intercultural competence on a 5-point scale, from a "monocultural mindset" that totally denies differences, to a fully adapted "intercultural mindset" that not only comprehends but also bridges across differences. Minimization, fittingly, is halfway between denial and adaptation.

us see where we can jump in and help our teammates. In addition to strengthening one-on-one relationships, aligning on a shared, collective purpose is critical to building a healthy team culture. (For more about collective purpose and healthy culture, see Chapter 11.)

Summing Up the Four Elements

Healthy working relationships have a balance of all four elements, which react to and reinforce each other. To cultivate authenticity, you must build trust and create space for difference, lest you end up with a homogenous team of people who look and sound just like you. To build trust, you must wield your power responsibly and demonstrate integrity (a close cousin to authenticity). And finally, alignment about shared purpose helps you harness the power of the other elements to do the work that brought you together in the first place.

RELATIONSHIP-BUILDING CHECKLIST FOR MANAGERS

Ask yourself these questions to reflect on your relationship-building:

Do you consistently. . .

- Build trust by. . .
  - Demonstrating care?
  - Being true to your word?
  - Demonstrating competence in your work?
- Create space for authenticity by. . .
  - Engaging with warmth and kindness?
  - Expressing interest in others?
  - Checking in about boundaries?
  - Inviting vulnerability without demanding it?
- Effectively navigate power and difference by. . .
  - Asking for and incorporating other perspectives?
  - Celebrating differences?
  - Owning and asserting your power thoughtfully?
  - Using your power and authority to *conspire and align*?
- Align on shared purpose by. . .
  - Reiterating your values and strategy?
  - Setting clear goals and role expectations?

MANAGING SKIP-LEVEL RELATIONSHIPS

If you're a manager at a multilayered organization, you should also build relationships with the people whom your staff people manage. Strong skip-level relationships have enormous benefits:

- Healthy relationships across lines of authority can promote equity and belonging.

- You're more likely to spot upcoming talent.

- Knowing their staff members can help you support your direct report in their management.

    Here are three tips for navigating skip-level relationships.

Go to Them

Your staff member's direct reports might not feel comfortable popping into your office or sending you an out-of-the-blue email. Be proactive about connecting. When you do, be clear about your intentions. You can get to know them by:

- Conducting regular skip-level meetings.[8]

- Having getting-to-know-you meals or meetings with staff (including new hires).

- Connecting informally during staff retreats or gatherings.

Don't Short-Circuit the Manager

In a skip-level check-in, invite the staff person's feedback about how they're being managed. When you do this, be careful not to undermine the person you manage by making on-the-spot decisions. Instead, steer people back to their manager unless it's a grave concern. For example:

- If the staff member comes to you for approval on a proposal for a new system, you might say, "I'm so glad you're thinking about this. Since this is Cam's realm, why don't you propose this to them and see what they think first?"

- If that staff member just wanted your input, share it and reiterate that it's ultimately Cam's decision. In this case, you're just acting as a resource.

- If that staff person proposed something that goes beyond their manager's realm, you could say, "This is an interesting idea. Why don't you talk it over with Cam

---

[8] Check-ins to connect personally, hear how they feel about their work, and get feedback about the organization or their manager.

first? If they decide to move forward with this, Cam and I would need to discuss further before taking action."

Handle Critical Feedback Thoughtfully

You might hear critical feedback about your direct report from their staff person. First, thank the person for their feedback, knowing that it takes courage to share critical feedback, especially across lines of difference or power. Focus on listening, and don't jump to problem-solving. From there, you have two options:

- Steer the person back to the manager to resolve the issue on their own. You can coach the staff member to give direct feedback (see Chapter 7) or manage up (see Chapter 10).

- If the issue requires your intervention, reflect and decide on next steps. Then communicate them to the staff person *before you take action.*

RESOLVING CONFLICT AND REPAIRING RELATIONSHIPS

Conflict can feel terrible. Like effective management, how we handle it is a skill few of us learned or saw modeled well. Plus, many of us come from communities with different approaches to conflict, which can sometimes create *more* conflict when those approaches don't align. As a result, most organizations don't have the practices or processes we need to move through conflict. But conflict, reconciliation, and repair are essential for healthy relationships and teams.

We believe that conflict doesn't always have to feel like a setback.[9] It can sometimes be the gateway that leads to "aha!" moments—breakthroughs that shift how we work with others, leading to better relationships and outcomes. As a manager, part of our job is to boldly pass through that gateway.

Here are some tips for navigating conflict:

- **Reflect before taking action.** What feelings or memories does the conflict bring up for you? What's in your *sphere of control?* What resources do you have to draw from to navigate it?

- **Name the tension.** If you feel like something's "off," don't push past it or ignore it. Sometimes, just calling it out is enough to release the tension and start a conversation to get back on track.

---

[9] Note that if there has been a pattern of disrespectful, discriminatory, or abusive behavior, it may simply not be reparable. This is another place where healthy boundaries are key. If someone has done irreparable harm to you, you are not obligated to pretend everything is fine after they apologize—and if you're the one who's harmed someone else, they are not obligated to forgive or forget.

- **Acknowledge your feelings.** It can seem like there's no room for feelings in professional environments. But people and relationships are *full* of feelings, and we can't have authenticity without emotional honesty. Plus, they affect how we show up, even (especially!) when we ignore them.

- **Look for an iceberg.** Sometimes conflict is just a simple disagreement. Other times, there's an iceberg underneath—a bigger issue that needs to be addressed. (We'll talk more about this in Chapter 7.)

- **Be accountable for your part.** How did you contribute to the conflict? Is there anything you need to apologize for?

- **Take meaningful action.** Action can look like a heartfelt apology, changing your behavior, or finding a way to repair the harm caused. Here are examples:

  - *Apologize*: "I'm sorry that my tone was harsh. I was frustrated, and I took it out on you."

  - *Change your behavior*: "I know when I show up unprepared for our check-ins, we don't have as much time to cover the most important things. From now on, I'll block off 30 minutes before each check-in to prepare."

  - *Repair*: "Is there something I can do to set things right between us?" (It's good to aim for repair, but remember that sometimes the process of mending feelings and rebuilding takes time. Go back to our advice on cultivating trust!)

- **Do a stepback.** Sometimes, conflict builds up so much it's not just about working through a single incident. Something about your entire dynamic has shifted (or maybe wasn't quite right to begin with). In these cases, try a stepback, where you take stock of your relationship and air grievances. Ideally, you'll leave the conversation with an agreement about how to move forward. If you do this, it might help to get a mediator or facilitator.

NAMING THE TENSION

When Jasmine started managing a former peer, it was rocky. She couldn't put her finger on it at first; their relationship had been great before, but the added layer of positional power shifted the dynamic. In addition, they were two women of color in a predominantly white organization, and it often felt like they were being compared to each other.

During one of their check-ins, Jasmine said, "Hey, sometimes it feels like we're competing, and I know it's not because either of us wants that. What do you need from me to feel supported?" Naming the tension she sensed was a turning point for their relationship—like breaking a spell. They still sometimes experienced conflict after that point, but they were able to name it more quickly. They saw themselves as partners supporting each other and getting the work done.

PERSPECTIVE-TAKING

A natural part of the human condition is that we are the main characters in our own lives. It's easy to get sucked into our stories, forgetting that other people are the main characters in their lives, too—not just side characters in ours.

Perspective-taking is the practice of putting yourself in someone else's shoes.[10] While you can never completely understand someone else's experience, trying to see their perspective can be a powerful step toward reducing bias, resolving conflict, and building empathy. These are the keys to building healthy relationships and working effectively with others across lines of difference.

We find that perspective-taking can be most useful in conflict or when you feel frustrated. Here are things to reflect on:

- **The other person's strengths.** To understand someone, we need to appreciate their strengths (yes, even when they're getting on our nerves). Ask yourself: What are some things they excel at? What do I appreciate about them?

- **The pressures or challenges they face.** What gets in the way of their success? These can range from macro-level challenges like systemic oppression to smaller-scale or temporary obstacles, like having a project partner who's been out sick. Pressures can include feelings of responsibility and accountability. Ask yourself what the other person might be worried about or which stakeholders they feel most concerned about.

- **The *impacts* of these pressures.** Don't presume to know the full story, but try imagining how the pressures might play out for them. Do your staff person's feelings of accountability to community members manifest as anxiety about letting people down? Is your colleague more likely to forget details when they feel overwhelmed? Do you have a teammate who frequently has to rearrange their schedule because of caregiving responsibilities?

- **Your sphere of control and possible next steps.** How you approach this depends on the relationship. As a manager reflecting on a direct report, you might provide support or coaching. If you're in a tricky situation with a manager or colleague, consider strategies for managing up and sideways (see Chapter 10).

To be clear, perspective-taking is *not* a way to talk yourself out of your feelings or perceptions. You don't have to forgive someone if they've harmed you. It also doesn't let you off the hook from sharing feedback or holding someone accountable if their

---

[10] Perspective-taking is a skill typically learned in childhood, but it still needs to be encouraged—and it can be developed and cultivated at any age. It "goes far beyond empathy: it involves seeing things as others would see them: their likes, dislikes, feelings and thoughts." From Mind in the Making: https://www.mindinthemaking.org/perspective-taking

behavior negatively impacts you. Perspective-taking *can* help soften your frustration and help you deliver feedback effectively.

The Ladder of Assumptions

We must acknowledge and release our assumptions, biases, and beliefs to do perspective-taking well. You don't have to let them go forever, but check your biases and short-circuit the automatic process of climbing the "Ladder of Assumptions"[11]— the often-unconscious process by which we draw (or jump to) conclusions. Many interpersonal conflicts, microaggressions, and inequities stem from jumping to incorrect or unfair conclusions about others.

The Ladder of Assumptions has seven steps:

1. We **observe,** experience, or learn something.

2. We **filter** out whatever data we think is irrelevant based on our prior beliefs and experiences.

3. We **make meaning** from our filtered observations based on personal and cultural norms and values.

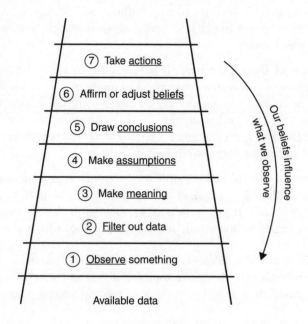

---

[11] Or the "ladder of inference," a term coined by organizational psychologist Chris Argyris and later popularized by Peter Senge in his book *The Fifth Discipline* (Doubleday, 2006).

4. We make **assumptions** based on those meanings.

5. We draw **conclusions** and/or react emotionally based on our interpretations and assumptions.

6. We affirm or adjust our existing **beliefs** based on these conclusions.

7. We take **action** based on our beliefs. These actions create new circumstances (and observing or experiencing those circumstances can start the whole process over again).

With practice, we can cultivate more awareness of each rung of the ladder and pause before climbing to the next level.

SELF-REFLECTION QUESTIONS

Ask yourself:

- What beliefs am I holding onto? Where do they come from?
- What data did I filter out because of these beliefs, and why?
- What assumptions can I set aside for now? What meaning did I make that I can reconsider?

KEY POINTS OF RELATIONSHIP-BUILDING AND CHECK-INS

Here are the takeaways from the chapter:

- Effective management is built on strong relationships, which help us *conspire and align.*

- Check-ins are the soil in which a *conspire-and-align* management relationship takes root, grows, and thrives. They provide a regular space to get to know each other, get aligned, troubleshoot problems, and share feedback.

- There are four main elements to building strong relationships:

    - Cultivating **trust**, which involves demonstrating care, integrity, and competence;

    - Practicing **authenticity**, which involves letting yourself be genuine and vulnerable—within healthy boundaries!

    - Navigating **power and difference**, which involves being honest and mindful about differences in power and identity. It also involves wielding your power responsibly by neither clinging to power too tightly nor hiding from it.

- Aligning on a **shared purpose**, which involves working toward something meaningful together.

- Cultivating skip-level relationships with the people your direct reports manage has many benefits, including new insights for you and a greater sense of belonging for them.

- Learning to resolve and recover from conflict is essential to healthy relationships. Some principles and tips for navigating conflict or repairing relationships include:

  - Be honest about your feelings and the tensions you perceive.

  - Be accountable for your part in a conflict, and apologize or change your behavior if warranted.

  - Use perspective-taking to build empathy for the other person.

  - Check your biases and avoid jumping to conclusions (or climbing the "Ladder of Assumptions") about another person's motivations or character.

APPENDIX TOOLS

TOOL 2.1

CHECK-IN MEETING AGENDA SAMPLE

Quarterly Priorities	Annual Goals	Backburner
• Send survey to coalition members • Lead 15 tenants' rights webinars • Hire housing rights coordinator by Q3	• Recruit 3 local organizations that work with communities not currently represented in our coalition. • Train at least 2,500 people (of which 40% identify as BIPOC) through our leadership development programs.	• Volunteer leadership team retreat planning (postponed until Q3) • Revamp train the trainer curriculum • Online advocacy center overhaul

Personal check-in

- Highs: We got a puppy!
- Lows: I'm moving and it's stressful.

This week will be successful if. . .

- All materials for training finalized by Thursday night.
- Conference presentation on track to be done by end of next week.
- Newsletter draft complete.

Key updates / FYI

- Training: outline completed, materials for training about to be finalized.
- Housing: new member orientation completed and members have been plugged into working groups.
- Outreach: newsletter and social media on schedule.

Feedback & Learning

	One success	One area for improvement
Staff member self-reflection	I set up a volunteer call to go over our resources and answer questions. Since then, the volunteers seem more confident and connected.	Our volunteer show-up rates have been below average. I'll have to do at least one round of confirmation calls before each action.
Staff member feedback for manager	I appreciated the pep talk you gave me last week. You knew I was stressed, and you reminded me that I know what I'm doing.	Can you share more of your bigger picture thinking and planning for the rest of the year? I know what I'm responsible for, but it feels disconnected from our team priorities.
Manager self-reflection	I was able to support you this week when you were anxious about the training.	I haven't done the best at communicating some broader organizational shifts. I'll incorporate more updates into our check-ins.
Manager feedback for staff member	Coalition meetings have been efficient. Great job setting a clear purpose and agenda for each meeting! Even our newest members have been contributing.	I've noticed that you tend to spend more time with volunteers you already know. Now that our team is growing, it's important to make sure that everyone has a similar experience of belonging.

Items for discussion
- Program associate opening — Can we brainstorm candidates/sources? I've already posted on the usual lists, but could use help thinking of ways to build the pool.
- Coalition—getting pushback from AWM; let's talk this through.
- Conference talk debrief.

Manager's list:
- Mid-year evaluations.
- Partnering with XYZ organization—what do you think?
- Questions about the leadership team's announcement at last staff meeting?

Next steps
- Set up connector calls with Carlos and Madison.
- Schedule mid-year evaluation conversation.

CHAPTER

3

DELEGATING EFFECTIVELY

In Chapter 1, we talked about management as a practice. Delegation, or assigning work to others, is a building block of that practice—one of those fundamental skills we repeatedly use, like the two-step in dance. Delegation is the primary way we get things done with and through others.

While we often talk about delegation in managerial relationships, delegation happens in all directions. Everybody delegates: managers to staff, staff to volunteers, project managers to team members, peers to peers, and executive directors to board members.

When we delegate effectively, we strengthen relationships, results, and equity. But *effective* delegation is much more than giving someone a to-do list. It requires *conspiring and aligning* on what success will look like and how to achieve it.

For instance, do either of these scenarios sound familiar to you?

- You ask a staff person to plan a stakeholder meeting. They've never planned an event like this before, so you get nervous when they present you with an incomplete project plan. Unsure they'll pull it off, you decide to "help." You give them a venue contact, tell them what to order from the caterer, and send a guest list. You write to-do lists and send weekly reminder emails to complete the tasks. The staff person, who started off feeling excited about the assignment, is now frustrated that they're just implementing your ideas and constantly being checked on. "It feels like you don't trust me to handle this," they say.

- You ask a staff person to drive a new video project. You're not 100% sure what success looks like, but they have previously taken on new projects without a hitch.

You're behind on your work, so you don't check in until they complete the project a month later. The final product was executed well, but it's completely different from what you'd imagined. You're afraid it won't go over well if you share it more broadly with your membership, so, unfortunately, you have to start over.

These scenarios represent two extremes we sometimes see managers defaulting to: micromanaging and barely managing. On one extreme, you're too closely involved, undermining your team member; on the other, you've neglected them entirely.

In this chapter, we talk through what you need to find the right balance that keeps you meaningfully involved in, but not *doing,* your team member's work.

PRINCIPLES OF EFFECTIVE DELEGATION

Our three principles of effective delegation are:

- Guide more, do less.

- Notice choice points.

- Use comparative advantage.

Guide More, Do Less

Delegation should *transfer the weight* of the work from you to the other person. As a manager, you're like a coach and spotter for a weightlifter. You're not lifting the weight yourself—you're providing support so your team member can do it successfully. When you do it well, your team member can build their muscles—the skills and experience that help them do the job more easily.

On the flip side, if the spotter tries to lift all the weight themselves, the weightlifter doesn't get a good workout. Plus, it's not sustainable for the spotter to lift everyone else's weights all day!

Let's be honest—sometimes, we avoid delegation because we don't want to burden others. Other times it's because we don't trust them to handle the task. And sometimes, we don't delegate because it would be easier or faster if we did it ourselves. But here's what happens when we never transfer the work:

- We don't get to work on the things we are uniquely positioned to do.

- Our teammate never gets to rise to their full responsibility, power, and potential.

- We don't fulfill our duty as managers to get the results we need to achieve our mission.

Effective delegation also gives people ownership over their work. It's an investment of time, energy, and trust—trusting them to meet the challenge and giving them the support they need to be successful. And like any investment, it has compounding effects over time. (We'll talk more about investing in people in Chapter 8.)

Notice Choice Points

Transferring responsibility involves sharing power. This can mean giving the other person decision-making authority, co-creating a vision of success, and ensuring they get credit for the work.

It also involves *choice points*. Ask yourself: Who do you trust with big, high-stakes projects? Who do you assign an exciting or challenging task to when you could do it yourself in less time? Who do you trust to make decisions? And who might you *pass over* for those opportunities or avoid delegating certain tasks to?

Use Comparative Advantage

Comparative advantage in management boils down to this: do what only *you* can do (most of the time). Our time and energy are limited resources, and we must spend them wisely.

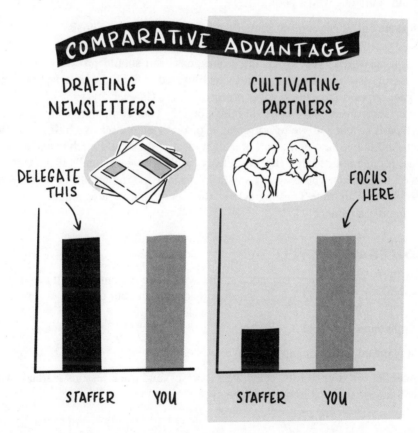

Here's an example: As an organizer, Bex was *excellent* at making flipcharts. They could crank out a beautifully illustrated flipchart for a training in under 30 minutes—something that took others twice as long. But even though they were great at it (and enjoyed doing it!), when they started leading a team, they had to stop making flipcharts. Those 30 minutes were better spent working on things they were uniquely positioned to do, like strategy and management.

Comparative advantage isn't about everyone *only* doing what they're best at. It's about playing to each person's strengths and position in a way that will make the biggest collective impact. Applied correctly, it helps you be strategic about what to prioritize and what to delegate.

To identify your comparative advantage, think about everything on your plate and consider whether the following criteria apply:

- **Role:** Does it fit your role expectations and position in the organization?

- **Strengths:** Are you excellent—not just good—at the thing? (Alternatively, are you the only one who's good at it?)

- **Impact:** Will it get you substantially closer to meeting your goals?

If you answered "yes" to all three questions, you should probably do the task yourself. But, if you have too many responsibilities that fit all the criteria, you'll have to delegate or prioritize. (We'll cover prioritization in Chapter 5.)

Note: Sometimes, you *should* do things outside your comparative advantage. We all have parts of our job we're not great at or don't enjoy, but we have to do them anyway. And sometimes, being part of a team means you should pitch in and help. For example, Monna noticed that Bex was always willing to get on calls if the team was behind on their goals. There wasn't any task Bex was too important for. But Bex still spent most of their time working within their comparative advantage—remember, management is a balance!

THE DELEGATION CYCLE

Effective delegation is a *process*, not a single action. We recommend a three-step process for delegation, each of which you should adapt to fit your context.

1. Align on expectations.
2. Stay meaningfully engaged.
3. Account for your results, celebrate successes, and track lessons learned (which will inform the next iteration of the cycle).

Picture this: Brandon is the senior program manager at a leadership development nonprofit. He manages Katherine, a program coordinator. Every year, one of Brandon's priorities is to oversee an annual national conference for organizers.

Brandon has a lot on his plate with high-level planning and programming decisions. So he delegates conference logistics, communication, materials, and onsite conference troubleshooting to Katherine. In the next few sections, we discuss the delegation cycle using their experience planning this conference.

See Tool 3.1 at the end of the chapter for a filled-out "Delegation Worksheet," a tool you can use to reflect on and plan out the steps of delegation.

Step 1: Align on Expectations

For the first step, we use an English class throwback: the five Ws—who, what, when, where, and why—and a bit of H (how). In journalism, the five Ws give readers the information they need to follow a compelling story. In management, the five Ws provide someone the information they need to successfully complete an assignment.

THE FIVE WS (AND AN H)

Before you delegate a task, be prepared to discuss the following:

Who should be involved?

What does success look like?

When is the project due?

Where might they go for resources?

Why does this work matter? Why them? Why now?

And a little bit of. . .**How** to approach the work.

As you go through the first step, *make the implicit explicit* and *seek perspective*. It could be as simple as going through each of the five Ws and saying, "Here's what I'm thinking. What do you think?"

You might also consider asking questions like these:

- Have you done something like this before? What worked? What didn't?

- What are you excited about? Anything you're nervous about?

- Is there anything else you want to discuss?

What *Does Success Look Like?*
Picture what it'll be like when the project is over. What will you have accomplished? How will you be closer to achieving your goals? Share your idea of success, ask for the other person's thoughts, and agree on what success will look like.

Many managers avoid sharing too much information because they worry about micromanaging. But sometimes, this has the opposite effect—staff wishing you were *more* involved because the lack of clarity leads to frustration and wasted efforts. And sometimes, we micromanage *because* we weren't clear enough about the "what" in the first place.

When you define the "what," consider the quantitative ("Raise $5,000") and qualitative ("Community members feel like their input was heard and valued") measures for success. Be explicit about what you care most about—to figure out what this might be, ask yourself, "What am I worried might get done incorrectly?"

Language is subjective, so define terms. For example, let's say you're asking a staff member to write a rough draft of an email blast. Which of the following two options sounds like a "rough draft" to you?

- The content is presented in complete sentences with placeholders where further discussion is needed; the draft contains only a few typos.

- It's an outline with a brain dump of the main ideas so you can check to see that you're on the same page before investing more time. Errors will be edited out later.

Both options qualify as a "rough draft," right? But what if you expected option A, but your staff person turned in B? Would you judge their writing to be sloppy and unprofessional? Or, what if you expected B, but they thought you meant A, so they prioritized it over projects that were actually more important?

Now imagine that you gave this direction to two people. One is a junior team member with less educational experience; the other has been on staff for years and graduated from the same training program as you. Who was more likely to guess what you had in mind? Who would you be more likely to assume the best about if they had guessed wrong?

This is why delegation must start with a *conversation*, not a dictation. In the rough draft scenario, you could get to alignment by saying, "To me, a rough draft is a thorough outline with all of the main ideas. We'll review it and make sure we're on the same page before you invest more time in it. What do you think?"

When Brandon prepared to delegate conference logistics and materials to Katherine, he wrote down his ideas about what success would look like before their conversation. He considered *choice points* in logistics—like accessibility, dietary needs, and language access—and included them in his definition of success. His ideas included:

- "Participants have no issues with logistics, so they can focus on learning."

- "All attendees' dietary restrictions are met."

GOLD STAR VS. GOOD ENOUGH

When defining success, align on the *degree* of excellence needed. Specify what "gold star" (their strongest work with all the bells and whistles) and "good enough" (solid work that hits the must-haves) would look like. Then, decide what to aim for.

For example, with the email draft, option A could have been the "gold star" version of the assignment, and option B could have been the "good enough" version. You could tell the staff person, "To me, a 'good enough' rough draft is just a thorough outline."

To be clear, this isn't about passing off low-quality work as "good enough." It's about strategically using your time and energy, holding yourself and others to a realistic standard, and aligning with your staff by *making the implicit explicit*. Remember that those most likely to stretch themselves to deliver a gold star product are newer, more junior, and/or more marginalized staff. So, you can promote equity by being explicit when good enough is *actually* good enough.

- "All conference venues are wheelchair accessible."

- "We provide ASL and Spanish language interpretation for participants who request it."

Why *This, Why You, and Why Now?*

When we understand why something matters, we're more motivated to do it. Under a *conspire-and-align* approach, motivation and buy-in from your team are crucial. Understanding the *why* helps you both feel like you're working toward something together, not just handing off work so they can execute your to-dos. You should be able to answer the following questions when you assign work:

- **Why does this matter?** How does this work connect to your broader mission or goals?

- **Why you?** Why does it make sense for *this* person to be responsible for the work? How does it fit within their comparative advantage?

- **Why now?** Why does the work need to happen now?

Brandon gave Katherine two reasons why solid logistics and clear communication with participants were crucial:

- The participants' first impression of the conference would be via Katherine's communication. She'd set the tone for their experience.

- Many organizers covered their own conference costs. This learning experience needed to be worth their time and money. Smooth logistics would enable participants to focus on learning—not handling hotel mix-ups or finding food they could eat.

When *Is It Due?*

Share the deadline and check if they can realistically meet it. The "when" can present tensions for effective management. On the one hand, you're after great results, which are often time-sensitive. On the other hand, you care about sustainability, which means not pushing people beyond their capacity, driving toward unreasonable deadlines, and getting swept up in urgency.

To balance these tensions, remember these three things:

- Be **honest** about what success really looks like and why.

- Be **explicit** about where there's flexibility and where there isn't.

- Be **supportive** with troubleshooting and reprioritizing. (See Chapter 5 for more on reprioritization.)

If you have a firm deadline, explain why. Don't soft-pedal the importance of it. Instead of: "Hey, it'd be great if you could send me that agenda by Friday," try "I need to send all of the materials for the advisory board meeting by 5 p.m. on Friday, so I need the agenda by 3 p.m.. Is this doable?" If the answer isn't a clear "yes," follow up by restating why it's important and asking questions to help troubleshoot. You could say, "This is a top priority. What would it take to make this deadline work? How can I support you?"

Sometimes you don't have firm external deadlines, but must create benchmarks to keep the work moving. Be clear about how flexible deadlines are, but set guardrails. For example, you could say, "We don't have a firm deadline. But if we don't complete the project by June, it might create a crunch during our summer recruitment drive. How about we set a deadline of end of May and check in on whether that still feels realistic in early March?"

Brandon and Katherine had six months to plan the conference. They scheduled deadlines and debriefs for each work stream (applications, hotel logistics, and conference materials).

Having trouble figuring out what the real deadline is? Ask yourself: At what point would I be upset if this still wasn't done?

Where *Can You Go for Resources?*

Resources include the following:

- People you can turn to for help or input.

- Templates or samples from other projects.

- Articles, videos, or other places to get more information.

- Your budget.

The conference was 15 years old, and Brandon had run it for a decade, so he had many resources to share with Katherine. He didn't want to send Katherine off to re-learn lessons that others had already learned through trial and error. Brandon gave her the previous year's templates, debrief notes about what had worked, and old checklists of tasks. He told her about history and constraints relevant to her tasks and facilitated introductions to vendors.

Who *Should Be Involved?*

Have you ever been to a kids' soccer game? If so, you've probably seen a dozen 7-year-olds descending on a soccer ball at once. It's adorable, but that strategy doesn't score goals. Like those kids, your team needs clear roles to avoid stepping on each other's toes. We use MOCHA.

MOCHA

MOCHA stands for:

Manager: The Manager assigns responsibility to the Owner, supports them to be accountable, and serves as a resource. They're the spotter who intervenes if things are off-track, but they don't do the work directly. This person may or may not be the Owner's supervisor. They may also be an Approver.

Owner: The Owner is responsible for the project's success or failure. They ensure all the work gets done, drive the project forward, and coordinate steps to complete it. They may do the work directly or by delegating to Helpers, and they may consult others along the way. *There should only be one Owner.*

Consulted: Consulted people don't do the work directly but provide input and perspective. Often, Consulteds are key stakeholders, either because they have expertise to offer or will be directly impacted by the project. They may share resources, referrals, or input. They should be kept in the loop and updated as the work progresses.

Helper: Helpers do part of the work by taking on specific tasks assigned by the Owner. For complex projects, Helpers may also own workstreams or mini-projects with their own MOCHA (we call this a cascading MOCHA).

Approver: The Approver signs off on the final product or key decisions in the process. They may also be the Owner, Manager, or a separate person or group with a decision-making role on the project, such as the executive director, principal, or a committee. Sometimes, there are multiple Approvers on a project. Be explicit and avoid having hidden approvers.

Here are a few important reasons to MOCHA:

- MOCHA can help establish *role clarity*, especially when multiple Helpers are responsible for significant work streams. MOCHA is especially helpful for more complex projects, like running a conference in Brandon and Katherine's case.

- It helps build *meaningful inclusion and collaboration* by specifying who is responsible for what, whose input is needed, and who has final approval. When creating a MOCHA, get consent from the people involved and give credit where it's due.

- It can promote *equity* by reducing hidden labor, responsibility, and authority. It makes each person's contributions visible—like the credits reel at the end of a film.

Usually, when you delegate a project to a team member, they're the Owner, and you're the Manager. Sometimes, the Owner will be responsible for work where they won't have complete decision-making authority. This is normal, but always *make the implicit explicit*. During your delegation conversation, share what decisions the Owner will make, who they'll need to consult, and what decisions need to be approved by someone else. And if you find yourself with a MOCHA where the Owner doesn't have *any* decision-making power, reconsider—remember that transferring responsibility also means sharing power.

In the Brandon and Katherine scenario, they had a top-level MOCHA for the conference. Here's what it looked like:

Table 3.1 Sample Conference MOCHA.

Manager	Owner	Consulteds	Helpers	Approvers
Executive Director	Brandon (Senior Program Manager)	Finance Director—Budget	Katherine (Program Coordinator)—Logistics and communication	Executive Director

In this MOCHA, Brandon was the Owner, and Katherine was a Helper. Brandon was responsible for running a successful conference that maintained the organization's strong relationships with its movement partners.

In the cascading MOCHA that covered logistics, Katherine was the Owner. On her MOCHA, Katherine had a Helper who created name tags, assembled binders, and ensured the food arrived on time. Brandon was the Manager and Approver on most of Katherine's logistical work—with a few exceptions, like signing the venue contract. When they went over the MOCHA, Brandon and Katherine aligned on what decisions Katherine was responsible for (like conference meals and participant room assignments) and what Brandon would decide (like the conference venue).

(A Little Bit of the) How

If you want to avoid being a micromanager, don't delve into every detail about how to do the work. Instead, share and discuss:

- The **overall approach and values** they should bring to the work. For example, you could say, "I want to bring a value of inclusion to this project—we want our stakeholders to feel meaningfully engaged."

Table 3.2 Sample Cascading MOCHA.

Manager	Owner	Consulteds	Helpers	Approvers
Brandon	Katherine	Finance director—Budget	Intern—Binders, name tags, food	Katherine—Logistics Executive Director—Venue contract, hotel rate

- Existing **processes, systems, or tools** they should use or refer to. For example, you might encourage them to use fair process to engage stakeholders (see the "Using Fair Process for Inclusive Decision-Making" section in Chapter 5). You can also refer them to a teammate who worked on a similar project.

- Anything **critical** to the "how," such as accounting standards, legal requirements, or grant deliverables.

- Important **lessons learned**. Some lessons aren't worth learning twice—if you have insights from previous experiences, share them.

Figuring out how much of the "how" to share is part of the balancing act of management—give enough to be clear and helpful, but not so much that you dictate their every move.

To balance this, go back to *PTR* in the "Preferences, Traditions, and Requirements" section in Chapter 1. Drill down on the requirements, name your preferences

DON'T TAKE BACK THE WORK!

The "delegation boomerang" is a common challenge. It happens because we like being helpful, hate seeing people struggle, or feel we could do it better ourselves. Sometimes, if the project is in serious trouble and you can't afford to fail, you *do* need to take the work back. But, in most cases, the delegation boomerang can undermine your team member and your long-term results.

Here are some tips for turning the boomerang into a Frisbee®:

- **If helping out feels good:** Rethink what it means to "help." As a manager, helping means guiding more and doing less.

- **If you hate seeing people struggle:** Recognize that they might be in the learning zone, where a bit of struggle is part of the process. If you take over, they won't learn.

- **If you love solving problems:** Recognize that you don't have to stop problem-solving—you have to stop being the first person to come up with solutions. Put your staff in the driver's seat—ask them to come up with possible solutions (you can share your thoughts after).

- **If you don't think you have time to let somebody learn as they go:** It may be faster in the short term to do the work yourself, but in the long term, your staff's ability to do the work frees you up to do yours. (Remember comparative advantage!)

Note: If you regularly hesitate to delegate to someone who *should* be able to do the work, you might have a performance problem, not a delegation problem. (If that's the case, turn to Chapter 9 on addressing performance problems.)

and traditions, and state where there's room to depart from them. Hidden preferences and traditions can become expectations that prevent us from finding new (and potentially better) ways to meet the requirements, which can hinder results, equity, and inclusion.

In Brandon and Katherine's case, Brandon did give Katherine resources from previous years—but he also had to check his urge to tell Katherine exactly how he'd done it in the past. After all, he had a decade of experience (and built-up preferences and traditions) in planning this conference. For example, Katherine was responsible for conference recruitment, including tracking applications. The organization had historically used a specific survey platform to collect conference applications. But Katherine found a different one with an auto-translate feature, making the form more accessible for Spanish speakers. Brandon agreed to try it out because he knew it better met the requirement of having a user-friendly application process.

Use Repeat-Backs to Check Alignment

To round out the first step of the delegation cycle, lean on a best practice from the food service industry: the repeat-back. At a restaurant, the repeat-back saves you from the disappointment of getting a side salad when what you wanted was garlic fries. In management, the repeat-back confirms your alignment on the five Ws.

Try putting it this way: "To make sure we're on the same page, can you do a repeat-back of what we just agreed on?" If it helps to have it in writing, you could ask, "Will you jot down what we just aligned on in our check-in document?" (If you feel awkward about asking for a repeat-back, tell them that TMC made you do it!)

WHAT HAPPENS IF YOU DON'T KNOW WHAT YOU'RE DELEGATING?

Delegating starts with being clear about success, but if you're not exactly sure what that looks like, be honest. Then, try this:

- **Do a brain dump.** You might say, "I know it needs to achieve X, and we have to be careful about how we handle Y," or "I picture so-and-so reading it and thinking, 'Wow, this is powerful.'" If you have inspiration to draw from, share it.

- **Brainstorm together.** Even if you can't identify exactly what you need, your staff member might be able to. Or, it could emerge through your discussion.

- **Seek and share resources.** If someone in your organization has done a similar project, connect your staff person to them.

- **Delegate the final figuring-out.** Ask your staff member to think about everything you've discussed and come back to you with a proposal.

Step 2: Stay Engaged

Delegating and disappearing is one of the easiest ways to lose trust and set yourself up for failure. Step 2 of the delegation cycle helps maintain momentum while building your relationship. It's also your chance to get things on track if you didn't align well on the front end.

The "staying engaged" part happens in a few ways: during team meetings, in check-ins (see Chapter 2), through written reports, and through "slices."

Ask Probing Questions

Ask probing questions to dig deeper and understand how the work is progressing. In their weekly check-ins, Brandon asked Katherine questions like these:

- What's something that's going really well?

- What would you like my support or perspective on?

- What challenges have you encountered? What are you worried about?

For more probing questions, see Tool 3.2 at the end of this chapter.

Review "Slices"

Slices are small samples of the work in progress. In the first year of planning the conference together, Katherine's slices included drafts of emails she prepared to send to participants. These slices helped Brandon and Katherine stay aligned about what information they needed to communicate to attendees. It also let Brandon see they were on track to meet their deadlines. For big projects, slices break down the work into more manageable chunks and help sustain momentum.

Take slices early. These help you surface the following:

- Points of misalignment.

- Questions you missed answering in Step 1 of the delegation cycle.

- Preferences and traditions you weren't aware of when you delegated.

As much as you can, try to build slices into your plan from the beginning, so that you can both expect them. (When managers frequently request slices out of nowhere, it can feel like a pop quiz, signaling a lack of trust.)

Use "I Do, We Do, You Do"

"I do, we do, you do" is a teaching strategy that gradually moves the responsibility from one person to another. Here's how it works:

- **I do:** Model the skill and have the person observe you. Then, debrief it. The first time Brandon and Katherine met with the conference caterer, Brandon led the meeting. In their debrief, he asked Katherine what she had noticed. He also shared the rationale behind his questions and decisions in the meeting.

- **We do:** Have the other person do the task with you and then debrief. Before the next meeting with the caterer, Katherine and Brandon aligned on what to cover. Katherine took the lead in the meeting itself, with Brandon chiming in occasionally. When they debriefed, Brandon shared feedback—including things he thought Katherine did well and suggestions for next time.

- **You do:** Have them do it on their own and then—you guessed it—debrief! Katherine led the third meeting independently and shared her reflections with Brandon at their next check-in.

See the Work in Action

Find opportunities to observe your team member in action (also known as "shadowing"). Seeing someone's work firsthand is more illuminating than hearing a report. Shadowing allows you to see—and appreciate—how your teammate makes decisions, what obstacles they encounter, and how they behave in real-time.

Shadowing can also help you gather more information or diagnose problems if you're worried that something's off-track. For instance, let's say your staff person is working on publishing a considerable backlog of articles to your website. It's taking them twice as long as you expected, so you ask to shadow them to understand their process. When you do, you notice that they're also proofreading the articles before publishing—which is another person's responsibility! You realize that you didn't clarify this in Step 1, so you inform them that they don't need to proofread. The staff person can now save enough time on the remaining articles to finish by the expected deadline.

Remember that you want shadowing to feel like observation, not surveillance or scrutiny. Do what you can to put your staff person at ease when you shadow them. Get consent and be explicit about your intentions.

Step 3: Create Accountability and Learning

When you're done with a project, don't just move on to the next thing! The third step of the delegation cycle is about looking honestly at the results (compared to expectations) and the overall process. Whether it was a success or failure (or something in between), this step is where you each take ownership of your parts, share feedback, and document lessons learned. Then, if the results were good, celebrate!

Set aside time to debrief. One reason managers don't debrief with their team is that as soon as the project has wrapped, they want to go on to the next thing. Put a debrief on the calendar *before* the work is finished so you don't skip this step.

Here are some suggestions for what to cover in a debrief conversation:

- Compare results to expectations. Ask questions like:
  - What were our expectations? How well did we meet them?
  - How did our results contribute to our overall goals?

- Celebrate wins and unpack their best decisions. Ask questions like:

  - What were the biggest factors that contributed to the results?

  - What went well? What should we celebrate?

  - What would it take to replicate or build on that success next time?

  - What was the best decision you made? What can we learn from it?

- Capture lessons learned and think about what you would do differently next time (focusing on progress and growth, not perfection). Ask questions like:

  - What didn't go well? What needs to improve next time?

  - What would it take to prevent or mitigate the obstacles we ran into?

  - What else have we learned?

  - How well did the MOCHA work? Did everyone have the right role and responsibilities?

- Seek and share feedback on the process and each person's involvement.

  - What feedback do you have for me about how I managed you?

  - What did you learn about your skills through this project? How did you grow? What do you want to build on or develop?

Brandon and Katherine did a full debrief with their key stakeholders at the end of the conference. Each person went through the participant survey results and shared their impressions of the program. Along the way, Brandon and Katherine also debriefed the different stages of the work during their check-ins. For example, after the recruitment stage, they spent 15 minutes in a check-in sharing appreciations and noting lessons learned for the next recruitment cycle. In the first year, Brandon also took Katherine out to lunch to celebrate a successful first conference.

Adapt to Fit the Context

Because we're working with humans and not robots, and in the real world and not a lab, we must adapt to fit the context. In management, "context" includes the following:

- **The staff person's skill, will, and capacity regarding the task.** How motivated are they to do it? What's their capacity in terms of time and energy?

- **Our capacity.** How much time, energy, and willingness do you have to support them?

- **The importance and complexity of the work.** How high-stakes is it? How does it stack up against your organizational or departmental priorities? How many stakeholders does it involve? How much of the work is new or unpredictable? How high-quality does the final product need to be?

- **External circumstances.** What else is happening within the organization or in the world that might affect your staff's ability to complete the project successfully? What support might they need from you?

These factors can help you figure out how "in the mix" or "out of the mix" of the project you should be, helping you maintain the balance between micromanaging and undermanaging. The more complex and/or high-stakes a project, the more involved you should be. (See Figure 3.1.)

Brandon was very "in the mix" with Katherine in their first year. In particular, he took more slices and double-checked any work involving many moving pieces because Katherine wasn't as detail-oriented as the previous coordinator. But when it came to working with vendors and caterers, Brandon was less involved—Katherine was an excellent relationship builder.

Their context also changed as Katherine gained more experience. During her first year, Brandon offered more help with troubleshooting—every emergency had to be solved together. For example, Katherine might have texted Brandon: "SOS! Someone's flight got canceled, and they're stuck in Oakland!" In the second year, Katherine would have come to him and said: "Someone's stuck in Oakland, and here's what I'm going to do about it."

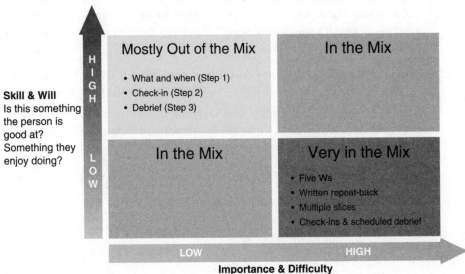

FIGURE 3.1 *Context Chart: How involved should you be in this project?*

Nothing about management is "one-size-fits-all." This overarching principle of the delegation process helps us take the fundamentals—like the five Ws and MOCHA—to the next level.

KEY POINTS OF DELEGATING

Here are the takeaways from the chapter:

- Delegation is assigning work to others. It helps us *conspire and align* on what success looks like and how to achieve it.

- Guide more and do less. When you delegate work to someone else, you're like a coach and spotter for a weightlifter.

- What, how, and to whom you delegate involves several *choice points*. Delegating equitably can build relationships and leadership, leading to better results.

- Use *comparative advantage* to do what only you are positioned to do (most of the time).

- Effective delegation is a process, not a single action. Use the three-step **delegation cycle** to stay aligned and engaged with your team member, making sure to adapt to fit your context along the way:

  - **Step 1: Align on expectations** by defining the **five Ws** and an **H** of the work (who, what, when, where, why, and a little bit of the how). Remember to *make the implicit explicit* and *seek perspective* from the person you're delegating to.

  - **Step 2: Stay engaged** by asking probing questions, reviewing slices of the work, and looking for opportunities to observe your staff member in action.

  - **Step 3: Create accountability and learning** by debriefing after the task or project is complete to assess how things went, learn from the experience, and apply those lessons to the next project.

APPENDIX TOOLS

TOOL 3.1

DELEGATION WORKSHEET

A preparation tool for project leaders and managers to set people up for success

I am assigning Mattie the responsibility of the reproductive justice video project.

Step 1: Getting Clear on Your Expectations (the five Ws and how)
We sometimes call this part the five Ws (what, why, where, when, who). Always discuss your thinking with your staff member or team, seek perspective, and check your PTRs before you delegate.
Begin at the end: **What** outcomes are you looking for? What would success look like? How will you make the implicit explicit?   • Produce 5 short (under 5 min) videos that respond to our most frequently asked questions about the issue.   • Engage team members in a way that feels meaningful to them (bonus if they have fun!).   • Learn about the process of creating content in this way.   • We're not looking for super high-quality production for this test, but it can't have any obvious errors (to the viewer) and the look and feel should be consistent across all videos.
Why is this task important? Why X [name of staff person]? Why this? Why now?   • Not everybody learns best by reading, so we want to experiment with video to reach a broader audience.   • This project is timely given current events; we want to have it ready to launch by the start of the legislative session.   • Why Mattie: Given your role on the team, you have strong relationships with the team members we'll engage to produce the videos, and you have experience with video production.
When does it need to be completed by? What are benchmarks along the way?   • Final deadline: Mar 20—roll out in our newsletter in time for the start of the legislative session   Benchmarks: Feb 10 - confirm MOCHA   Feb 15 - script finalized, start recording   Mar 1 - videos recorded and sent to editor   Mar 15 - videos finalized and ready to be uploaded
Where else can they go for resources, examples, or advice?   Amy has videography experience.   Look at orgs X, Y, and Z for examples of videos that match our tone and content.

Who else should be involved? The MOCHA for this task is:	Manager	Owner	Consulted	Helper(s)	Approver
	Lawrence	Mattie	Amy Carmen Ben	Jasper Carmen Lyell	Lawrence

Are any specific approaches (mindsets, values, etc.) needed for this assignment? *Remember to distinguish requirements from preferences or traditions.*

- Go for experimentation and learning, not perfection.
- Bring spirit of inclusion and collaboration, including having team members lead when possible.
- Go for little wins that build on each other and create a strong foundation.

How will you seek their perspective and adapt to input?
Ask Mattie how she's approached similar projects in the past—see if there's anything she's especially excited to try.

How will you make sure you and your staff member are aligned on key points and next steps?

- Verbal repeat-back
- **Written repeat-back**
- Other (specify):

Step 2: Stay Engaged

What specific products or activities (e.g., outlines, data, drafts, etc.) will you want to review or see in action to monitor progress?

Early Slice	Midstream	Back End
Draft of storyboard & script	First drafts of videos	Final videos
Date: 2/12	*Date: 3/5*	*Date: 3/15*

Step 3: Debrief

Create a plan for accountability and learning—yours and theirs.

When and how will you **debrief** how things went? What **questions** will you ask? What **feedback** will you seek or offer about what went well and what could be improved?
Debrief on 3/22 about:

- Process (team engagement, video recording and editing)
- Product (metrics, feedback from team, etc.)

Step 4: Adapt Your Approach

Given the difficulty and importance of the task and my staff member's will and skill for this project or assignment, my approach should generally be:

- Very in the mix
- **In the mix**
- Mostly out of the mix

TOOL 3.2
PROBING QUESTIONS

General questions
- What indicators are you looking at to see if things are on or off track?
- How are you handling X [a specific element]?
- What seems to be working well? Why?
- How is this impacting you, your work, or your relationships with colleagues/partners/members?

Getting aligned
- Can you help me understand what X means to you?
- When you say Y, I'm picturing ABC [impact, steps, etc]. How do you see it?

Anticipating challenges
- What could go wrong? What do you have the most concerns about?
- Have you thought about what you'll do if Y happens?
- What are some pitfalls you've seen in projects like this in the past? How have you dealt with them?
- Do you anticipate any disparate impacts based on identity?
  - How do you plan to mitigate them?
  - Do you have any suggestions for how to mitigate them?

Strategy and approach
- What led you to make that decision? How are you making sure that the process and outcome will be equitable?
- Can you share your thinking about this? What else did you consider/are you considering?
- Are there any new approaches or tactics you're trying out?
- Of all these potential approaches, which do you think might be most effective?
- Is there any bigger picture context I should keep in mind as I work on this?

Your role
- How else can I best support you with this?
- What else do you need (from me) to make that work?
- Is there anything you'd like me to do differently to support you?

CHAPTER

4

DEFINING
ROLES AND GOALS

In the previous chapter, we explained how to delegate projects and tasks. This chapter is about two bigger-picture types of assigning work:

- Creating meaningful *roles* that make clear which individuals are responsible for which broad categories of work.

- Setting *goals* that help us make our intended impact.

If you own a bakery, delegating would be asking someone to bake a cake. Creating a role would be hiring a pastry chef. Setting a goal would be deciding to sell 10,000 cakes next year.

Roles help people understand the bottom-line expectations of what they should deliver and how they contribute to the whole. They're like positions on a sports team—with clear roles, everyone has a meaningful and distinct part to play in helping the team win. (Without well-defined roles, your team looks more like the chaotic kids' soccer game from Chapter 3!)

Setting goals helps ensure that we don't leave it to chance whether our work makes an impact. And when goals connect to our overall mission, they keep us focused, energized, and motivated to do an excellent job.

Roles and goals are both critical to a *conspire-and-align* approach. They help bring purpose and clarity to our work with our co-conspirators. And when we craft roles and goals with an eye toward equity and sustainability, we ensure people have both significant responsibilities and balanced workloads.

HOW TO CREATE CLEAR AND MEANINGFUL ROLES

Clearly defined, meaningful roles give people agency and purpose, let everyone focus on their comparative advantage, and are a basis for accountability. (This will be important when we discuss feedback and evaluations in Chapter 7!) When we create meaningful roles for people, they hold the weight of work, responsibility, and power so that we managers can focus on being spotters.

When Valerie, TMC's first full-time talent person, came on board as our head of talent, she had her work cut out for her. She was responsible for setting a vision for the talent team and implementing it. She also owned day-to-day tasks, like scheduling and conducting interviews. Eventually, as the organization grew and we increased our hiring goals, the work became unsustainable. Valerie did the math: to get applicants through the process in a timely manner, she needed 25 hours per week just for interviewing—and that wasn't counting bathroom breaks! Then, she paused and considered her comparative advantage. Did it make sense for her to spend hours putting holds on calendars? What priorities was she neglecting as a result?

So, she advocated for hiring a director of talent—someone who would take over recruiting, screening, and scheduling, and manage a caseload of searches. This hire would free up Valerie to build the vision and strategy for the team and support hiring managers in more complex hiring processes. She needed someone who could take the initiative and drive the work (with her guidance)—which also meant she had to craft a role with meaningful responsibilities and powers.

Here's what makes a role meaningful:

- The responsibilities are **specific enough** to be understood by everyone on your team, but **broad enough** that there's room for initiative and flexibility.

- The person has the **authority and power** to carry out their responsibilities and feel ownership.

- The role connects the person to the **bigger-picture purpose** and vision of the team and organization.

Try the following three-part exercise to set role expectations. Use it for yourself or someone you manage, whether you're creating a brand-new role (as Valerie did) or clarifying an existing one.

Step 1: Craft a CEO Statement

What's the headline of what you're responsible for on a broad and fundamental level? That's what a "CEO Statement" is—a high-level summary of a role's purpose in an organization. When people own a distinct body of work—an area they make decisions about and are responsible for—they have more agency and feel more invested in their work.

As the [Role], I am the CEO of _____.

You might fill in the blanks of the CEO statement like this:

- As the Chief Operations Officer, I'm the CEO of maintaining our organization's cultural, financial, and operational health.

- As the Operations Coordinator, I'm the CEO of supporting staff to meet their operations needs so they can succeed in their roles.

- As the General Counsel, I'm the CEO of ensuring we meet all ethical and compliance standards.

- As the Organizing Director, I'm the CEO of building grassroots political power for immigrant youth in Texas.

Your CEO statement doesn't have to be punchy or poetic; it needs to be clear and memorable. If you'd like, inject some humor and personality. For example, as the development director, you could be "the CEO of making it rain!"

Valerie landed on this CEO statement for the talent director role: "Ensuring our recruiting and hiring processes yield the amazing talent we need to achieve our mission."

Step 2: Define the "What"

What is this role on the hook for? Think about the *outcomes* the person will be responsible for and the specific *activities* they will do to get those outcomes. Refer to the job description if you have one. Then, define three to five "buckets" of work, focusing on the broad categories of activities that will lead to the outcomes that the person is responsible for.

When Valerie defined the buckets of work for her director of talent, she chose:

- Candidate screening.

- Owning hiring processes for the admin team.

- Hiring logistics for all roles.

- Cultivating prospective candidates.

- Partnering with the talent head to improve hiring systems and processes.

Remember to consider the requirements of the role and not just the current skills and capacity of your existing staff.[1]

When designing a role, think about power *and* responsibility. What will be in this person's *sphere of control*? What do they have the authority to decide?

Note: If the role involves managing—*especially* if it's managing a team—"management" should be a bucket of work! Too often, we see people treating management as the thing they do in between their individual contributor work. But checking in, delegating, preparing feedback, conducting evaluations, and hiring require your time and resources—and you should account for that in your role expectations.

Step 3: Define the "How"

Whether we intend to or not, we evaluate people's work based on what they do *and* how they do it. So it's essential to *make the implicit explicit* and align on the "how." Think about five values, mindsets, or approaches that would support someone to be successful in the role and organization. For example, some "hows" for an organizer might include adaptability and flexibility, given the fast-paced nature of organizing.

These were some of the "hows" Valerie came up with for the director of talent role:

- Relationship-building: Build strong relationships with prospective candidates (across racial, gender, and class identities, among others) and connectors in the field. Cultivate relationships to find candidates for entry- and mid-level roles, and engage effectively with our diverse team to generate ideas.

- Strong problem-solving: Anticipate challenges and devise creative, pragmatic solutions to help us move forward.

- Fast-paced and detail-oriented: Be able to handle large volumes of work. Prioritize the most important and impactful projects while keeping other items moving.

Don't forget to *check your PTR!* Our expectations about how people approach their work often come from our preferences and traditions. For example, a training participant asked Jakada whether they should hire someone who seemed good for the job but was "not very warm and fuzzy." The role they were hiring? A pet surgeon! Jakada said, "As long as they can save the lives of your fuzzy friends, they don't have to be warm and fuzzy. But if they can't work effectively with the other people at the

---

[1] If you discover a gap between what's needed and what the person is delivering, check out Chapter 8 for ways to develop their skills.

clinic, that might be a problem." "No," the person replied, "it was nothing like that—the candidate just wasn't someone they'd want to hang out with." This brings us to another reminder: while it's delightful to genuinely like the people you work with, your teammates don't have to be your friends.

Defining the "how" (and making sure it's based on requirements) is a *choice point* because it's an opportunity to pause and reflect on our biases and expectations. For instance, if a "positive attitude" feels essential for success, what does *positive* mean to you? How might someone with a different racial, cultural, or even regional background understand it differently from you?

One of our trainers had a Black woman co-worker at a previous job who was excellent at her job. But one day, a white client complained that this co-worker wasn't "friendly enough." So, our trainer asked some follow-up questions. "Was she rude?" "No," the client admitted. "Did she ignore you?" "No." "Did she greet you and help you with your request?" "Yes." "So, what was the problem exactly?" The client couldn't answer. We're willing to bet that this client's reaction came from her ideas about "friendliness" alongside "angry Black woman" stereotypes.

Still, you might be confident that you want your client intake specialist to have a positive attitude. After all, they're the CEO of ensuring clients can access the services they need and have a stellar first interaction with your organization. Is there a more precise or inclusive way to describe what you're looking for? Perhaps instead of a "positive attitude," you're looking for someone who demonstrates "attentiveness and empathy," which looks like being able to make every person feel welcome.

For a sample role expectations sheet, check out Tool 4.1 at the end of this chapter.

Don't Set It and Forget It!

Things change. Sometimes you'll need to update your roles to respond to shifting circumstances. For example, managers commonly revisit role expectations when a staff person's work changes for the long term or when staffing shifts create ripple effects.

HOW TO DEFINE THE "HOW"

Here are some examples of approaches you might find valuable:

- **Continuous learning:** You strive to learn and grow. If something doesn't make sense, you ask questions until it does. You apply your learnings to your work.
- **Attention to detail:** You notice and fix errors that others might overlook. When mistakes happen (which they will!), you address them quickly and look for ways to prevent them.
- **Relationship-building:** You build authentic, reciprocal relationships with teammates, members, and donors, particularly across lines of difference.
- **Strategic thinking and judgment:** You guide priorities, practice discernment, and deftly balance tensions and multiple viewpoints to make sound decisions.

If you revise role expectations, *make the implicit explicit* about changes and *seek perspective* from the staff person about their evolving role. And don't forget to communicate the changes to everyone else!

WHY GOALS MATTER

At TMC, we *love* goals. Goals are a North Star—a guiding light and a vision to *conspire and align* around. When we use them at all levels—from the organization to the team to the individual—they help us ensure that each person's work adds up to meaningful collective results. They're an essential way to *make the implicit explicit* about what we're working toward.

Here are a few other reasons why we love goals:

- **They define progress.** Goals provide a shared and transparent definition of success, so we all know what we're reaching for. They give weight to the work.

- **They support focus and prioritization.** They articulate what's important and what's not, helping us manage our resources wisely.

- **They promote rigor, accountability, and learning.** Goals help us know how well we met our expectations. They also provide a basis for reflection that helps us learn and improve.

- **They can advance equity and inclusion.** Goals help us notice *choice points* about how we define success and where we direct resources. They also prompt us to *seek perspective* from those most impacted and mitigate disparate impact.

Some clients meet resistance from their teams when they try to set goals for the first time. We get it—change is hard, and adding structure can ruffle feathers. We've also found that resistance to goal-setting is often related to a lack of trust. If staff don't trust their leaders or feel like their leaders don't trust them, it's hard to believe that the goals won't be unrealistic or micromanage-y.

But goals are an essential tool for everyone—including leaders. So to get people on board with setting goals for the first time, remind them that *goals are not the enemy*. Focus on how goals make it easier to *conspire and align* on meaningful, well-defined work.

Rather than being constraining, goals free us from:

- **Task management.** With goals focused on outcomes, staff members have greater autonomy over tactics. Managers can let go of managing individual tasks and, instead, support staff to drive projects and broader responsibilities.

- **Uncertainty.** With clear goals, there's no question about what we're all working toward and why it matters.

- **Disunity.** With a shared purpose, we're less likely to work at cross-purposes.

- **Distraction.** Many things can pull us away from our work—the latest emergency, a political scandal, and even the most recent social media trend. Goals provide focus.

- **Missed opportunities.** When we're clear on what we're after, we can spot and prioritize opportunities that help us get there.

How to Set Effective Goals

Essentially, effective goals help us answer two questions: What does success look like? And how will I know when I see it?

You've probably heard the acronym "SMART," which usually stands for "Specific,[2] Measurable, Achievable, Relevant, and Time-Bound." At TMC, we've added our own spin: SMARTIE.

STRATEGIC	Reflects an important dimension of what your organization seeks to accomplish.
MEASURABLE	Includes standards by which reasonable people can agree on whether the goal has been met.
AMBITIOUS	It's challenging enough that achieving it would mean significant progress.
REALISTIC	It's not so challenging as to indicate lack of thought about resources, capacity, or execution; it's possible to track is worth the time and energy to do so.
TIME-BOUND	Includes a clear deadline.
INCLUSIVE	Brings those most impacted or most often left out into activities and decision-making processes in a way that shares power and fosters belonging.
EQUITABLE	Seeks to address systemic injustice, inequity, or oppression.

---

[2] We prefer *strategic* over *specific* because you can have a specific goal that doesn't get you closer to your mission. For example, you can set a specific goal to raise $10,000. But if what you *really* need is $100,000 to avoid a layoff, $10,000 isn't enough to make your desired impact.

Table 4.1 Sample SMARTIE goals.

Not-So-SMARTIE	SMARTIE Glow-Up
Advocate for fairer housing policies and lead the state-wide coalition table.	By 8/31, recruit 3 organizations that work with communities most impacted to join the housing rights coalition. Get each organization to lead one neighborhood action in its city council district.
Clean up digital filing system in Q4, so we're ready for the new staff.	By 11/1, revamp technology orientation so that all staff can use our systems to do their jobs more effectively, with no gaps in race or age, as measured by a yearly survey.
Reduce administrative costs by 10%.	Lower overhead costs by $X by [date], with quarterly check-ins with frontline staff to check for unintended disparate impact of cost savings.

When we set goals intentionally using SMARTIE, we:

- Make it easier to know when we've achieved them because they're *measurable* and *time-bound*.

- Make real progress without jeopardizing our sustainability by ensuring they're *ambitious* and *realistic*.

- Embed *strategy*, *inclusion*, and *equity* into our idea of success.

Consider the differences in Table 4.1. The "goals" on the left side might be missing critical information that could lead to misalignment and inequities. On the other hand, the goals on the right side have gotten the SMARTIE glow-up. See Tool 4.2 in the Appendix Tools at the end of this chapter for more sample goals.

So, how do you do it? Let's look at each of these components more closely.

Strategic

Goals should reflect a person, team, or organization's most important work. They help advance your team or organizational priorities and mission when you achieve them. Strategic goals answer the question: "What do we need to accomplish?"

Goals are strategic when organizational goals "cascade" down to team and individual goals. That way, someone owns each piece of work needed to accomplish the goal. On the flip side, every individual should be able to trace their goals to at least one organizational goal. Ask yourself: "Do the parts add up to the sum total we aim to achieve?"

TOUGH STRATEGIC CHOICES AT THE ELLA BAKER CENTER

When Jakada was the director of the Ella Baker Center (EBC), his team had an incredibly ambitious goal: close California's abusive juvenile detention system. After over a decade, they achieved that goal through their "Books Not Bars" campaign. It took difficult, deliberate work, and they often had to make heartbreaking choices.

The campaign created the first statewide network of families with incarcerated children, known as Families for Books, Not Bars, which grew to over 1,400 family members. Early on, many members pushed the organizers to fight for improved prison conditions. How could they not? Conditions were horrible; the kids weren't getting a proper education, and sometimes they didn't even get basic healthcare and nutritional needs met. In addition, the campaign exposed the human rights violations committed inside the prisons, including the death of six young people in just two years: Dyron Mandell Brewer, Roberto Carlos Lombana, Durrell Feaster, Deon Whitfeld, Hector Rodriguez, and Joseph Maldonado. So the pull to reform conditions was strong. It was a matter of life and death.

However, Jakada and his team benefited from the hard-earned wisdom of their movement elders. While it was tempting and morally righteous to fight for improved conditions, doing so would work against the long-term goal of closing the prison system entirely. Making the prisons more tolerable might ease some kids' suffering in the short term. But it would also create the illusion that change had come—while prolonging suffering for many more kids and families and costing more lives for decades to come.

So, instead, the campaign pushed for a bill to reform family visitation practices to ensure kids were jailed reasonably close to their parents' homes. This was important because, under the status quo, visitations presented a challenge to many parents, who had to take a whole day off work to drive up the length of the state—only to be denied visitation (usually for a ridiculous reason) once they arrived.

This bill eased some immediate suffering, helped build their base, gave them a win to celebrate, and served the long-term goal. When more family members were close enough to witness the abuses their kids suffered, they became better advocates. Ultimately, it helped the Books Not Bars campaign build the power and visibility needed to shut it all down.

Measurable

Consider the difference between an aspiring baker who says, "I will learn to make pastries," versus one who says, "By the end of this month, I will learn to make beautifully laminated croissants that my pickiest foodie friends will love." Or the budding writer who says, "I want to start writing," versus, "I will write 11,000 words by the end of this month." When goals are measurable, there's no question about whether you've achieved them. TMC trainer José Luis says, "When you can't make goals with a precise number, make it something that can still be answered with a 'yes' or 'no' when asked if you've met it."

When the goal is quantifiable, pick a measurement that indicates real progress—you should see the results of your activities and tactics add up. If they're not adding up (or adding up fast enough), you can course-correct by adding resources or changing tactics.

Sometimes, an effective goal focuses on quality rather than quantity. For example, let's say you're a community organizer whose priority is building engagement among your membership base. You *could* set a goal for increasing the number of members from X to Y, but more people doesn't always mean more engagement. Instead, you want to set a goal that measures progress toward deepening investment and participation.

Here are some ways to define your goal to measure progress:

- Every membership meeting is productive and engaging. It's productive in that you garner enough input to make decisions and engaging in that participants feel more connected to each other and the work.

- By the end of the year, you can identify at least 10 members to ask to take on leadership positions within your membership structure.

Remember that goals don't always have to involve going bigger and doing more. For example, when Jakada was at EBC, it was common for staff to be grumpy and burned out by the end of every campaign—even when they won, morale and relationships suffered. So one year, the founder set a goal for the staff to end the next campaign cycle with a better working relationship going into the next one. The dynamic shifted when everyone agreed that strong staff relationships were necessary, not expendable.

Ambitious and *Realistic*

Make your goal ambitious enough to mean something—as in, accomplishing it gets you closer to fulfilling your overall mission and vision. Then, ask yourself, "What would it take to make this possible? What would we have to prioritize? What resources would we need?" These questions help you craft a goal that's not just wishful thinking—it's something you can realistically achieve with what you have.

WHAT CAN A GOAL-SETTING PROCESS LOOK LIKE?

Who gets to decide what goals to set, and how should they do it? See Table 4.2 for a few tips. Chapter 5 also has more on decision-making processes.

Table 4.2 Methods of Setting Goals.

Method	Use this when. . .	Execution
Write them yourself: You write the first draft and explain the rationale. Then, your staff asks questions and makes suggestions, and you align on the end product.	You have strong opinions about what the goals should be and/or the other person lacks the context or knowledge to write a first draft.	Explain your choices and ask the staff member to offer thoughts or feedback.
Delegate to Owner: The Owner writes the first draft, you provide feedback, and you align on the end product.	The person has been in the role for a while (or has done similar work), and has the context and knowledge to write a solid first draft.	Be clear upfront about who the final decision-maker is and share any initial thoughts you have so they're incorporated. Once they've completed the first draft, share your feedback and ask probing questions to get aligned.
Collaborate: Engage in a collaborative process (lock yourself in a room and knock out the goals).	It's a new initiative, or you're both unsure and you need to puzzle through it together from the start.	Be clear on the front end about who the final decision-maker is. Circle back to those whose ideas aren't represented and explain your choices.

If you've accomplish it through your regular course of work without setting a goal, it might not be ambitious enough.[3] But, on the other hand, if you don't have a plan to achieve it, or if it involves more time, people, or energy than you have, it's likely *too*

---

[3] We say *might* because there are many things that are worth setting goals around, even if they happen year after year, such as running a clean financial audit or putting out monthly newsletters.

SEEKING PERSPECTIVE

Getting input during goal-setting is a *choice point*. Bake inclusion into your goals by *seeking perspective* from relevant stakeholders, especially those who are:

- Most impacted by the problems you're trying to solve.
- Most often left out of decision-making processes.
- Most likely to be involved in achieving the goal.

Talk to the people on the MOCHAs, especially the Owners and Helpers. Check in with your manager or someone who has the vantage point to see how your goals fit into the broader context of your team and organization.

ambitious. Goals that are ambitious and realistic feel like a gentle stretch—they push you to the edge of your ability, but not so far that you tear something.

We recommend occasionally setting "stretch goals" that challenge you to reach farther in terms of effort, tactics, or creativity. Stretch goals can help drive progress and facilitate evolutionary leaps for our teams and organizations. But beware—when every goal is a stretch goal, you're on the fast track to burnout (remember, you don't want to tear something!). One approach is to differentiate between "base" goals (the bare minimum you need for success) and "stretch" goals. For example, at EBC, Jakada's team had a base goal of getting one legislator to introduce their bill. Their stretch goal was to get a legislator in each house to introduce the bill. (This is similar to the idea of differentiating between "good enough" and "gold star," which we discussed in Chapter 3.)

Time-Bound

On a practical level, deadlines can be an excellent motivator. The loftier your vision, the more helpful it is to chunk out goals over time. They should function like mile markers in a marathon. It's much easier to think about getting from mile 8 to mile 9 and then from mile 9 to mile 10 than to look ahead to the finish line and despair that you're not even halfway to mile 26 yet. When goals articulate bite-sized chunks of your vision, they keep people sustainably involved in the work.

Another way to think of goals is "roles played out over time." Goals establish what it looks like when you and your team perform your roles well during a specific period.

Inclusive and Equitable

Think about how your goals could potentially deepen or disrupt existing inequities. For example, if you run a leadership development program for Asians and Pacific Islanders, you could set this goal: "Increase the number of youth trained by 20% from the previous year's results." But let's say that based on previous years' data, most program participants are East Asian, cis young people with middle to upper-class backgrounds. For some reason, Pacific Islanders, South Asians, Southeast Asians, trans folks, and youth from poor or working-class backgrounds don't participate in your program. So setting a general "20% increase" goal might get you higher numbers, but it might also deepen those existing disparities.

What if, instead, your goal was "Increase the number of Pacific Islander (PI) youth trained by 20% from the previous year's results"? This goal aims to address existing disparities and serve *more* people in your community. It will also change *how* you go about achieving your goal. If you're specifically looking to attract more PI participants, you won't just do the same outreach you've always done. Instead, you might take another look at where you do outreach, who your trainers are, and whether your curriculum speaks to PI youth.

Your top-level goal statements don't always have to spell out how you'll promote equity and inclusion. (They also don't have to be as long as the ones in the SMARTIE glow-up chart.) But if they don't, you should specify how you plan to incorporate equity and inclusion into your tactics and metrics. For example, if your development team aims to raise $X by Y month, one of your tactics might be "recruit, retain, and develop 30,000 dues-paying members, at least X% of whom identify as BIPOC." Another might be "host an event for LGBTQ major donors."

Beyond Tokenism

Tokenism is representation without real power, influence, or inclusion. To be genuinely inclusive—meaningfully involving people enough that they can actually shape or influence something—we need to proactively address inequities, shrink disparities, and build power with those on the margins.

For instance, with the example of the leadership development program, you might consider adding to the goal of increasing the number of PI youth by 20% in any of the following ways to go beyond tokenism:

- Post-program survey scores should indicate no disparities in the quality of their experience.

- By the end of the program, at least X% of PI participants decide to join the alum group.

- Expand our training team to include at least X PI facilitators.

SMART	SMARTIE
Increase the number of youth trained by 20% from the previous year's results.	Increase the number of Pacific Islander (PI) youth trained by 20% from the previous year's results. • Post-program survey scores should indicate no disparities in the quality of their experience. • By the end of the program, at least X% of PI participants decide to join the alum group. • Expand our training team to include at least X PI facilitators.

Ready to start writing your own SMARTIE goals? See Tool 4.3 at the end of the chapter for a SMARTIE goals worksheet!

HOW TMC USED GOALS TO ADVANCE DIVERSITY, EQUITY, AND INCLUSION

While we're pretty proud of TMC's work over the last decade and a half, we haven't always been as thoughtful as we needed to be regarding equity and inclusion. Here's a story about how goals helped us in our racial equity journey.

Shortly after joining TMC in 2013, Bex grew concerned about how well our trainings served clients. At the time, we didn't have advice for managers about navigating issues of race, gender, and other identities. In addition, we didn't address the unique challenges that BIPOC face in predominantly white organizations. For example, when a queer Black woman asked for advice about experiencing bias at work, Bex could only offer thoughts based on their experience as a queer person of color.

Bex brought this concern to Jerry, our co-founder and CEO. They said, "I know we care about supporting people of color, but that's not coming through in our content—it feels like a liability." Jerry wholeheartedly agreed to explore solutions to the problem.

After six months of wrestling with ideas, Bex came up with a proposal: What if we piloted a training for BIPOC leaders? We could provide a space just for them, test our content, and learn more about how to serve them better. Unfortunately, the post-training survey scores from that pilot were a painful reality check. While TMC routinely saw about 70% of respondents say they were "very satisfied" with the training, only 13% of the pilot participants reported the same.

This pilot training in 2014 led us to confront the disconnect between what we *said* we valued and what we delivered. From that point on, TMC staff worked to understand and close this gap. We learned about equitable management practices and developed new content (much of which is in this book). We wrestled with questions about our identity and strategy—questions that led to some knock-down, drag-out battles. (Bex and Jerry once got into a two-hour debate about our equity goals at a Nando's restaurant!) We asked ourselves: What does it mean for TMC to be committed to racial equity? What do we need to do to live out that commitment? Slowly, we moved through the conflicts and discomfort that came from those conversations.

The tide turned, in part, when we started setting race-explicit goals (the precursor to SMARTIE goals), like "train 1,200 managers, with at least 35% of training participants who identify as BIPOC. Ensure no gaps in satisfaction." In 2015, the team worked to create another three-day training just for BIPOC managers. This time, 95% of participants rated "very satisfied" in their surveys.

(continued)

(continued)

Every time we were explicit about racial equity, it drove new actions. Our goals, activities, and rationale ratcheted each other up as we went, creating a cycle of progress. For example, on its surface, our training satisfaction goal was about wanting all participants to have a similarly positive experience—but it had a more profound impact. This goal forced us to revisit two things:

- Our content and curriculum, to make sure it felt relevant to BIPOC participants' experiences.
- Our trainer competencies, to set the expectation that trainers should effectively build trust with participants of all racial backgrounds.

In 2017, TMC embarked on a massive hiring push. In preparation, we incorporated racial equity and inclusion competency as a must-have for most roles. This push resulted in a wave of new staff (including Jakada and Monna) aligned with TMC's commitment to racial equity. During Jakada's interview, he was pleasantly surprised when he asked about racial equity, and the hiring manager pulled up her SMARTIE goals. These hires further pushed for cultural and programmatic changes that better served BIPOC managers and staff.

TMC is now a majority-BIPOC organization that better serves the full breadth of leaders in our sectors and movements. And, as our sectors and movements evolve, we also continue to learn and grow (and struggle!).

More Tips for Setting Goals

Here are some additional tips for setting goals.

Leave Space in the Suitcase

Approach goal-setting as if you were packing for a trip. If you stuff your suitcase so much that only a Tetris master can close it, you'll have no room for souvenirs, and you'll end up scrapping things anyway. We recommend no more than three to five big goals for each person or department. Going over isn't a disaster, but too many will lead to less focus and flexibility. Remember that goals are supposed to help you prioritize—when everything is equally important, nothing is truly important.

Don't Let the Perfect Be the Enemy of the Good

When the world and work constantly evolve, there's no point in perfecting your goals down to the last word and metric. Instead, focus on capturing what you want to accomplish and getting aligned with your team. Then, plan to revisit your goals throughout the year.

And if you're setting goals for the first time, give yourself a lot of grace—sure, it might feel more like a "SMTI" goal than a "SMARTIE" goal, but it's better than nothing.

Focus on Outcomes

Focus on what you aim to *achieve*, not just what you'll *do*. It's helpful to outline some of the activities you'll do to achieve the goal, but above everything, the goal should specify your desired results. Focusing on results allows room for new or different approaches and helps you *check your preferences and traditions (PTR)*.

For example, if you're a legislative director, you might set a goal of getting 10 legislators to co-sponsor your bill instead of holding 10 meetings with legislative staff. You could tell your staff, "Traditionally, we try to get co-sponsors through legislative meetings, but if you think there's a better way, try it." Your staff might decide legislative meetings and lobby visits will work for some legislators, but others need more constituent pressure. Outcome-oriented goals help align managers and staff on what they want to accomplish and give staff the responsibility and freedom to figure out the best way to get there.

Watch Out for Implicit Spending

Anytime you do something new, budget for more resources—time, energy, money—than you'd expect. In personal finance, there's a concept called "implicit spending." For example, if you're buying a new car, you'll factor the price of the vehicle into your budget. But you'll overestimate how much you can afford if you don't also budget for insurance, repairs, and the occasional parking ticket. Similarly, if you don't consider things like administrative tasks and hiring, you'll overestimate your team's capacity. Plus, if you're amid significant transitions or dealing with unexpected crises, there are the added emotional costs of coping with change and simply getting by.

Budgeting for these costs can look like the following:

- Setting a later deadline than you normally would.

- Making hiring an explicit, stand-alone goal if you know you'll need to add staff capacity to achieve your goals.

- Setting aside time in your work plan for research, testing, and input-gathering.

Don't Forget to Celebrate

So you meet a goal and then move on to the next thing—you're busy, and time's a-wasting, right?

Wrong!

Management isn't just about working hard—it's about creating opportunities for joy, celebration, and appreciation. Getting to celebrate success and hard work is one of the best things about goal-setting. It's also essential for instilling a sense of teamness and belonging, reinforcing shared purpose in relationship-building, and contributing to a healthy culture. Plus, having a treat at the end can be motivating. For example, Jerry once begrudgingly agreed that if TMC met a hiring stretch goal, he'd sing at a staff karaoke night (something he'd vowed *never* to do). While everyone was committed to reaching the goal anyway, the promise of "Jerryoke" at the end of it made the process and outcomes much more exciting.[4]

Celebrations don't have to be over the top. They just have to be a chance for people to appreciate everyone's efforts. Here are other ways to celebrate that don't involve rocking a mic:

- Offer appreciations in a team debrief.

- Share a celebratory meal or throw a party (even virtually!).

- Give time off to rest after a sprint.

Tools for Staying on Track to Meet Your Goals

Like roles, goals are useless if you set and forget them. Instead, use goals to check on progress, make course corrections if needed, and prioritize your time and energy (more on this in Chapter 5). Here are some tools to help you stay on track:

- **Check-ins.** Make your annual priorities and goals a standing agenda item so you can track progress.

- **Stepbacks.** Stepbacks are moments to pause and look at the bigger picture. We recommend quarterly or semiannual stepbacks with your staff to assess progress toward goals, reflect on what's working, share feedback, and reprioritize if needed.

- **Red light/green light.** You can use red light/green light in stepbacks to indicate whether you're on track to meet your goals. At TMC, "green" means on track to meet or exceed the goal, "yellow" means not yet on track or not started yet (but still likely to meet the goal), and "red" means you're off track and need to course correct or reprioritize. See Tool 4.4 at the end of this chapter for a stepback worksheet (you can use the "current status" column for red light/green light).

KEY POINTS OF DEFINING ROLES AND GOALS

Here are the takeaways from the chapter:

- Roles and goals are critical to a *conspire-and-align* approach. They help bring purpose and clarity to our work. When we craft roles and goals with an eye toward equity and sustainability, we ensure people have both significant responsibilities and balanced workloads.

---

[4] In case you're wondering, Jerry sang "The Joker" by the Steve Miller Band.

- Clearly defined, meaningful **roles** give staff members a true sense of agency and ownership.

- To create a new role, or revamp an existing one, use a three-step process:

  - Craft a "CEO statement" (As [role], I'm the CEO of [responsibility]") to broadly define the role's purpose and context.

  - Define the "what"—the three to five "buckets" of work where this person is on the hook for the outcomes.

  - Define the "how"—the values, mindsets, and approaches it takes to succeed in the role.

- Setting **goals** helps ensure that we don't leave it to chance whether our work makes an impact. Goals are the North Star that guides and focuses our efforts.

- The most effective goals are created by thinking through the acronym **SMARTIE: Strategic, Measurable, Ambitious, Realistic, Time-Bound, Inclusive,** and **Equitable**. This ensures that:

  - We know when we've achieved them because they're *measurable* and *time-bound*.

  - We make real progress without jeopardizing our sustainability by ensuring they're *ambitious* and *realistic*.

  - We embed *strategy*, *inclusion*, and *equity* into our idea of success.

- The *I* and *E* must go beyond tokenism. Goals should meaningfully involve and build power with people on the margins.

- When setting goals, focus on outcomes, not just activities. Also, don't overload yourself with too many goals, and don't forget to celebrate your achievements!

- Use check-in and stepback meetings to stay on track to meet your goals.

APPENDIX TOOLS

TOOL 4.1

ROLE EXPECTATIONS SAMPLE

Name:	Job Title: Senior Programs Director

Overall Headline

I'm the CEO of. . .making sure our programs have the biggest possible impact.

Areas of Responsibility

Recruit, train, and mentor staff:
- Ensure that managers effectively recruit and manage staff.
- Ensure there are no gaps in development opportunities by race or gender.

Equity and Inclusion:
- Monitor program results by race and gender to spot gaps and disparities.
- Make sure all staff (especially those on the margins) have the support they need to thrive.

Compliance:
- Ensure that all reporting is correct and done on time.
- Make sure partner organizations understand their roles in this and have the tools to deliver.

Leadership team
- Give input on strategic decisions and collaborate on other issues as needed.
- Be a thought partner to the ED on key questions.
- Ensure that all organizational decisions are translated to and through the program teams.

The Approach

- **Inclusive leadership and management:** Brings a clear vision and recognizes the value of divergent perspectives. Approaches leadership with a mindset of "power with" rather than "power over" and regularly includes others in decision-making. Able to make and communicate difficult decisions in the organization's best interest.
- **Attentive, empathetic leadership:** Enthusiasm for meeting and engaging with people. Empathizes with the communities we serve. Able to put people at ease, especially across lines of difference. Listens closely to understand needs or concerns. Gets back to people in a timely manner.
- **Proactive problem-solving:** Develops solutions to challenges, including by constantly looking at big-picture progress on the programs team, and by flagging any potential upcoming challenges.
- **Applies best practices in equitable management:** Translates equity and inclusion into plans for staff development, retention, strategy, and improving culture.

TOOL 4.2
SAMPLE GOALS

Advocacy, Organizing, and Policy Change

- Get X legislation passed in at least two of our five target states.
- Increase the percentage of Nevadans who believe X from 40% to 46%, and track these results by [race, gender, income level, etc.].

Community Impact

- Involve 50 family members in making key decisions about school priorities this year, with at least X families who are [part of Y neighborhood, on free/reduced lunch, Asian or Pacific Islander, etc.].
- Train 75 Spanish-speaking public health navigators to conduct phonebanking in X county to connect Latinx communities to affordable healthcare before the registration deadline.

Culture

- In a year-end survey, X% of staff agree or strongly agree with the following statement: "Our organization has a culture of [fill in the blank]."

Information Technology

- By [date], conduct an audit of our digital security practices, publish a revised security policy, and implement at least one new procedure for safeguarding staff, client, and volunteer information.
- By the end of first quarter, identify three office procedures that could be improved through IT solutions. Work with relevant departments to implement improvements and train staff.

Office Administration/Finance

- Manage the office to make it an inclusive and welcoming space for all staff, visitors, and clients—particularly those from traditionally marginalized backgrounds—and receive at least XX unsolicited raves (praise) over the course of the year.
- Find a new office location that is fully ADA accessible and public-transit friendly, and move for under $X and by [date].

Operations / HR

- Complete an audit of our benefit plans to make sure that we provide benefits that cover the needs of LGBTQ staff. If we identify any problems with our current plans, we will implement solutions by X.

Strategic Communications & Digital Strategy

- By [date], at least X of the Y spokespeople we train and feature in our communications will come from communities whose experiences are often marginalized or invisible when it comes to our issue.
- By end of 20xx, explore four new forms of audience engagement. At least two should improve accessibility and/or the experience of our most marginalized audiences (along lines of race, class, gender, and ability) audience members.

TOOL 4.3
SMARTIE GOALS WORKSHEET

Use this template to write a goal for yourself or a team member.
Time-Bound: My goals between *(start date)* and *(end date)* are to achieve this **Strategic** and **Ambitious** outcome:
I will know success when I see it using these **Measurable** standards:

A **Realistic** plan to achieve this goal includes these tactics/activities (consider time, resources, capacity):

	By *(date)*
	By *(date)*
	By *(date)*

Thinking about **Equity and Inclusion**: Can you imagine any unintentional *disparate impact* along the lines of power and identity? How might inequity or exclusion show up? For whom?

How could you *change the goal* to either mitigate that disparate impact or make **Equity and Inclusion** more explicit?

TOOL 4.4

GOALS STEPBACK WORKSHEET

Use this worksheet to track progress and share updates about your team or individual goals on a regular basis. Use the questions below to discuss progress and next steps with your manager. You can also check out our Red Light/Green Light Goal Tracking Tool to track progress year-round[5].

Quarter X Stepback (as of mm/dd)			
Goal	**Current Status (On track / Not started yet / Not on track)**	**Updates**	**Key Next Steps**
Grow the grassroots power of our membership base. By end of year, at least 2,500 people (of which 40% identify as BIPOC) will have been trained through our leadership development programs. At least 80% of participants will answer "yes" to the statement "I would recommend this program to a friend."	*Not yet on track.*	*We should have enough trainings scheduled in the second half of the year to hit our overall goal, but need to do additional outreach to get to 40% BIPOC.*	*Reach out to Maria and Cynthia about recruitment; make a push on social media channels.*

Questions for Discussion

- What else needs to happen to achieve _____?
- Is there anything you should start now, in anticipation of what's coming up?
- *(For goals that are not on track)* What happened to throw us off-track? What are you doing to restrategize?
- What could go wrong? What worries you? What can you do now to plan for those possibilities?
- Are there things we've deprioritized that we should move to the front burner? Are there items that we should focus less on now, in favor of higher priorities?
- What has been going well that you want to continue doing?
- Do you need any additional support or resources to meet your goals?

---

[5] See our website: http://www.managementcenter.org.

CHAPTER

5

MAKING DECISIONS AND PRIORITIZING

"In a fractal conception, I am a cell-sized unit of the human organism, and I have to use my life to leverage a shift in the system by how I am, as much as with the things I do. This means actually being in my life, and it means bringing my values into my daily decision-making. Each day should be lived on purpose."

—*adrienne maree brown, author of* Emergent Strategy:
Shaping Change, Changing Worlds

What have you eaten today? Which friends have you texted? Which messages have you left unread?

We face countless choices every day. We decide how we spend our time, what emails to respond to, and how to spend money. Everything within our *sphere of control* is a potential decision that could impact our teammates, culture, and results.

For managers, our positional power raises the stakes. Positional power means more *choice points,* authority, and responsibility to make bigger decisions. We are responsible for the consequences of our choices on our staff, results, and organization. And, as managers, *how* we make and communicate decisions can make or break people's trust in us.

Oh, and let's not forget that no matter our positions, we rarely have all the information we need. We grapple with change and uncertainty, which bring instability and self-doubt, making it harder to be clear, confident, and decisive.

How we approach decisions is what separates *conspire-and-align* from command-and-control. The most effective managers and leaders conspire with our teams to make great decisions, and align around those decisions clearly and swiftly. We engage our teams meaningfully without collapsing from indecisiveness or shirking our authority. Effective managers make decisions we're willing to take responsibility for, and do our best to build power and alignment with our teams. We also know when we should follow someone else's lead and trust them to decide.

This chapter shares tips and tools to help you make decisions (and support your staff to do the same). Of course, you can't make the "right" decisions every time, but you *can* be more considerate, inclusive, and transparent in your decision-making. We offer tools and advice about making all kinds of decisions, from the high-stakes and complex to the seemingly mundane (but still necessary!).

HOW TO MAKE DECISIONS EFFECTIVELY

An effective decision gets you the outcomes you want using an inclusive process that builds trust, relationships, and culture. Your decisions are more likely to be effective if you:

- Examine choice points.

- Know and share your decision-making mode.

- Make a "pros/cons/mitigations" chart.

- Know when to delegate a decision.

Examine Choice Points

Even small decisions can have big impacts. Pay attention to those little forks in the road that give you a chance to perpetuate the status quo or find alternatives that lead to greater equity.

For instance, say you're hiring a program manager. You need input on the job description. Who do you reach out to? You know you need feedback from your manager and the two colleagues who will work with the new hire. Do you also invite the program coordinator (your most junior staff person) to weigh in? Even though they won't work closely with the program manager, the coordinator will occasionally support their projects. Getting their input early in the process is one way to include their perspective, communicate that you value their ideas, and get better outcomes.

Know and Share Your Decision-Making Mode

Isn't it annoying when someone asks you to "weigh in" on a decision when they've already made up their mind? Avoid being *that* person by sharing your decision-making mode. Essentially, a decision-making mode tells people what type of input you're seeking, how you'll engage with it, and how open you are to ideas.

The spectrum in Figure 5.1 (adapted from a similar framework created by Monitor Consulting) offers one framework that anyone can use—whether you're a sole decision-maker or a group working toward consensus. Before you seek input, ask yourself: What mode am I in?

Joint: The team is the decision-maker and will decide through voting or consensus. Questions you can ask your team to build consensus:

- What do you think we should do?

- What ideas do you have?

Consult: The decision-maker(s) will use new ideas or feedback to shape the final outcome. Brainstorming questions you can ask:

- What could make this better?

- If you were in my shoes, what would you do?

Test: The decision-maker(s) have an idea or draft and want to see how it lands on different audiences. Questions you can ask to get reactions:

- One option we're considering is A. How does it land on you?

- What could you imagine going wrong with how we're approaching this?

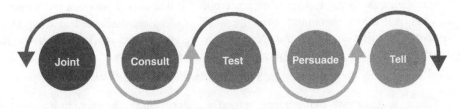

FIGURE 5.1 *Decision-Making Spectrum. Choose one of these decision-making modes to let people know what type of input you're seeking, how you'll engage with it, and how open you are to ideas.*

Persuade: The decision-maker(s) have a proposal and want to build buy-in. Concerns raised will inform improvements and might even change the decision. Questions you can ask:

- What would it take to implement this well?

- What would make you really excited about this path or proposal?

Tell: The decision is made. The decision-maker(s) are sharing information. Questions you can ask to promote understanding or aid implementation:

- Do you have any questions about how we are moving forward?

- What do you need from me to implement this?

Make a "Pros/Cons/Mitigations" Chart

Stuck between two (or more) options? Level up your typical "pros vs. cons" list by adding a "mitigations" section, where you list ways to minimize the downsides or risks of your options. This tool can be handy for teams or organizations that make consensus-based decisions. Think through what it would *really* be like to move forward with a proposal—how would you deal with the downsides? This tool helps push you past "either/or" thinking and gives you a better sense of the risks and benefits of a decision.

Make your process more inclusive and surface more solutions by *seeking perspective*—especially across lines of difference—in thinking through pros, cons, and mitigations. See Table 5.1 for a completed sample chart.

Know When to Delegate a Decision

As managers, there are plenty of decisions we have the *authority* to make but might not be in the best *position* to make. That's when we need to delegate.

Delegating decision-making is a *choice point*. It helps us share power, communicate trust, and affirm ownership over the work. And as we discussed in Chapter 3, effective delegation is about transferring the weight of the work—which should include the weight of making important decisions about that work.

Consider making someone else the decider if any of the following apply:

- There is someone with more expertise, experience, or proximity to the issue than you.

- There is someone with the skills and expertise, *and* more bandwidth or capacity to be thoughtful about decision-making.

- You're managing someone who already owns significant pieces of the work.

Table 5.1 Pros/Cons/Mitigations Chart.

Option	Pros	Cons	Mitigations
	Actual or potential upsides	*Downsides, costs, risks*	*Ways to minimize the downsides or risks*
Keep current office space	• Cheaper! • Less hassle—no need to pack up • Easy commutes	• Gloomy appearance isn't great for staff recruitment • Two more hires and we run out of room	• Shift to rotating desk system—we're rarely all here on the same day • Create a "spillover" fund so we can rent temporary (day rate) space when needed • Set aside small pool of $ to invest in sprucing up the office
Move to larger space	• Brighter space, boost to morale • Lots of room to grow	• Locks us into a big expense • Not sure how fast we'll grow • Slightly harder commutes	• If we do move, seek subtenants for first two years, at least • Create taxi fund to reimburse staff when they have to work late • Schedule move to happen after board meeting

When you delegate a decision, support your team member to do it effectively. Ask them to consider their choice points; think through pros, cons, and mitigations; and be clear about their decision-making mode.

USING FAIR PROCESS FOR INCLUSIVE DECISION-MAKING

Think about one of the trickiest decisions you've made. Why was it challenging? Maybe the consequences of that decision were far-reaching, long-lasting, or hard to reverse (or some combination of all three!). Maybe it had huge equity implications. Maybe there were a lot of stakeholders. Perhaps you didn't have enough time, information, or trust to lead an effective process.

Many of these things are out of our control. But what we *can* control is our approach. Enter: fair process, a tool that helps managers navigate complex decisions.

With fair process, we're clear about who the decision-maker is, invite input from those who will be impacted, explain the decision, and outline expectations once a decision has been made. Fair process promotes equity by authentically engaging the people who'll be most impacted by a decision or are closest to the work.

Fair process has three mutually reinforcing elements: engagement, explanation, and expectation clarity. You can also add a bonus *E*: evaluation.

Before you get started, answer some key questions:

- What **question**, **problem**, or **decision** are you wrestling with?

- Which **stakeholders** do you need to prioritize, and **what** do you need their input on?

- Who is the **decision-maker?** If the decision-maker isn't the same person driving the process, how will the decision-maker and process owner coordinate?

- What is the **deadline** for the decision? What is the **timeline** for gathering input?

- What **criteria** (values, guiding principles, must-haves) will be used to decide?

Like many nonprofits, TMC went remote at the start of the COVID-19 pandemic in March 2020. As the world began to open up in 2021, we received more requests from clients and staff to consider returning to in-person work. As you can imagine, this was a complex decision. With so many unknowns about COVID-19 and a geographically dispersed, diverse team, there was no easy way to meet everyone's needs.

We formed a committee to create a policy to provide guidance for in-person engagements. The "reopening crew" included our chief of staff, our vice president of HR and staff experience, the managing partner of our coaching team, and a managing partner from our training team. They used fair process to decide on the first iteration of our reopening policy, which was released in summer 2021.

At the beginning of the process, the reopening committee developed three guiding principles for crafting the policy. They were committed to:

- Promoting safety, which meant following the available scientific guidance and protecting staff health.

- Being mindful of equity, which meant not distributing benefits or burdens unevenly.

- Avoiding unintended pressure on people to do things they were uncomfortable with, with careful attention to race, gender identity, ability, and caregiving status.

Engagement

Engagement can mean the difference between people feeling valued and respected, and feeling overlooked and marginalized. We've mentioned *seeking perspective* a lot—decision-making is one of the most important places to use this fundamental tool that invites other people's knowledge and experience. Seeking perspective brings people in as co-conspirators and problem-solvers.

For engagement to be meaningful, it needs to be:

- **Timely.** People share input when it matters, not just as a perfunctory step or an afterthought.

- **Appropriate.** People are in a position to give helpful feedback, whether because of their experience, expertise, or vantage point.

- **Open.** People feel like they can freely engage without encountering judgment or defensiveness.

Identifying the right stakeholders is a crucial part of engagement. Think about the following when you consider whom to engage:

- Who will be most impacted by the decision (in particular, who is most likely to experience *negative* impacts)?

- Who has experience with the problem?

- Who's most likely to anticipate risks and concerns that you might miss?

- Who might have desires or considerations that differ from yours?

- Who has identities, experiences, or roles that may be on the margins of your team?

- Who has been historically left out of similar decision-making processes?

Here was the reopening committee's engagement process, during which the committee:

- Met to discuss the pandemic phase, review client and staff requests, and brainstorm ideas.

- Consulted with key stakeholders—our client support, operations, coaching, and training teams.

- Took a draft proposal to TMC's leadership team for review and input (in "test" mode).

- After weighing input from the leadership team, sent out an all-staff survey and held office hours for input (in "persuade" mode).

Invite Dissent

Try taking seeking perspective to the next level: invite dissent. The higher the stakes, the earlier you should surface differing opinions. In the cascading MOCHA for TMC's reopening policy, Jessica (managing partner on our training team) owned getting input from trainers. Trainers were key stakeholders for two reasons:

- They would be most impacted by changes to our in-person policy (pre-pandemic, all of our trainings were in-person).

- The training team is one of TMC's larger and more diverse teams with varied opinions about in-person work.

Jessica said to trainers in their check-ins: "I'm looking for complete honesty about your needs and concerns. In fact, I'm asking you to be selfish." The policy needed to work sufficiently for a diverse team of over 50 people. The committee needed to consider not only race, gender, and other identities, but also geographic locations, family structures, and health concerns. Jessica especially needed to hear from people who were differently situated from her. She said, "If no one tells me what really matters to them, we might end up with a policy that only works for the Jessicas at TMC. A Jessica policy will only serve people who live alone in a progressive metropolitan area, don't have day-to-day caregiving responsibilities, and aren't immunocompromised."

In collecting input from trainers, she knew—and reminded people—that she wouldn't be able to address every concern. There was no way the committee would land on a policy that'd please everyone 100%—and that wasn't the goal. The goal was to collect enough information to make a thoughtful and fair decision.

Explanation

Once you make a decision, explain how you got there. Share the following:

- The context.

- The criteria, values, or guiding principles used to make the decision.

- Appreciation for those who shared input.

- Anticipated drawbacks or risks and how you plan to mitigate or avoid them.

- When you might revisit the decision (if relevant).

With the reopening policy, the committee revised its proposal based on input from the surveys, check-ins, and the leadership team meeting. They submitted this revision to Jakada. Once he approved it, they shared the policy via email and presented it at a staff meeting. They also previewed the policy at a TMC managers' meeting so that managers could ask questions, learn the policy, and talk through potential scenarios.

The written policy included the following:

- A reminder about the guiding principles.

- Details about the policy.

- An overview of the process.

- An appendix of resources, including a summary of feedback and how it was incorporated.

Expectation Clarity

Once you've decided, get buy-in, set and align expectations for moving forward, and implement it. Many organizational or team-wide decisions will affect how people do things (new practices, systems, or policies) and what success looks like. *Make the implicit explicit* about what will be different moving forward, like updated role expectations, goals, processes, or procedures. Finally, be honest about what you don't know. Clarity doesn't have to mean certainty. If there are things you're still unsure about, share what they are.

The committee ensured expectation clarity by supporting managers in understanding the policy. They even developed case studies to help managers think through potential decisions they'd need to make based on the policy.

Bonus: Evaluation

You don't have to debrief every decision. But, the bigger it is or the more likely it will recur, the more important it is to evaluate its outcome and identify lessons learned.

As always, check for equity in the results! Use whatever data is available to evaluate the outcomes. If you don't have data, consider sending out a quick survey or having managers check in with staff and report back. In reviewing it, you'll look for evidence of negative consequences, particularly for marginalized team members.

After sharing the policy, the reopening committee scheduled quarterly meetings to check in and revisit the policy. At these meetings, they discussed changes in Centers for Disease Control and Prevention (CDC) guidelines, reviewed input and feedback from staff, and considered further updates to the policy.

MAKING DECISIONS ABOUT YOUR TIME AND ENERGY

For every big decision involving stakeholders, fair process, and pros/cons/mitigations charts, you likely make 100 microdecisions about how you spend your time and energy. While relatively small, these choices add up—and they're unending!

Being strategic about how you spend your time and energy is critical for sustainability and results. In this section, we share strategies for managing your time, systems, and energy.

Focus on Your Big Rocks

The basic idea of big rocks[1] is this: Imagine you have a one-gallon mason jar, and you fill it to the top with baseball-sized rocks. The jar isn't "full" at that point; there's still plenty of room between those big rocks. If you add some smaller pebbles, you can fill

---

[1] The idea of "big rocks" as a metaphor for your most important priorities was popularized by Stephen Covey in *The Seven Habits of Highly Effective People* (Free Press, 1989).

in those cracks. And once you've done that, there will still be room for sand. But this doesn't work in the opposite direction—if you start by filling the jar with sand or pebbles, there's no room for bigger rocks.

The jar is your time and energy—a finite resource. Your "big rocks" are the major priorities that determine whether your day, month, or year has been successful. Everything else is proportionately less important. Try identifying 1–3 big rocks daily or weekly and tackling those before you do anything else.

Test for alignment about your staff's big rocks, too—they might prioritize sand or pebbles without knowing it. (You can list big rocks in our check-in agenda template in Chapter 2.)

Also, remember that you're a manager, so *you should spend time managing*! This might seem obvious, but many managers forget to make it a big rock because of everything else we're responsible for.

Separate the Important from the Urgent

Struggling to identify your big rocks? Take a lesson from former President Dwight D. Eisenhower, who once said: "I have two kinds of problems: the urgent and the important. The urgent are not important, and the important are never urgent."

Author Stephen Covey took this quote further with the Eisenhower Matrix, also known as the Urgent-Important Matrix (See Table 5.2). This framework helps you prioritize (or even eliminate) tasks. An important task enables you to make progress

Table 5.2 Urgent-Important Matrix.

	Important	**Not Important**
Urgent	Do it	Delegate it, do it, or say "no"
Not Urgent	Schedule it	Don't do it (or limit it)

Source: Stephen Covey, *The Seven Habits of Highly Effective People*, Free Press, 1989.

toward results. An urgent task demands your immediate attention—but if we only focus on urgent tasks, we risk filling our jars with sand and crowding out our big rocks.

Here are the types of tasks according to the Eisenhower Matrix:

- **Important but Not Urgent:** Tasks that are essential for moving the work forward but don't have clear or imminent deadlines. These include long-term goals that get lost in the daily shuffle if you don't prioritize them. Examples of important but not urgent tasks include strategic planning, goal-setting, and using your vacation time. Block off time to do these.

- **Important and Urgent:** Tasks with specific deadlines and consequences for not being met (e.g., processing payroll, meeting publishing deadlines, and communicating with job candidates). Do these right away. Try to limit the number of things that go from "important but not urgent" to "important and urgent" by planning your work in advance.

- **Not Important but Urgent:** These are usually tasks that need to be done but aren't *your* big rocks. Either they don't fit within your comparative advantage, or they're someone else's priority that may require your help. If possible, delegate these to someone better positioned to do them. If you have the capacity to help, do it—but make sure these types of tasks don't overload your plate. If it's truly not that important, set a boundary and say no.

- **Not Important and Not Urgent:** Tasks that are usually distractions or things you do for fun, like scrolling social media. Avoid these or set clear parameters ("I'm going to take 10 minutes to watch this video of unlikely animal friends and then get back to work").

Distinguish between "Gold Star" and "Good Enough"

To use your time wisely, get clear about what priorities must be "gold star" and what can be "good enough." If it pains you to give less than your best, remember that distinguishing between gold star and good enough helps you be more discerning, strategic, and sustainable. It's also a valuable tool for coaching staff who struggle with perfectionism—people whose "good enough" is already "gold star."

You can also use gold star and good enough to align expectations with your manager or a teammate. One of our colleagues does this by naming the amount of time and effort required to achieve each standard: "I can get this to 85% with 8 hours of work. It'd take about 16 hours total to get to 100%. Do you think it's worth it?"

Work Your Calendar

These days, people commonly have viewing access to their colleagues' calendars. This means that our calendars are a tool for organizing our time and also convey important information to our teammates. Calendars help us to track important deadlines and tasks and to communicate priorities and boundaries.

Use these tips to make your calendar work for you:

- **Use work blocks.** Schedule blocks of distraction-free time on your calendar to focus on your most important work. Encourage your staff to set work blocks, too—and don't schedule over them. Model setting boundaries by being explicit: "I'm reserving Fridays this month for goal-setting, so I won't be taking meetings then. If it's urgent, chat me. If not, email me and expect a response on Monday."

- **Add breathing room.** Use your calendar to maintain balance. Schedule time off, set working hours, and calendar times to walk the dog. Include buffer time between meetings so you can catch a breath, prepare, or jot down follow-up notes.

- **Audit (and declutter!) your calendar.** Do a monthly or quarterly review of your calendar and ask yourself: Do I need to be at that meeting? Are my recurring meetings useful? Are there upcoming deadlines that I need to create work blocks to meet? Do I have enough breaks? Use audits as a management tool, too—try doing one at your next check-in, where you review an upcoming week on your staff's calendar and find things to declutter.

Set Boundaries

"One of the things I remind myself—and my loved ones remind me when I forget—is that my no isn't just a no, it is also a yes. When I'm clear enough to say no to what I don't want, then I have more room to say yes to what I do want. I can't have my true yeses without the nos."

—*Mia Birdsong, author of* How We Show Up: Reclaiming
Family, Friendship, and Community

In Chapter 2, we talked about setting emotional boundaries. Here, we're talking about boundaries around your time and energy. When your to-do list, calendar, and inbox are perpetually overstuffed, color-coding won't quell the overwhelm. Boundaries are the glue that holds our systems together.

For managers, supporting staff to set and assert boundaries is one of the most important management moves we can make to increase equity, sustainability, and results. The people on our teams most likely to overextend themselves and accommodate others are those who feel they need to "earn" their place—whether because they're new, more junior, or have marginalized identities. Setting boundaries is always easier in a culture that normalizes and celebrates it.

Here are some tips for setting boundaries:

- **Share the why behind the "no."** "To make sure I can deliver on X, I can't do Y right now." Or, "I'd really like to support X, but XYZ is happening, and I need to focus on that." When you say "no" to someone you don't work with closely or who has less positional power than you, sharing the rationale is more than a matter of courtesy. A task, meeting, or request may not be your big rock, but it might be the other person's. Communicating your "no" with a rationale shows respect and consideration for the other person.

- **Make proposals.** For requests that need to be deferred or rescheduled, share your context, make a proposal, and check in. "I have an important deadline this week that's taking more time than expected. I'd like to push back our meeting by two weeks. How does that sound to you?"

- **Mind the impact of your "no."** The more power you have within your organization, the more important it is to understand how your actions impact others. Two things are true: first, setting boundaries to protect your time and energy is important; second, when the work is interdependent or collaborative, our "no" can create more work or barriers for others (often those with less power than us). How you allocate your time and resources is a *choice point*, so check for patterns in whom you say "no" to (or whom you make exceptions for).

MAKING DECISIONS IN TIMES OF CHANGE AND UNCERTAINTY

Change is a constant. While some changes are good, a lot of the change we encounter these days is the debilitating and destabilizing kind—like a pandemic, setbacks in legislation, and acts of violence. Even instability at the organizational level—like drops in funding, shaky leadership transitions, and political disagreements—can be highly disruptive.

In these moments, our decisions—and how we go about them—make a difference. When managers navigate challenging circumstances well, their teams are better off. People feel connected, build trust and resilience, and are grounded in purpose—and they're more likely to stick around and do great work.

Here are some tips for making decisions in times of crisis or uncertainty:

Lift Up Purpose, Agency, and Connection

To be okay, humans need to feel a sense of control over their lives. Unfortunately, many of us already live with trauma, violence, oppression, and other forms of disempowerment that limit our choices and safety. So when we make decisions that support purpose, agency, and connection, we make it easier for our staff to navigate change and uncertainty. Here are some ways to do it:

- **Purpose:** When communicating decisions, connect them to your mission, vision, and goals. Remind people why you're all here, what you're working toward, and why their contributions matter. For example, you could say, "Your work helps us keep parents and guardians informed so they can feel assured that their kids are safe with us."

- **Agency:** Help staff focus on what's in their *sphere of control*. Align on the big rocks and let them figure out the how. Involve people in the decisions that affect them. If you can, offer more flexibility and control over how they spend their time and energy.

- **Connection:** During hard times, moments of genuine care and connection are like air pockets in an avalanche—they help you survive. Learn how your staff members prefer to connect. Where you can, inject joy, play, and silliness—anything from taking 10 minutes to learn a dance move to hosting a virtual costume contest.

Reprioritize

Knowing when and how to shift your priorities is just as important as prioritizing in the first place. It's not always easy to let go of well-laid plans, but sometimes it's the only way to manage your time and energy well. As our colleague Court likes to say, "Let go or be dragged."

While reprioritizing can trigger feelings of scarcity, remember that it's not just about setting aside prior commitments because you don't have *enough* (time, energy, people power). Instead, you're *making room* for the most important things (and modeling being flexible and strategic!).

When you reprioritize, don't forget to renegotiate with your stakeholders. Most likely, your priorities overlap with your teammates', and changing them will have ripple effects. When you communicate with stakeholders, share your rationale and make a proposal to revisit priorities later (see Chapter 10 for more about "making proposals").

Reprioritization is *most* important during times of uncertainty and crisis. Knowing what's most important helps everyone stay focused, agile, and grounded in purpose. In addition, it gives you a sense of agency when things feel out of control.

Sometimes, the best way to reprioritize is to *deprioritize* work. Court, our colleague mentioned earlier, recalled a time when her mental health was spiraling. Her counselor recommended a full-time 6–12 week program to let her focus on recovery and healing. Unfortunately, she didn't feel she could take time off work—we were in the thick of audit season and had an all-staff retreat to plan. And as our chief of staff at the time, these were time-sensitive big rocks for Court. Her counselor asked her to consider mentioning the program to Jerry, her manager. She brought it up during their check-in and listed all the reasons she couldn't take time off, but Jerry pushed back. "He told me my life was more important than any job," she shared. "And his words matched his actions. During that check-in, we planned for me to be out starting the following day."

KEY POINTS OF DECISION-MAKING AND PRIORITIZING

Here are the takeaways from the chapter:

- How we approach decisions is what separates the *conspire-and-align* approach from command-and-control. The most effective managers and leaders conspire with their teams to make great decisions, and align around those decisions clearly and swiftly.

- An effective decision gets you the outcomes you want using an inclusive process that builds trust, power, relationships, and culture.

  - Always examine your *choice points*.

  - Share your **decision mode**, which tells people what type of input you're seeking, how you'll engage with it, and how open you are to ideas.

  - Make a **pros/cons/mitigations** chart to get beyond "either/or" thinking and better understand the full risks and benefits of a decision.

  - Don't be afraid to **delegate** decision-making.

- Use **fair process** for inclusive decision-making, which entails:

  - **Engagement** with stakeholders by seeking perspective and inviting dissent.

  - **Explanation** of the decision after you've made it.

  - **Expectation clarity** about what will be different moving forward, like updated role expectations, goals, procedures, or policies.

  - **Evaluation** (optional) to debrief the decision and analyze the outcomes.

- To make decisions about prioritizing your time and energy, use these concepts:

  - Focus on the **big rocks** before the "jar" of your time and energy gets filled by pebbles and sand.

- Consider the level of **urgency** and **importance** of each task or project. The highest priorities are important; the lowest are not important and not urgent.

- Know when something needs to be "**gold star**," and when "**good enough**" will suffice, to be more discerning, strategic, and sustainable.

- Schedule distraction-free **work blocks** on your calendar designated for you to work on particular projects or tasks.

- Set and honor boundaries around your time and energy.

- In times of crisis and uncertainty, lift up **purpose, agency, and connection**, and **reprioritize** as needed.

CHAPTER

6

HIRING AND BUILDING YOUR TEAM

In Chapter 4, we talk about Valerie, our head of talent, who needed to hire a director of talent. When she finally hired someone—Breanna—the results were incredible. To say that Breanna was a good hire would be an understatement. In just under a year at TMC, Breanna:

- Helped us fill 12 roles.

- Set standard practices around hiring processes and got hiring managers aligned on them. These practices improved candidates' experiences, mitigated bias, and ultimately, made everyone's job easier.

- Created a way for finalists to share feedback about equity, accessibility, timeliness, and overall experience of our hiring process.

- Was promoted because of all of the above (and much more!).

Beyond owning—and improving—the day-to-day work, Breanna contributed to TMC in other ways. She showed up ready to be a team player, from sharing ideas about our brand refresh to judging our admin team's annual gingerbread decorating contest. In addition, Breanna gently pushed and supported Valerie to buck traditions that got in the way of equity, sustainability, and results.

When we make great hires, *everything* gets better.

- Our results are stronger because of the added talent and capacity.

- We get to spend our time and energy more strategically.

- Our teams benefit from a new colleague's fresh perspectives, experiences, and energy.

- As managers, we get a new partner in the work—someone to *conspire and align* with.

Hiring well is one of the most important things we do as managers. Unfortunately, it's also one of the places where managers struggle the most. We get it—it's time-consuming work. Paradoxically, we often hire when we're already understaffed, while hiring demands staffing capacity. And often, we don't make it a big rock, so we fail to dedicate the appropriate time and capacity to do it. But it's worth investing the resources to create an effective hiring process. It's worth prioritizing, even if that means scaling back on other work to make it happen. In the long run, an excellent hire saves time and energy. A bad hiring decision, on the other hand, will leave you further behind than when you started.

An effective hiring process helps you find what you're looking for while showing your candidates who you are as a manager and as an organization. It lets people imagine how they'd fit in—and ideally gets them excited about joining your team. A well-designed process brings in a great pool of candidates, minimizes angst and extraneous work, and enables you to find a superstar. And when that person finally starts, they will help you take your work to the next level, just like Breanna did for Valerie and TMC.

In this chapter, we explain how to:

- Define the role and write a great job posting.

- Build a robust, diverse pool of candidates.

- Conduct the interview process.

- Choose your top candidate and make a strong offer.

- Onboard and train your new hire.

. . .all while spotting choice points, checking your biases, and examining your PTR!

CREATING THE ROLE

Before you write your job posting, reflect on why this hire is important. Whether filling a vacancy or creating a role, you should know how your work will benefit from having someone great in it. How will they add to the diversity of your team? Will having additional capacity get projects off the back burner? Will a new hire increase sustainability for people by taking things off overflowing plates? Will a fresh perspective energize your team?

Once you know the "why," figure out the "what." Outline the duties and responsibilities of the role and the skills and approaches needed to succeed in it. (Refer to Chapter 4 for more advice on how to define role expectations.)

Figure out which buckets of work the person will own. If they were to call themselves the "CEO of ____," what big-picture responsibility would go in that blank? You can use previous job descriptions as a guide, but don't assume everything should be the same.

Separate "Must-Haves" from "Nice-to-Haves"

PTR check! Think through the requirements, or "must-haves," for the role (we recommend four to six). You will refer to them at every step of the hiring process. (You'll also refer to them later when you evaluate the staff person's performance—see Chapter 7.)

Must-haves are competencies[1] that someone needs from day one. They're role requirements because they would take more time or resources to develop than you're willing or able to spend on teaching a new hire. Must-haves often include hard-to-teach skills or qualities like critical thinking, empathy, or attention to detail. "Nice-to-haves" are what they sound like—competencies that are nice to have but aren't essential to the person's success.

Check if your "requirements" are just preferences or traditions in disguise by asking yourself: Is this competency *really* needed to do the job well? If so, is it a skill they need to have *right now*, or can it be picked up along the way?

The following are a few common "must-haves" to be cautious about because they frequently reinforce existing inequities. Consider excluding these from the job listing:[2]

- **Educational requirements.** Unless you're in a field where a special license or certification is required to do the job, educational requirements create barriers that limit your pool of candidates. Seriously—no one needs a bachelor's degree to be an excellent organizer.

- **Years of experience.** Here's our beef with years of experience: it tells you how *long* someone did something without telling you how *well* they did it. That's a

---

[1] A competency is a skill, quality, mindset, or knowledge base that someone needs to do a job well.

[2] If you do list one of these criteria as a must-have, make sure you have a clear and specific reason.

pretty cheap proxy for skills and expertise! Also, marginalized people already have inequitable access to job opportunities—years of experience requirements only perpetuate that cycle. (It's hard to gain the years if you can't get in the door in the first place!)

- **Written communication skills.** While some roles rightfully require strong writing ability, we've found that people tend to overemphasize writing ability in hiring. This can happen even when it's not an explicit must-have—have you ever judged someone because of a typo in their cover letter? It's also an equity issue. If you judge people's writing skills harshly, you might pass up great candidates who are English language learners or have language processing issues. Trust us—in many cases, it's okay if someone sometimes confuses "your" and "you're."

Removing unnecessary barriers for candidates helps make your process more equitable. It also makes it less likely that you'll accidentally weed out candidates who don't fit the traditional profile but could otherwise do an excellent job. For instance, some research indicates that women are less likely to apply for jobs than men if they don't meet all of the qualifications listed on a posting.[3] We've experienced and witnessed this ourselves. In fact, Monna probably wouldn't have applied to work on TMC's content team if the job description hadn't said, "You don't need to be a writer to be considered for this role."

Talent often trumps experience. Just ask one of our clients, who hired a head of finance who had no accounting experience. The client needed someone who could see the bigger picture and how everything fit together, but also zoom into the nitty gritty details. She needed someone who could explain complicated financial ideas in layperson's terms. Ultimately, the candidate she hired was a data person who had no finance experience, but had many transferable skills and a drive to learn. This person nailed the must-haves, which included things like critical thinking, problem-solving, and comfort with numbers. When our client decided to hire them, she said, "finance is just data with dollar signs."

To see a sample of our "Figuring Out the Role" worksheet, see Tool 6.1 in the Appendix Tools at the end of this chapter.

---

[3] An often-cited statistic claims that women only apply for jobs if they meet 100% of the criteria compared to 60% for men, but the source of that is a Hewlett Packard internal report with no hard quantitative data. However, an analysis by LinkedIn ("New Report: Women Apply to Fewer Jobs Than Men, But Are More Likely to Get Hired," 2019) of its job search data does back up the idea that women are more selective about which jobs they apply for; women applied to 20% fewer jobs than men, and were 16% less likely than men to apply to a job after viewing it.

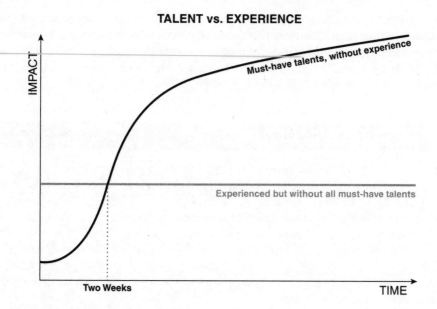

TALENT vs. EXPERIENCE

Equity and Inclusion Competency

We recommend including equity and inclusion competency as a must-have for every role.[4]

At TMC, here are a few equity and inclusion must-haves we've used:

- Effectively develops and builds relationships across lines of difference and power.

- Able to build an inclusive culture.

- Demonstrates self-awareness: understands their limits and biases and knows when to seek other perspectives.

- Leverages positional (and other) power to lift up and value the work of others, particularly those with marginalized identities.

- Able to set, own, and deliver on organizational equity and inclusion goals.

In addition, think about the specific *choice points* someone might encounter in their day-to-day work. For instance, imagine that you run a communications

---

[4] When TMC started doing this in our own hiring, it led to some remarkable organizational changes and growth; refer back to Chapter 4 for more on that story.

department for a national reproductive justice organization. Let's say you want your organization to represent the most marginalized people in your community, including queer and trans people, immigrants and refugees, and disabled people. In that case, everyone on your team should also be knowledgeable about web accessibility best practices, bias-free writing, and inclusive design.

WHAT ABOUT "CULTURE FIT"?

We've moved away from using the term *culture fit*, a common must-have in job descriptions. Here's why: it too easily lets our biases get in the way of equity and results. When we search for "culture fit," we're asking, "Will this person fit in with our organization as it is now?" And that question gets us dangerously close to "like me" and "I like you" bias.[5] With "like me" bias, we evaluate people favorably because they're similar to us. With "I like you" bias, we do it because we get along with them (remember that training participant who was hesitant about hiring someone they wouldn't want to hang out with?). When these biases drive our hiring decisions, we end up with teams that lack diversity in identities, backgrounds, and perspectives.[6]

On the other hand, we want every new staff person to work well with our team and be aligned with our organizational values. After all, our team has an existing culture, and we can't pretend it doesn't exist.

So what can you do? We have a few recommendations:

- **Be explicit about your values.** Test for values alignment in the hiring process. For example, at TMC, we value learning and growth—a true must-have. One way this shows up is that we strive to be accountable when we cause harm. So, one of our common interview questions is, "Tell us about a time when you caused harm to someone with less positional power than you. What did you do?"

- **Look for "culture add."** Culture isn't static, and we all aspire to grow and improve our cultures (we hope!)—which means we should hire people who can help us do that. What do you need more people to embody so the organization can realize its values or strategic direction? Is it a highly collaborative spirit? A drive toward results? Culture add forces us to be honest about those aspirations and helps us see how a candidate might challenge the status quo of our existing culture.

---

[5] The tendency to judge in favor of someone we like. "Bias from Liking/Loving: Why We Comply with Those We Love," Farnan Street, fs.blog/mental-model-bias-from-liking-loving

[6] Outside of hiring, we've also seen "culture fit" weaponized against marginalized people within organizations—most commonly against BIPOC in predominantly white organizations who didn't code-switch well enough.

Write the Job Posting

Once you've defined the role and identified your must-haves, use them as your guide to writing the job description.

You want your most promising candidates to read the posting and think, "Wow, this job was made for me!" To do this, you should use clear language, avoid jargon, and not get too bogged down in the details. Be inspirational and honest—don't just list out a bunch of responsibilities, but also don't just highlight the exciting parts of the job.

Recheck your PTRs when deciding what materials you'll require for an application. What must-haves are you looking for in the first stage of the process? What will help you test for them? If you know you'll need to see work samples, ask for them with the application—but make it easy by requesting existing work.

We also recommend sharing information about the process so that candidates can understand the steps and how much time they'll invest.

Your job description should contain the following:

- A high-level summary of your ideal candidate.

- A brief overview of your organization.

- An overview of the role's major responsibilities.

- Four to six must-haves.

- Compensation, benefits, and other enticing qualities about your organization.

- Information about how to apply and what to expect from the process.

Salary (and Other) Transparency

Making the implicit explicit in job postings can have major equity implications. Some of you might be legally obligated to disclose a salary range in your posting. Even if you're not, we recommend being as transparent as possible about salary and benefits. If your organization doesn't negotiate salaries, share that upfront.

Legalities aside, it's good to be honest about compensation early in the process for the following reasons:

- Reducing the need for negotiation makes it more likely for women and BIPOC to receive equitable pay. Research shows that gender and race influence candidates' willingness to negotiate for higher salaries.[7] They also impact how candidates are received when they do, with women and BIPOC being judged more harshly the more they negotiate.[8]

---

[7] Kerry Jones, "Gender Can Be a Bigger Factor than Race in Raise Negotiation," *Harvard Business Review*, 2016, hbr.org/2016/09/gender-can-be-a-bigger-factor-than-race-in-raise-negotiations

[8] "Counteracting Negotiation Biases Like Race and Gender in the Workplace," Program on Negotiation Daily Blog, Harvard Law School, 2020, www.pon.harvard.edu/daily/leadership-skills-daily/counteracting-racial-and-gender-bias-in-job-negotiations-nb

WHAT DO YOU MEAN BY "DIVERSITY"?

Hiring can be a crucial lever in advancing diversity, equity, and inclusion because the make-up of your team impacts your organization's mainstreams and margins. Every new person adds new perspectives to the mix. Research shows that diverse teams get better outcomes in decision-making, problem-solving, and employee experience.[9] And for many of us, it aligns with our values to build organizations where people from various backgrounds feel welcome and included.

If you're looking to increase diversity through hiring, first be explicit about what type of diversity you want to build and why. Then, focus on building your pool and reducing barriers in your application and interview process. Don't lower the bar on your must-haves or let demographic criteria outweigh competencies. (Aside from being illegal, it's unwise.)

Also, don't focus on hiring as your primary (or only) strategy for diversity, equity, and inclusion without laying a foundation first. It can result in marginalized staff feeling tokenized and exploited. In addition, it usually means that your "firsts" (e.g., the first Black person, the first queer person, the first Indigenous person) end up doing the work of educating and advocating—often on top of their regular duties and without extra compensation. While it's normal for organizations to evolve their policies, practices, and systems as their teams grow and change, it's *not* okay to do a diversity bait-and-switch. Don't hire people with marginalized identities and expect them to transform your organization (unless this is an explicit part of their job). It's like inviting someone to dinner and making them clean, cook, and serve.

- People working in social change aren't just doing it for the good feelings—most of us need to make a living! Posting salary information helps candidates make informed decisions about whether to apply. You don't want to wait until you've invested weeks (or months!) to discover that the most you could offer is far below your first-choice candidate's needs.

- Transparency builds trust, and your job posting is the first opportunity to do it. Start your relationship off on the right foot by being honest.

BUILDING A STRONG, DIVERSE POOL OF CANDIDATES

The quality of your pool determines the quality of your hire. You can spend hours crafting the job description, designing great interview questions, or refining your rubric.

---

[9] "Why Diverse Teams Are Smarter," *Harvard Business Review*, 2016, hbr.org/2016/11/why-diverse-teams-are-smarter

Still, if you don't also spend time and energy building your pool through proactive outreach, your other efforts won't matter.

We rely on three tactics for building our candidate pools: mass marketing, talent scouting, and finding connector sources.

Mass Marketing

Of course you'll post your job listing on your website as well as online job boards and networking sites. But also think about the spaces where people congregate, such as schools, faith communities, professional groups, and mailing lists. Post to lists that serve marginalized communities, such as LGBTQ jobs boards, professional networking groups for specific BIPOC groups, and affinity groups on college campuses. In a world of social media and the mixing of the social and professional, it's easier than ever to go beyond the usual suspects to get more diverse pools of applicants.

Note: Mass marketing helps cast a wide net, but it should never be your *only* outreach tactic.

Talent Scouting

Go beyond mass channels and proactively look for people to recruit, including by working your personal connections. And to diversify your pool, encourage other people on your team to do the same. People are more likely to do anything when they're personally invited by someone they know (Bex recruited Monna to apply to work at TMC!).

Remember that you can find potential talent everywhere. Once, a few TMC staff took a cardio fitness class together—the instructor was so engaging that our colleague Deb considered recruiting her to apply to be a trainer!

Finding Connectors

Do you know a social "hub"—someone who seems to know everybody? Part of talent scouting involves digging into your networks and finding people who can connect you with potential candidates. Reaching out to a diverse set of connectors is essential for building a diverse pool.

Think of people in your networks who are highly connected. Reach out to them directly to tell them about the role and ask for specific recommendations or ideas for potential applicants. To help you brainstorm contacts who might be good connectors, think about your networks in terms of three categories:

- **Professional:** Past jobs, partnerships, professional memberships, your field/sector.

- **Educational:** High schools, colleges, universities, school networks.

- **Personal:** Personal networks and communities (religious, recreational, volunteer, friends).

Here's a quick sample email you might send to a connector:

Hi X!

I'm reaching out because I know you're connected to lots of people, and I thought you might have ideas for candidates for a role I'm hiring.

The role is a receptionist for our school. This is the first person community members see and talk to. We're looking for someone who is highly organized, has strong follow-through (especially with tight deadlines), and communicates well (they'll be interacting with many people—including other staff, students, and caregivers. We are especially looking for candidates who can model the respect and care we have for our school and broader community members.

The salary range is $62–68K and includes a generous benefits package. The full details about the job are attached and linked here.

If anyone in your network is a good fit, please let me know (I may ask you for an email introduction). If it'd help to chat more, I'm happy to give you a quick ring!

Thanks,
Y

WHAT ABOUT HIRING OR PROMOTING FROM WITHIN?

You might have great candidates right under your nose. Here's our best advice for approaching an internal hiring process:

- **Explicitly inform staff about the role and process.** Either before or at the same time as you post the job, let staff know. If you have very promising internal candidates, you might consider sharing internally first and then posting the job if those candidates don't pan out. Or, you can cast a wide net and simultaneously have internal and external candidates in the mix.

- **Don't test for competencies you already know they have.** Think about their competencies (referring to previous performance evaluations or their existing role expectations if needed) and consider what must-haves you still need to test.

- **Modify the process for internal candidates.** With the possible exception of senior-level roles, internal candidates should ideally go through a shorter process than their external counterparts, especially if you've removed extraneous questions or assignments. Instead of checking external references, use internal references (discreetly).

- **Respect their privacy.** Keep your internal candidates confidential and on a need-to-know basis. Be mindful of their privacy when you create calendar invitations for interviews or share hiring rubrics with your hiring team.

DESIGNING THE HIRING PROCESS

There's no way around it—the interview process takes time. You must figure out the must-haves, write interview questions, recruit interviewers, screen applications, and fill out hiring rubrics. You need to check in with your team along the way to make sure you're aligned. You also need to check in with yourself to examine your biases, assumptions, and preferences.

But like we said, it's *really* worth investing the time upfront to create a thorough, equitable, and values-aligned process. Again, the time wasted with a poor hiring decision will far outweigh the time you save by cutting corners in the hiring process.

From start to finish, your overall interview process might be broken into the following phases:

- Résumé/application submission.

- One to three interviews (depending on the role).

- Paid exercise (this might come before, after, or in between interviews).

- Reference checks.

- Offer and acceptance.

We often remind clients that with the interview process, you're not just in evaluation mode—you're still in recruitment mode, too. The process should help candidates understand what the job will entail, whom their colleagues will be, and how they'll feel about showing up to work. To avoid a long, arduous process that leaves everyone exhausted, be strategic about what you test and when. And no matter your decision, make sure to communicate with people promptly and kindly at every stage.

Assembling Your Team

Hiring is a team sport. As the hiring manager, you're the captain. You'll make the decisions, but need helpers to balance your perspectives and provide insight. That's where your hiring team will come in—they'll provide input on the must-haves and role description, participate in interviews, and evaluate candidates. Your hiring team should comprise people who understand what's needed in the role, will work closely with the hire, and bring diverse identities and perspectives.

Creating a Hiring Rubric

Make sure your hiring team is aligned on the must-haves (and how you'll test for them!) by creating a hiring rubric. Rubrics are key to equitable hiring because they provide clarity and minimize subjective assessments. For instance, "strong project management skills" might mean different things to different team members. Do you need somebody who can hold people to deadlines? Somebody who has great instincts for stakeholder inclusion? Something else?

To create a rubric, list your must-haves and their associated "look-fors."[10] You might also want to list yellow or red flags and qualities you *aren't* looking for.

For example, in hiring a curriculum designer position at TMC, one must-have was project management ability (defined in the sample rubric in Table 6.1). We *weren't* looking for someone who was a project management software expert. If the candidate lacked self-awareness or focused solely on logistics and task management without attention to relationships (and vice versa), those were red flags.

Table 6.1 Sample Hiring Rubric.

Must-have	Rating (1–4)	Comments, examples, and evidence
Must-have #1: Curriculum design skills. • Able to design curricula that meet the needs of adults with multiple learning styles. • Uses different modalities (facilitated, experiential, workshop, and direct instruction). • Understands online learning platforms and can make strong recommendations. • Writes clear, comprehensive talking points.	2	Hasn't designed for others to facilitate, and I think this showed up in his work sample, which was an agenda outline without nuance about how the session was constructed. He had a strong grasp of interactive learning styles and was able to articulate learner outcomes. Because he has no experience designing for others and didn't submit a work sample that demonstrates this, I can't say that he can write clear, comprehensive talking points or trainer guides.
Must-have #2: Commitment to racial justice and equity. • Has intersectional understanding of oppression, identity, and power through lived and learned experience. • Able to foster learning experiences that center those traditionally marginalized in workplace trainings—such as BIPOC, neurodivergent folks, disabled people, and early career staff.	3	Strong answer on incorporating racial or disability justice in design. For example, suggested that when designing, ask how the design might be received by a new educator, or by the only Black teacher at an all-white school.

(Continued)

---

[10] "Look-fors" are your must-haves in action—how you'll know when you see, hear, or experience it in the interview process.

Table 6.1 (Continued)

Must-have	Rating (1–4)	Comments, examples, and evidence
Must-have #3: Project management skills. Able to: • Drive a project. • Hear input from a variety of stakeholders (truly welcoming viewpoints that differ from their own) and decide the best course of action. • Communicate effectively across differences in identity, power, and position, and build rapport and trust with others. • Set and meet realistic deadlines and reprioritize when faced with unexpected challenges.	3	In one example, it was clear he took responsibility to spot issues with the existing curriculum and offer solutions or new paths. He was nervous to share with program leaders, but built rapport and buy-in. When there was participant feedback he couldn't accommodate around asynchronous learning, he decided to hold off, showing prioritization.

Include a numerical score and space in your rubric to support the rating with examples and observations. Here's a snippet of a sample hiring rubric.

Every interviewer should fill out a rubric after every stage—including you, the hiring manager! When it's time to make your final decision, you'll need them to look at the bigger picture and see where your candidate met the must-haves (or didn't).

Planning Interview Questions

You'll generally ask two types of questions in any interview: questions to probe prior experiences and scenarios or simulations of actual job activities. Unless you're testing the candidate's ability to think on their feet, consider sharing some (or all) of your interview questions in advance. Here are the benefits of sharing questions in advance:

• It helps people who need more time to process.

• It helps people who process information better when it's written.

• It can reduce nerves, which will help them perform better. (Unless you expect them to be anxious every second on the job, this will give you better insight into how they'll actually perform.)

• It gives you insight into *how* they prepare.

RECOGNIZING YOUR BIASES

At the beginning of this book, we said that bias is like dental plaque—we all have it. It's our job to keep an eye on it and take basic precautions to ensure our biases don't get out of hand. Yes, hiring rubrics are helpful tools for mitigating bias because they force us to slow down and look for evidence to back up our scores—but they're not enough. If we don't recognize our biases, they'll still show up in our assessments, and we might miss out on qualified candidates.

Our biases are shaped by our upbringing, culture(s), and experiences. They're influenced by the dominant culture and mainstream norms. And they show up in many different ways for each of us. We've already mentioned two types of biases that commonly show up in hiring: "like me" and "I like you."[11] Here are two questions you can ask yourself to identify and examine your biases:

- What identities, experiences, and qualities do I most identify with? Why?
- What identities, qualities, or experiences do I most admire or judge favorably? What do I judge harshly? Why?

At TMC, we share our more complex interview questions with candidates in advance and foreshadow what topics we'll cover. For example, we mentioned earlier that we sometimes ask candidates to tell us about a time they caused harm to someone with less positional power than them. This question requires self-reflection and can bring up some—potentially hard—memories that might be difficult to process on the spot. Sharing this question in advance gives the candidate space to prepare a thoughtful response.

With that said, there *are* times when it's helpful to ask an on-the-spot question. This is where follow-up questions come in handy—they help you get past the surface of a polished (possibly rehearsed) answer and check for depth. For example, with the question about harm, one follow-up question could be, "What, if anything, did that

---

[11] To be clear, having these biases isn't an inherently *bad* thing—sometimes, these biases can even help us appreciate things in candidates that others might overlook, especially if the "like me" part is a marginalized identity or experience. But we need to be able to recognize our biases to avoid having them be the deciding factor in our hiring decisions, which should be based on how well the candidate meets the must-haves.

experience lead you to do differently in your other working relationships?" Always be prepared with follow-up questions to dig deeper.

Probing Prior Experiences ("Tell us about a time when. . .")

It's important to explore a candidate's actual prior experiences. Probing prior experiences lets you see how they approach their work and how self-aware they are about their actions and choices.

Let's use racial equity and inclusion competency as an example of the must-have you're testing for. You might ask, "Can you talk about a time you navigated tricky dynamics around race or other identities in your work? What did you do?" Some follow-up questions could be, "What do you think were the root causes of those dynamics?" or "What lessons did you learn?"

Realistic Scenarios and Simulations

"Let's say you have the job. XYZ happens. What do you do?" Questions like this are useful for two reasons:

- They help you understand how your candidate would respond to situations that may crop up on the job. This is especially helpful if they haven't been in a similar role.

- They help the candidate better understand the role.

In our experience, the best scenario questions are complex and realistic. There's no single correct answer, and the challenges presented have multiple factors to consider. They help you better understand someone's analysis, skills, and approach when faced with a challenge. And the closer the simulation or scenario is to an actual situation they might encounter in the role, the better.

Here are three examples of scenario questions:

- For a finance manager position: "Let's imagine you're starting in this role at the beginning of October. Your new manager (our head of finance) has a list of items on the back burner this year that she'd like your help with. How would you prioritize this list? Please come prepared to discuss the order of prioritization and why."

- For a political director position: "Assume you were working within a coalition of several nonprofits. If you disagreed with a strategy the coalition wanted to pursue, how would you navigate that?"

- For a communications role: "Here's a blog post we wrote about an issue that's very important to our audience. What are three to five suggestions you'd make for how we could improve it?" In this question, one of your "look-fors" might be their ability to spot places where the article is race-silent or uses biased language.

See Tool 6.2 in the Appendix Tools at the end of this chapter for sample interview questions.

Exercises

Exercises and simulations are incredibly helpful for evaluating candidates outside of interviews (which means less time spent scheduling!). There are two kinds of exercises:

- **Bite-sized simulations.** Simple, small assignments are best at the beginning of the process. For example, we give coach candidates a short assignment of responding to a sample email from a client with a management challenge. These simulations should be easy for candidates to produce and even easier for you to evaluate.

- **Full-blown assignments.** Use these to see what a promising candidate can deliver with more time and effort. For example, suppose you're hiring a writer. In that case, samples of their work might not help you gauge their fit because you won't know how well they can adopt your organization's voice. So you might ask candidates to write the first draft of an article (making sure to share your organizational style guide and guidance on what you'd expect from a first draft). Assignments also help you compare apples to apples by letting you see how different candidates deliver the same work product.

When requesting an exercise, tell the candidate how much time you expect them to spend on it. Make sure that the scope of the assignment is reasonable for the time limit, and be explicit about the degree of completeness you're looking for. For example, in asking for a writing exercise, you might say, "We're not looking for more than 300 words. Think of this as a first—not final—draft. We're just hoping to get a sense of your approach, so please don't spend more than an hour on it."

Pay the candidate for their time if the exercise will take more than an hour. If you think seeing more involved work would help you make a better decision, you could make it a paid freelance project.

For legal and ethical reasons, *do not* ask candidates to do unpaid work that you might use. For example, you can ask candidates to write a sample press release about a fictitious or past event. But if there's any chance you'll use their work, pay them and share how it might be used. Finally, give ample time to complete the exercise (we recommend at least one week). Also, be flexible if they need to negotiate the deadline because of other commitments or priorities.

See Tool 6.3 at the end of this chapter for sample exercises.

Conducting Interviews

Do your best to put the candidate at ease—you're hiring, not hazing! Job interviews are already stressful; don't make it more so by keeping candidates on edge.

You might ask some initial "getting to know you" questions earlier in the process, like in a phone screen or in the first interview, but save the bulk of your interview time for the deep-dive questions about prior experience and/or scenarios.

A one-hour first interview might go something like this:

- Welcome and introductions—3 minutes.

- General question about their interest in the role—5 minutes.

- Three to four questions about prior experiences, hypothetical scenarios, and/or simulations (with follow-up questions)—40 minutes.

- Description of the job, culture, and organization (from you) followed by questions from the candidate, and any follow-up questions you have about the questions they ask—10 minutes.

- Wrap up, thank the candidate, and tell them when to expect to hear from you next—2 minutes.

Don't forget to leave room for questions from the candidate at the end of every interview. Taking questions from candidates gives you insight into what they care about and gives them the chance to learn more about you, the role, and your organization.

Reference Checks

Make reference checks a distinct step in the process, rather than a formality you check off before making an offer. Conversations with references can help you decide between two similarly qualified candidates—or surface red flags that might not have come up in your interview. Of course, most candidates only list people as references who will give them glowing reviews. Still, there are ways of reading between the lines of a reference's positive spin, and you can ask probing questions to get more nuanced feedback.

For instance, references might be reluctant to get specific about a candidate's weaknesses or growth areas. Here are some questions that might help:

- What kinds of jobs would you *not* recommend X for?

- Tell me about a time when X struggled with something. How did they resolve it?

- Let's say I hired X. If I called you in six months and told you that it wasn't working out, why do you imagine that might be?

If the reference conversations you have are unhelpful, you can ask candidates to provide contact details for additional references. For a sample reference check outline, see Tool 6.4 at the end of this chapter.

WHAT ABOUT "OFF-LIST" REFERENCES?

Sometimes clients ask us if it's okay to do "off-list" reference checks—reaching out to contacts outside their organization who weren't included on the candidate's references list. This is tricky! We believe in being honest with candidates, practicing consent, and respecting candidate confidentiality. Many people apply for jobs while still employed—you could jeopardize someone's job by disclosing to their employer or a mutual contact that they're job hunting.

Still, we know that it can be helpful to hear from someone you know and trust who isn't on the candidate's curated list. Sometimes you need more information or want to better understand a specific aspect of their work.

Here's how we'd proceed: be transparent and let the candidate know there's someone else you want to reach out to. You could say, "I know X person who worked with you at Y organization. I'd like to talk to them as an additional reference. Do you have any concerns about my reaching out?" You might also share why you're seeking the additional reference. You could say, "You're one of our finalists, and I want to make sure we have what we need to make a decision. I'd love to hear from someone who worked with you during your tenure at X organization so that we can learn more about your work [on Y issue/as Z role]. Can you send me one to two additional references?"

MAKING THE DECISION

Don't just go with your gut! Stick to your rubric, and focus relentlessly on the must-haves. Discuss it with your interview team or a trusted colleague, and check your biases. Really imagine what it will be like to have this person in this role. Consider:

- What will they accomplish within the first six months?

- What will they need the most support on?

- What will be most challenging?

After thinking through what it might be like to have them in the role, check in with yourself—how excited are you? What are you still concerned about?

If you need more information from the candidate to make your decision, such as additional references or work samples, ask for it.

At the end of the process, you should know what must-haves they hit and which ones they're shaky on. By then, you should also know which ones you need your new hire to have from day one and which ones (if any) you'll support them to strengthen.

If you choose to hire someone who needs extra development in certain areas, be absolutely clear about the following when you make the offer:

- What the development area is.

- The plan to help them grow.

- How much ramp-up time they'll have.

Finally, if you haven't interviewed anyone who clears the bar you've set, don't settle. We repeat: *Don't. Settle*. We know it's frustrating to go through an entire process without hiring anyone. But it will be infinitely more frustrating to hire someone who can't do the job well. In most cases, you'll be better off keeping the position open and bringing in temporary help, shifting responsibilities among your current staff, or focusing only on your highest-priority activities until you find a great fit. (See Chapter 5 for more on how to reprioritize.)

CASE STUDY: WHY YOU SHOULDN'T SETTLE

Nina was the chief talent officer at a charter management organization. She was hiring a director of HR and needed someone to start within weeks. Unfortunately, they didn't have a great candidate pool. Nina eventually decided to hire Betty, even though she felt iffy about her. Betty didn't quite meet the must-haves, but she was the best of the bunch.

Nina could see immediately that Betty was out of her depth. Betty struggled to keep up with the volume of requests—in her rush to finish tasks, she missed vital details, resulting in mistakes like employees receiving paychecks with the wrong amounts. One time, an employee took her newborn baby to the pediatrician only to find out that the baby wasn't yet covered under her health insurance!

As you might imagine, the impacts were significant and pervasive. Employees lost trust in the HR department. Nina spent inordinate amounts of time and energy fixing Betty's mistakes. Betty constantly felt like she was underwater. She repeatedly failed to deliver, felt terrible about it, and then struggled to improve. Nina fired Betty within a year.

After Betty left, Nina refused to make the same mistake again and decided to hold out for a great hire. When she finally hired a replacement who met all the must-haves, she rejoiced at the difference it made. Employees got paid on time (and the correct amounts!), Nina had time and energy to work on the things within her comparative advantage, and people started trusting HR again.

Making the Offer

For hiring managers, making the offer is usually the most exciting part of the process. It means you've (almost) made it! This is your final opportunity to "sell" the position and get your potential new hire just as excited as you are.

Here are some tips for making your offer:

- **Don't hold back your enthusiasm!** Tell the candidate how excited you are about working together, and share why you think they'd be a great fit.

- **Lead with a strong, clear offer.** The salary and benefits you offer should reflect your enthusiasm. If you have a great candidate, don't risk losing them by low-balling the initial offer. We strongly recommend *against* basing it on their salary history or desired salary (seriously, don't even ask for these things).

- **Give them time to think it over.** Be honest about your timeline if you have one, but be willing to be flexible (and communicate that willingness!). The last thing you want is to lose a great hire because you pressured them to make a decision too quickly.

- **Offer more information.** Sometimes, candidates need more information to confidently accept an offer. You can ask, "Would it help to speak to someone else on the team?" Or "Is there anything else you still have questions about?"

- **Get a sense of what they're thinking.** Ask what factors they're considering—and respond to them if it makes sense. You could ask, "So, what's your initial reaction?" or "Is there anything you're still wondering or concerned about?" or "What would it take to get you to a 'yes'?"

MAKING THE IMPLICIT EXPLICIT: REJECT CANDIDATES WITH KINDNESS

It's never fun to reject someone, especially when they made it pretty far in the process. But rejection is a part of every hiring process and should be done explicitly. It's disrespectful to leave people hanging when they're no longer being considered for the role, even if all they've done is apply.

Above all, be kind. Our movements and communities are big, but the world is small. So assume that every candidate is someone you might encounter again—as a candidate or connector for another role, a donor, a colleague, or even your future boss.

The more time and energy the candidate invested in the process, the more you should personalize your rejection. You should also personalize it if they were a referral from a colleague. For a finalist candidate, we recommend sending a personalized email with an offer to do a call if the candidate wants more feedback or information.

For a sample rejection email, see Tool 6.5 at the end of this chapter.

ONBOARDING

You only get one chance to start a new relationship. The best part of a new management relationship is that you get to set the tone and establish excellent practices from the start!

Use your onboarding process to create and reinforce good management habits:

- **Check in regularly.** You may want to do shorter check-ins daily in the first two weeks. After that, switch to weekly and have your new hire own the check-in agenda. In the first month, you'll spend a lot of time answering questions, sharing context, and debriefing. (See Chapter 2 for more on how to run an effective check-in.)

- **Systematize feedback.** Use regular 2x2s (see Chapter 7), where you and your staff give each other praise and constructive feedback in your check-ins. Do debriefs after completing projects or assignments. The more you can normalize feedback from the beginning, the better you'll be set up for your long-term relationship.

- **Use delegation tools.** Get into the habit of sharing the five Ws, doing repeat-backs, and checking your preferences, traditions, and requirements. (See Chapter 3 for more on delegation.)

Set and Align on Expectations

Nothing will matter more for the success of your new hire than being on the same page as you about what's expected of them.

Ask yourself: "What would success look like after 30, 60, and 90 days?" Then use the answers to outline your new staff member's 30-, 60-, and 90-day goals. Those goals will likely include completing specific work products, building relationships with key people, and learning. You can also invite your new hire to propose a few of their own.

As always, *reflect on your PTR* regarding communication, relationship-building, and the work itself. Share your preferences and traditions, get their perspective, and be open to reconsidering (or be honest if you're not).

No matter how qualified they are, your new hire (or newly promoted staff person) will need support to be successful. Balance learning and doing for the first few weeks and months, emphasizing learning in the early days. To help them ramp up the "doing" part, start with one or two assignments that allow them to get immersed in their role—with ample modeling and side-by-side work with you or a colleague.

Debrief early and often! Your new hire's learning will come from well-timed check-ins and debriefs (along with formal learning opportunities and side-by-side work). For example, if a stakeholder emails you with a frequently asked question, you can forward your response to your new hire. Then, at your next check-in, discuss the inquiry and your response. You can tell them about the stakeholder, your thinking behind the reply, and any context that would be helpful for them to have when fielding future inquiries.

Focus on Belonging

The more welcomed, respected, and valued people feel, the more empowered they are to contribute their best. This is especially important for those with marginalized identities, who often face the burden of code switching, compartmentalizing, or diminishing aspects of their identities to "fit in." As the manager, you have a unique opportunity and responsibility to cultivate and maintain a sense of belonging for your new staff member. See Chapter 11 for more on building a healthy culture and Chapter 2 for more on relationship-building.

Here are a few ways to cultivate belonging:

- **Check in about access needs.** Access needs are the things that people need to communicate, learn, or fully participate in an activity. Examples of access needs include: live captioning at a meeting for someone who's hard of hearing, seating with backrests for people with chronic pain, and extra time to process information at meetings before jumping to decision-making. Only ask people to share the access needs as they're comfortable, and don't press for details—especially about medical issues.

- **Be a bridge.** Your new employee will need help establishing connections across the organization. Support them by making introductions, sharing context about a contact before a one-on-one, or inviting them to join a conversation at the water cooler.

- **Share the playbook (and invite feedback and questions).** Share information to help them do their job well, but remember that you hired them to contribute insights to improve your work (not just carry out orders). As one of our recent hires shared, "My manager consistently asked me to share my perspective and thoughts in our check-ins. It made me feel like I had something to contribute regardless of tenure, and my voice was equally important."

- **Don't overreact to mistakes.** Feeling like it's okay to mess up is key to psychological safety, so watch how you react to mistakes. One colleague made their first consequential mistake two months into the job. Feeling embarrassed and nervous, they agonized over how to approach their manager. When they finally worked up the courage to do it, they expected her to be upset. Instead, she reassured them that it was okay and confessed to making a similar (and even bigger!) mistake in the past. They laughed about it, made a plan to fix it, and moved on.

KEY POINTS OF BUILDING YOUR TEAM

Here are the takeaways from the chapter:

- Hiring well is one of the most important things we do as managers, and it's worth investing the time and resources to run an effective hiring process.

- Define the role you want to hire for. Separate the **"must-haves"** from the **"nice-to-haves"** to avoid perpetuating inequities. Use must-haves as your guide to writing the job description.

- Build a robust and diverse pool of candidates through mass marketing, individual talent scouting, and using "connectors." Focus on proactive efforts!

- Design a thorough, equitable, and values-aligned hiring process. Your process should communicate and reflect the kind of manager, team, and organization you are. In the process, **probe prior experiences** and use **exercises** that simulate what the job will actually entail.

- Use a **rubric** to minimize subjective assessments. Assemble a diverse hiring team of people with a stake in the hire. Align with your team on what the "must-haves" and the "look-fors" should be.

- When making your decision, don't just go with your gut! Stick to your rubric, focus on the must-haves, and imagine what it would be like to have this person in the role.

- Don't settle for a hire who doesn't meet the bar of your must-haves. If you hire someone who needs extra development in certain areas, be clear about that when making the offer.

- During onboarding, align expectations for the first 30, 60, and 90 days, and work to cultivate belonging.

APPENDIX TOOLS

TOOL 6.1

FIGURING OUT THE ROLE—SAMPLE

State Health Care Now: State Policy Director

<u>This person is the CEO of...</u> Building power for our people by advancing our policy agenda

Areas of responsibility

- Build and maintain relationships with key actors in state—policy makers, nonprofit leaders, and constituents
- Lead implementation of state advocacy agenda
- Supervise 3 state-based project staff, 2–4 consultants, and 10–20 volunteers
- Monitor legislative proposals and trends
- Serve on the organization's leadership team

Specific things this person would be doing now

- Call Joan at Citizens United and convince her ED should speak at their state conference
- Manage development of c4 voter guide—get input from national team members and from allies
- Sit in on healthcare caucus retreat and give input on legislative strategy

Must-haves	Nice-to-haves	Not-haves
• **Relationship-building:** able to connect with individuals and build alliances among wide range of players in the state • **Results-oriented:** has a track record of producing results, perseveres despite obstacles • **Project management skills:** stays on top of multiple projects, plans backward, anticipates obstacles, identifies and involves stakeholders appropriately, uses resources wisely • **Commitment to social justice and racial equity:** recognizes role of race, gender, and other identities in shaping health disparities	• **Legislative experience:** this would be good to have, but we've seen that we can teach the general approach • **Writing:** should be good enough to send emails on our behalf, but does-n't need to be stellar • **Strategic thinking:** will be an important helper in spotting opportunities and thinking of smart ways to move our issue forward	• **Public speaking/ charisma:** we will use ED and/or allies for most major public appearances • **Research skills:** should become able to monitor trends and be fluent in healthcare policy and related issues, but can rely on research from our analysts and outside sources

One-sentence profile

- Relentless, results-oriented person who excels at building relationships and at managing complicated projects to advance equitable public health legislation.

TOOL 6.2

SAMPLE INTERVIEW QUESTIONS

Tell us about a time when you. . .

- Changed a policy, practice, or procedure in order to improve racial equity and inclusion in work experience or outcomes. What was the equity concern and what changes did you make (or propose)?

- Had to make an unpopular decision. What was the decision and how did you approach it?

- Managed someone who worked hard and had good intentions, but didn't consistently meet expectations of the role. How did you manage the situation?

- Inspired or motivated others during a time of change or uncertainty. What did you do to motivate others or boost morale?

- Worked to make sure your workplace/team/project was a place where everyone (especially those most marginalized) could participate and thrive. What was the situation and what was your contribution?

- Had to explain a complex idea in a simple way. Talk me through your approach, any challenges you faced, and the outcome.

- Met an ambitious goal. What was the goal, and how did you achieve it?

- Met a tight deadline. What was the project? How did you get it done?

- Had to change directions because your approach wasn't working or was getting inequitable outcomes. How did you know it wasn't working? What did you do?

- Had to make improvements to better serve marginalized communities, but you had limited resources. What was the situation? How did you handle it? What trade-offs did you have to make?

Scenarios

- Share a sample brief, report, email to stakeholders, phonebank script, or other content with the candidate. Ask them to participate in a mock meeting where they share two to three suggested improvements they might make before it's published.

- Provide candidates with an example of how a shared resource is organized now (e.g., student resource center, supply closet, spreadsheet, database, website, or filing system). Ask for three ideas to improve the system. Describe who uses the system. Provide a budget, if relevant.

- Invite candidates to spend no more than [X time] developing a program or project plan relevant to the role. Describe basic considerations or parameters (purpose, outcomes, audience, typical length or timeline), while leaving enough room to see how well the candidate knows the terrain and makes independent choices.

TOOL 6.3

JOB SIMULATION EXERCISES

Having candidates complete exercises similar to what they'd be doing on the job can give you a good idea of how they would perform if hired. This list of sample exercises tests for specific qualities.

Position	Must-have	Sample exercise
COO	Critical thinking, writing	Observe the organization in action (e.g., delivering a training session, staging a rally, holding a hearing, etc.) and propose recommendations for improvement in a one- to two-page memo.
Manager of programs	Strategic thinking	Read and analyze a set of goals and objectives, and come up with recommendations to pursue.
Director of communications	Public speaking, judgment	Role-play a press conference or a call with a reporter about a controversial program we support.
Communications associate	Writing, racial equity and inclusion competency	Share a newsletter or email blast and ask for their suggested edits, with at least two recommendations for ways to be more explicit about the organization's commitment to racial justice.
Director of policy and advocacy	Strategic thinking, interpersonal skills	Sit in on a meeting with a potential partner organization. Afterward, give feedback including a recommendation on whether and how to engage with them.
Senior associate for policy and advocacy	Ability to explain complex ideas in a simple way	Produce a visual outlining key players in the healthcare industry and the relationships among them.
Executive assistant	Fast-paced, attention to detail	Complete 15-minute scheduling exercise involving multiple meeting requests.

TOOL 6.4
SAMPLE REFERENCE CHECK OUTLINE

Introduction

I'm the legislative director at State Health Care Now. Thanks for agreeing to speak with me about your experience working with Avery. Before we start, I'd like to give you a quick overview of our organization and the position we are considering Avery for. We're a 20-person advocacy organization committed to enacting universal health coverage legislation in the state. The organization is growing, and Avery is a finalist for our new state policy director position. This director must be a pro at 1) juggling a lot of projects without dropping any balls; 2) working with a racially diverse group of partners and building alliances among them; 3) working in a fast-paced environment and getting results.

Overall Strengths and Weaknesses

- How long did you work together? In what capacity? What were the circumstances of their departure?
- What was it like to work with them?
- What parts of the job sound most like something Avery might succeed in?
- Can you describe their greatest strengths?
- Based on what I described, what are two areas where they might need help?

Role-Specific Traits and Skills

- Tell me about a time when Avery had to stay on top of a large volume of work in a fast-paced environment. How did they handle it? What did they do well, and what could have been better?
- One skill that's very important for this role is building alliances across different stakeholders from various backgrounds and identities. Can you talk about a time when Avery demonstrated this skill?
- To be successful in this role, we need someone who is exemplary at bringing a racial equity lens to their work. In this case, that means being able to 1) understand how racism, classism, and other forms of oppression intersect with our issue and impact the communities that we and our coalition partners work with; 2) communicate and manage effectively across lines of difference and power; 3) recognize how their identities and background influence how they show up to their work and relationships. How have you seen Avery demonstrate this competency?

Wrap Up

- If you were in the position to hire Avery again, what kind of role would you hire them for? What kind of job would you not hire them for? Why?
- What should I know about Avery in order to manage them effectively? What do they need from their manager to be successful?
- Is there anything else you would want to know about Avery if you were in my shoes?

TOOL 6.5

SAMPLE REJECTION EMAIL

The following is a sample rejection email to someone who made it through one or two rounds of interviews.

From: Barry Ruiz

Subject: State Health Care Now State Policy Director position

To: Dan Miller

Dear Dan,

Thanks so much for talking with Tracy and me last week about our state policy director position. We really enjoyed the meeting, especially hearing about your work with United Way, and we were impressed with your qualifications.

We've had a very competitive pool and have had to make hard decisions, and unfortunately, I won't be advancing you to the next round of interviews for this position. I have no doubt, though, that you'll be a real asset to an organization in the right position, and I wish you the best of luck with your job search. I also encourage you to check back on our website periodically, as our needs may change and there may be a position that better suits your skills and experience.

Best,

Barry Ruiz

Chief of Staff

CHAPTER

7

GIVING FEEDBACK AND EVALUATING PERFORMANCE

One day Monna was at brunch when she received a call from Lily, someone she had supervised as the executive director at Lavender Phoenix. They'd only been in touch a few times in the seven years since they'd worked together. Monna answered, expecting to hear the tell-tale rustling sounds of a butt dial. "Hello?"

"Hi! I'm just calling to thank you for some feedback you gave me once," said Lily. She reminded Monna what happened years ago: Lavender Phoenix was hosting a community event, and Lily was staffing it. Lily arrived in a visibly horrible mood after a difficult interaction with her sibling. She was short with her fellow interns and community members. She *exuded* grumpiness. Monna pulled Lily aside and said, "Hey, I think you're upset about something. I don't think you're trying to be hurtful, but I see you taking it out on people who care about you—and that's not okay."

When Lily finished, Monna thanked her and then asked, "Why was this moment so meaningful for you?" Lily replied: "Up until my internship, I had never received critical feedback that was direct and kind. I was used to people being passive-aggressive—or just plain aggressive—or not saying anything and letting resentments build up. In my household growing up, every little mistake was construed as a character flaw, so I'm sensitive to criticism. I didn't feel like your feedback was personal because you made it about the impact of my behavior, not my personality. Plus, I knew it was coming from someone who wanted the best for me. As an adult, I realize how lucky I was to have someone willing to give me honest and loving feedback."

Lily's previous experiences with feedback are unfortunately common. Many of us don't have good models for how to give feedback that's both honest and kind. Some of us fear conflict and avoid giving feedback about problems unless (or until) they can't be ignored. Some of us face conflict head-on but with our defenses up like we're entering battle. And many of us do both! To be fair, no one handles conflict ideally in every situation, and we all come by our communication styles honestly. After all, how we feel about giving (and receiving) feedback is connected to our upbringings, cultural norms, and past experiences. And differences in power, position, identity, and background make feedback in the workplace even trickier.

The good news is that we can all learn to give and receive feedback well. Maya Angelou wrote, "Do the best you can until you know better. Then when you know better, do better." Good feedback gets you to know better so that you can do better.

THE IMPACT OF FEEDBACK

In Chapter 6, we talked about what a great hire Breanna was. As it turns out, Breanna once had an awful experience with a manager that sometimes still makes her doubt herself. Here's her story:

I had a manager who was never on my side. When she had critical feedback, she'd say, 'Breanna, you messed up.' Instead of asking, 'How can I help you get better?' when I had growth areas, she punished me. And worst of all, she treated me differently than she did my colleagues. When others made a mistake due to an unclear process, she let it slide. When I made the same mistake, she reported me to our HR person (who dismissed the complaint and suggested we improve our processes). It was a classic case of confirmation bias. As the only Black staff person, I already didn't feel very comfortable in the organization, and my manager put me even more on edge. After I left that job, her criticism came with me. To this day, I stress about making the slightest mistake.

Valerie, however, sees things I don't see in myself. As a Black woman, she empathizes with my experiences in ways other managers haven't. She knows about the self-doubt I carry with me from my previous manager, so she works to help me build confidence in myself. This self-doubt is something I haven't shared with other managers because I was afraid they might use it against me, but I knew I could be vulnerable with Valerie. When she notices my attention to detail, she points it out. She validates me when I do a good job and is gracious when I make mistakes. When I do miss something, she reminds me that I'm just human.

And as people working for social change, we owe it to ourselves and our communities to always do better.

Feedback can happen in various ways: in writing, check-ins, and performance evaluations. And in the same way that it shapes our relationships, how we handle feedback (especially with positional power) has ripple effects on our team's culture. According to TMC coach Sarah, "good management is clear communication plus handling power well."

In this chapter, we give you the tools and tips to give feedback effectively and receive it graciously. We also talk about how to develop a culture of feedback and ways to systematize it, including a deep dive into one of the most important ways managers deliver feedback: performance evaluations.

PRINCIPLES OF EFFECTIVE FEEDBACK

All feedback can help us grow—done skillfully, it demonstrates care and investment. Giving feedback is always in your *sphere of control*. Often, the quality of your feedback reflects the quality of your relationship. Plus, feedback can influence your staff long after you stop working together (as we can see from Breanna's story).

Before diving into *how* to give and receive feedback, let's talk about some principles of effective feedback:

- **Give feedback early and often.** Giving it *early* helps ensure that good work keeps happening and problems don't snowball. Giving it *often* makes it a habit (and less scary!). Like most things, it gets easier the more we do it.

- **Make it routine.** Build feedback into your management structures by including it in your check-ins and project debriefs. It's not just about creating the habit—systematizing feedback also mitigates bias and helps you give feedback equitably. *Who* we provide feedback to is a *choice point* because we tend to feel more comfortable sharing feedback with people we're close to (remember "I like you" bias). So unless you choose otherwise, your staff with marginalized identities different from yours probably receive less feedback overall, which means they get fewer opportunities to grow. Making it routine ensures that you give your staff the same gift of feedback, regardless of the closeness of your relationship or their identities.

- **Treat praise like a must-have (and be generous).** For many people, positive reinforcement is equally, if not more, important than constructive feedback. Yet too often, we treat praise like a garnish when it's a key ingredient. Offering genuine, specific praise helps people feel valued, and expressing gratitude makes us feel good too. Praise is always a win-win.

- **Don't just dish it—ask for it!** In healthy relationships, feedback is a two-way street. Normalize receiving feedback so that you can also improve. And try asking for specific feedback. For instance, instead of saying, "How do you think I facilitated that meeting?" you could say: "I'd love your thoughts on what worked and what didn't. I think the activities were helpful, but I don't think I gave enough time for people to process. What would you have done differently?" One TMC colleague remembered when Jerry made it easy for her to share feedback by demanding it (jokingly!). In an evaluation conversation where she didn't offer constructive feedback, he said, "I'm not getting off the phone until you give me at least two things I could do better."

- **Make it part of your culture.** The more collaborative your team, the more important it is for people to feel comfortable giving and receiving feedback in all directions. Build feedback into team meetings and project debriefs, encourage direct one-on-one conversations, and incorporate it into your core values. (We talk more about culture in Chapter 11.)

CHECK FOR BIAS

Identity-based stereotypes affect our expectations of other people, and our biases influence the feedback we share. For example, research shows that men often receive more detailed, insightful feedback on technical skills. In contrast, women receive less specific feedback that's more about how they work with others.[1] Basically, women are expected to be more collaborative and less assertive than men, and that's reflected in the feedback they get. The result? Men get better feedback for improving their outcomes (as opposed to their likeability)—which gives them higher chances to advance to leadership. And, of course, when you add other dimensions of identity, such as race, it's even more complicated (remember our trainer's story in Chapter 3 about his Black woman colleague who wasn't "friendly" enough?).

To avoid giving biased feedback, check your assumptions, biases, and expectations first. Ask yourself:

- Would my expectations of this person change if they had different identities? If so, how?
- Would my feedback be different if I liked this person more? What if I liked them less?
- Would my feedback be different if they were more similar to me? What if they were less similar?
- Is my feedback tied to their performance and outcomes (not character traits)?

---

[1] Elena Doldor, Madeleine Wyatt, and Jo Silvester, "Research: Men Get More Actionable Feedback Than Women," *Harvard Business Review*, 2021, hbr.org/2021/02/research-men-get-more-actionable-feedback-than-women

TYPES OF FEEDBACK

Feedback can be praise, suggestions for improvement, or corrective notes (the last two are both forms of constructive feedback).

- **Positive** feedback is one of the best ways to supercharge someone's growth! Effective positive feedback doesn't just express appreciation for someone—it also spotlights their *specific choices* that had a positive impact. This helps reinforce the behaviors you'd like to see more of.

- **Developmental** feedback gives people suggestions for how to improve. The feedback could help someone take their skills from good to great or from meeting to exceeding expectations. It can also be about an improvement that isn't critical to the person's success in the role.

- **Corrective** feedback is for managers to communicate to staff when something needs to change for them to meet the agreed-upon expectations. If something doesn't change, there will be negative consequences.

Explain the three kinds of feedback to your staff, and *always be explicit about which type you're giving*. For example, you could say, "This is developmental feedback, so take this as a suggestion," or, "This is corrective feedback. If we don't see improvement in the next few weeks, I'll have to address this as a performance problem."

Notes on Corrective Feedback

If your bike starts to veer off the road, you need to turn the handlebar *before* you crash into a tree. Sometimes, our clients call us because they need help firing someone. Unfortunately, our coaches often quickly discover that the performance problem was, in fact, a management problem: the manager waited too long to give clear corrective feedback. By the time they did, the issue had grown to the point of raising serious concerns about the staff person's performance. When the feedback finally came, it was a surprise to the staff person.

Here are some things to keep in mind about corrective feedback:

- **Use feedback to *conspire and align*.** If there's a problem, feedback can help us get aligned on what's happening. When we talk openly about issues, we can surface assumptions and be honest about the stories in our heads. For example, suppose a staff member constantly turns in assignments late. You might assume they don't care about their work (remember the ladder of assumptions in Chapter 2?). When you talk to them about it, you learn that one manifestation of their ADHD is a profound struggle with meeting deadlines—despite their best efforts (and plenty of shame about it). Now you've got your stories straight—you're *aligned*. You have the same information, agree it's a problem, and *conspire* to find the best strategies to address it.

- **Don't use the "compliment sandwich" to soften constructive criticism.** If you try to "cushion the blow" of critical feedback by sandwiching it between two pieces of positive feedback, you risk misalignment. Some people won't process the criticism because it was couched between praise. Others will *only* hear the criticism and not the praise. If you have corrective feedback, make sure they actually hear it![2]

- *Do* **ground your feedback in care.** It's hard to hear when you're not doing something well, but just like with Lily, it's much easier to hear constructive criticism when you believe it's coming from a good place. Help them lower their defenses and hear your feedback by saying, "I care about you. That's why I'm sharing this feedback."

- **Focus on behaviors and impact (not character).** Corrective feedback should always be about a person's behavior and the effects of their actions—*not* judgments about their personality. And it should be about using past experiences to inform future behavior to get better results next time—*not* dwelling on or shaming someone for their mistakes. Think of giving constructive feedback like telling someone that there's broccoli between their teeth. You're sharing a (somewhat awkward) observation about something that could be better or different—not judging, insulting, or condemning them.

When deciding whether feedback should be corrective or developmental, ask yourself: If this behavior persisted for another three months, would it be a problem? If the answer is "yes," give corrective feedback.

TOOLS FOR GIVING FEEDBACK

I know that I'm ready to give feedback when. . .

I'm ready to sit next to you rather than across from you.
I'm willing to put the problem in front of us rather than between us (or sliding it toward you).
I'm ready to listen, ask questions, and accept that I may not fully understand the issue.
I'm ready to acknowledge what you do well instead of picking apart your mistakes.
I recognize your strengths and how you can use them to address your challenges.
I can hold you accountable without shaming or blaming.
I am open to owning my part.
I can genuinely thank [you] for [your] efforts rather than criticize [you] for [your] failings.
I can talk about how resolving these challenges will lead to growth and opportunity.
I can model the vulnerability and openness that I expect to see from you.
I am aware of power dynamics, implicit bias, and stereotypes.

—BRENÉ BROWN, *AUTHOR OF* DARING GREATLY: HOW THE COURAGE TO BE VULNERABLE TRANSFORMS THE WAY
   WE LIVE, LOVE, PARENT, AND LEAD

---

[2] If you have an established practice of sharing constructive feedback and praise in the same sitting, stick with it!

In this section, we share our favorite tool for giving feedback (CSAW), and a way to systematize giving and receiving feedback (2x2s).

CSAW

To give feedback, remember that it takes two to seesaw (CSAW): Connect, Share, Ask, and Wrap Up. While most of the examples in this section assume a manager/staff relationship where the manager shares feedback with the staff person, CSAW can be used in any direction.

HOW TO GIVE FEEDBACK

C ONNECT & GET CONSENT

S HARE OBSERVATIONS & IMPACTS

A SK QUESTIONS

W RAP UP

Connect and Get Consent

Our colleague Jami compares feedback to catch—your goal is to throw the ball so your teammate can catch it. So, instead of suddenly chucking the ball at them, wait for them to face you and make eye contact first. "Making eye contact" when it comes to feedback involves:

- Connecting over a value, goal, or experience.

- Being explicit that you have feedback to share.

- Getting consent to have the conversation.

The following are examples of ways to connect and get consent for each type of feedback:

- **Positive:** "You've been working so hard on the campaign rollout, and I've been really impressed! Can I share some praise?"

- **Developmental:** "Thank you for stepping up and facilitating yesterday's meeting! I have some ideas that might help you with facilitation next time. Would you like to hear it?"

- **Corrective:** "I know we both really care about this project's success—I've seen you demonstrate that in many ways. I have some feedback for you about some things to do differently. Is now a good time for me to share?"

Connecting and getting consent can be as simple as saying, "I appreciate the work you've done on this—is now a good time to share feedback?" Connecting is especially important for constructive feedback and when giving feedback up, sideways (see Chapter 10), or to someone you don't have a strong relationship with. The best time to share feedback is when the other person is open to it.

Remember that even explicit consent can be tricky when positional power is involved. Your staff person might feel obligated to say "yes" even if they're not in a good space to hear corrective feedback. You can help defuse this dynamic by naming it explicitly ("'No' is an acceptable answer!"). Of course, you shouldn't wait indefinitely to share corrective feedback for a direct report. Be firm about having feedback to share, but let them decide when to have the conversation.

Share Observations and Impacts

Share specific observations about the person's behavior and its impact. If it's part of a pattern or if you have a suggestion, share that too.

Examples:

- **Positive:** "The tutorial video you made for Nia was one of the most helpful learning tools in her onboarding. You showed awareness of her learning style, and it's made such an incredible impact on her experience so far."

- **Developmental:** "I noticed that you waited until halfway into the call to ask why they reached out for our services. Next time, you could raise the question earlier in the conversation so you can make a stronger recommendation for our offerings."

- **Corrective:** "I've noticed that you've turned in your expense reports late for the last few months. Can we discuss that? Being late on reports slows down our ability to bill for the work and increases the burden on our admin team."

Again, focus on the person's behavior, not their character. For example, there's a difference between saying, "I've noticed that you've been turning in expense reports late," and, "You've been such a scatterbrain."

Ask Questions

After you've shared your feedback, get their perspective. This is the aligning part, where you check to see if you have the right information and understand the problem so you can address it together. As Brene Brown put it, you're putting the problem in front of you, not between you. You're also willing to listen, ask questions, and accept that you may not fully understand the issue.

You can ask questions to do the following:

- Check for alignment: "What do you think is happening? What am I missing?"

- Unearth causes: "Why do you think this happened?"

- Surface solutions: "How do you think we should move forward?"

You can also keep it open-ended by asking, "What do you think about what I've shared?"

Wrap Up with Next Steps

Once you've both shared your perspectives, agree on what to do next. This is the place for you to make or reiterate specific requests.

Sometimes one (or both) of you won't feel fully resolved at the end of the feedback conversation—that's okay. If you're not totally aligned on how to move forward, or if one of you needs time to sit with what you've discussed, schedule time to revisit the conversation.

Examples:

- "So moving forward, can we agree that you'll set work blocks to do your expense reports and let our colleagues know if you need more time?"

- "How about we continue this conversation next week?"

THE 2X2 SYSTEM

The 2x2 system helps managers and staff members reflect, share feedback, and discuss how the work is going. The manager and staff each share two things that each person is doing well and two things they could do better, using concrete examples and observations. (It's more like two 2x2s—your self-reflection and feedback for the other person.) For the staff member, the focus is on their performance; for the manager, the focus is on their management.

If you don't already share two-way feedback at your check-ins (see Chapter 2), we recommend doing 2x2s quarterly, if not more. See Tool 7.1 in the Appendix Tools at the end of this chapter for a sample 2x2 form.

STRATEGIES FOR RECEIVING FEEDBACK WELL

Imagine someone coming up to you and asking, "Hey, can I give you some feedback?" How does it make you feel? Did your gut tense up and your heart rate increase? Are you nervous? Curious? Excited?

If you feel some anxiety or worry, you're not alone. Our amygdala, or "lizard brain," perceives critical feedback as potentially threatening to our need for social acceptance and group belonging. When we feel threatened, it can trigger a fight, flight, freeze, or appease response. Unfortunately, none of those responses will help us build trusting relationships or grow.

Monna's former staff person, Lily, learned at a young age to see feedback as an attack on her character. Lily could only hear Monna's feedback because she reminded herself that it was coming from someone who genuinely cared about her. This understanding allowed Lily to calm down and hear Monna's feedback.

To receive feedback well, remember the following:

- Feedback is the breakfast of champions. It helps you grow and get better.

- When shared with compassion, feedback is a sign of a healthy relationship. When someone is willing to give you feedback, they care enough about you to be honest. (They're not letting you go about with broccoli in your teeth!)

- How you respond is in your sphere of control. You can't control who you get it from or how they deliver it, but you can decide what to do with it.

When we respond well to feedback, we build trust and goodwill and contribute to a healthy team culture. The three steps for receiving feedback are listening, engaging, and deciding what to do with it.

Listen

Get your amygdala to chill out so you can hear what the other person is saying. Remember, the story in your head might be different from theirs! So pause, assess your feelings, and actually *listen*. You're more likely to react with defensiveness or jump straight to problem-solving if you don't.

When feedback calls up a body-level threat response, you might need a minute to calm down. Do you feel a knot in your stomach? Did your jaw tighten and your shoulders hunch? Relax and take deep breaths.

LET'S TALK ABOUT TONE

Have you ever heard someone say, "It's not what you said—it's *how* you said it"? *How* we deliver feedback impacts how people receive it. And like many aspects of communication, tone is subjective. Culture, social conditioning, and brain chemistry influence how we interpret others' tones and the tones we take ourselves.[3]

When you're receiving feedback, focusing on the feedback giver's tone can derail the conversation from the substance of the feedback. So try to hear the content of what they're saying, and don't dismiss it because you didn't like their delivery. Once you've had time to process the feedback, you might go back to them and share feedback on their tone. But do this sparingly and thoughtfully, knowing that marginalized staff—especially Black women and other women of color—tend to get tone-policed more often.

As a feedback giver, focus on being calm and kind in your delivery without ignoring your emotions. For some people, this might mean avoiding giving feedback in the heat of the moment. If you *do* give feedback while feeling upset, name your feelings calmly. For example, you could say, "Hey, I'm a little frustrated." If you can't be calm, ask for time.

Last, if people often misinterpret your tone, or if you can't hear or control it, be explicit upfront. You can say, "I'm not trying to convey impatience or frustration. Please focus on my words, not my tone, facial expressions, or body language."

Then, get meta:

- Think about how you're *thinking* about the feedback. Remember that feedback isn't an attack; it's a brave offering. After all, it's usually easier to say nothing than to say something (especially to someone with more positional power).

- Pause to consider the "why" behind a negative reaction. If the feedback struck a nerve, ask: Is this reaction about the specific feedback or my relationship with this person? Or is this about something else? When it comes to identifying and understanding triggers, our colleague Ebony likes to ask, "How old is that wound?"

Engage

Once you've prepared your brain and body, here's how to engage with the feedback conversation.

1. **Pause, acknowledge, and appreciate.** Let the feedback settle. You might say, "Thank you for this feedback. I'm taking it in." Don't push through if you're not

---

[3] Some neurodivergent people, especially people on the autism spectrum, cannot hear their own tone, discern others', or use tone to convey meaning. For additional insights, see: https://autisticscienceperson.com/2021/01/09/neurotypicals-listen-to-our-words-not-our-tone/

TAKING IN TOUGH FEEDBACK

A direct report once said to Bex, "I'm trying to lay down train tracks, but every time we talk, it's like you're trying to lift them up!"

That person wasn't wrong. Bex is always thinking about the big picture and looking to make things better—which means that they often step back to question the entire premise of an endeavor. That approach has many benefits for high-level strategizing. Still, it can be incredibly frustrating for teammates who feel like they have to rip up everything they've been working on and start over (ask us how we know!). Bex's team member was calm in her delivery, but Bex could tell she was angry and frustrated.

At first, Bex felt defensive—they were just trying to help! But before responding, they took a breath. When they stopped to reflect, they felt bad about making their staff person's job harder. Bex reminded themself that she was in the driver's seat, and Bex's job was to support her. Bex thanked her for the feedback and asked for time to process before responding. They sat with it all weekend.

On Monday, Bex returned and said, "I'm sorry about my impact on you. I know I can get carried away with the details and overlook the important work you've already done. So I'm going to try to do better at understanding your principles and approach." After that, they were more mindful about asking probing questions and reinforcing areas where she was the approver. They gave her more space to try things before jumping in and offering alternatives—even if that meant setting aside their reservations. And Bex was often pleasantly surprised by the results!

in a good place to continue the conversation. You could say, "Thanks for your feedback. I need to sit with that. Can we schedule a time to revisit this?"

2. **Ask questions to dig deeper.** If you engage further, ask clarifying questions like, "Can you tell me what you meant by X?" You can also use open-ended questions like, "Is there anything else you want me to know?" It can be helpful to ask for specific examples, but be careful about demanding evidence. If the feedback-giver is your manager, clarify the type of feedback by asking, "Is this feedback corrective or developmental?"

3. **Do a repeat-back.** The repeat-back is essential if you've just gotten corrective feedback from your manager. But in any situation, it's helpful to check for alignment. You can say, "I want to check my understanding. Can I do a repeat-back?" Then ask, "What did I miss?"

Decide What to Do

Feedback is information. You can usually learn from it, and you can always choose what you do with it. Typically, you have a few options:

- **Accept the feedback and change your behavior.** Sometimes the request is straightforward. For example, let's say you're responsible for facilitating staff meetings. Someone says, "Next time, can you invite more perspectives?" You agree, so you make a plan to do better next time. Even if there isn't an explicit request, if you agree with the feedback, think about what you could do differently. If you impacted someone negatively, acknowledge it, apologize, and seek to make amends. (See Chapter 2 for more on repairing relationships.)

WHAT TO DO WITH BIASED FEEDBACK

Feedback is biased when it's shaped by someone's assumptions and beliefs rather than observable facts and outcomes. For example, Monna once applied to be an organizing director at an organization for BIPOC youth. In the finalist stage, the hiring manager, a non-Asian woman of color, expressed concerns about Monna being an effective advocate in coalition spaces. She said, "You'd need to be assertive. We'd be counting on you to represent our youth." Monna was confused. She'd made it this far because she'd learned to go after what her community needed, which showed on her résumé. TMC coach Marissa, also an Asian American woman, has a similar story: she worked with a recruiter to apply for a senior position at a social justice organization. When it was time for reference checks, the recruiter and the hiring manager—both non-Asian women of color—questioned her "toughness" and leadership ability.

These concerns might seem valid at face value—*of course* you want someone who can be assertive and tough to lead important advocacy work. But for Monna and Marissa, this feedback echoed damaging stereotypes about "submissive" Asian women—stereotypes they'd faced (and flouted!) all their lives.

Even praise can be biased. Jakada, for example, often gets called "articulate" when he gives presentations. On the surface, this might sound great. Jakada is, in fact, a powerful and eloquent speaker. But it's also a microaggression—because when non-Black people tell Black people that they're "articulate," it's usually a reflection of their unconscious negative assumptions about Black people's intelligence.

When feedback is biased, your options are: accept (we don't recommend this), engage, or do nothing. You can also push back on the feedback, share feedback on the feedback, or talk to someone else at your organization (like a manager, HR person, or another trusted person). Regardless, take it as another data point and remember that when the feedback is biased, it's not you—it's them.

- **Engage further.** If you found the feedback surprising or confusing, or if you feel mixed about it, engage further. You could seek other perspectives and/or have a follow-up conversation with the feedback-giver. If there's a misunderstanding, offer clarification. You might even respectfully disagree and find a way to move forward anyway.

- **Take what serves you; leave the rest.** Feedback is like candy—you don't *have* to accept every piece you're offered. In some cases, like if the feedback feels biased or ill-intentioned, you might brush it off and move on. If you don't agree or can't act on it immediately, you can do nothing and file it away. But remember that if you do nothing, there might be negative consequences, especially if you've received course-correcting feedback from your manager.

What If There's an Iceberg?

Imagine this: you're the field director of a statewide LGBTQ organization, and you've spent the last two months working on your team's goals for next year. You've consulted with your staff and executive director and finally landed in a good place. Two days before your ED plans to present the goals for board approval, a field organizer approaches you and says, "I'm not sure that the goals are achievable." After you probe a bit, she shares that the goal you've set for turning out Latine people at Lobby Days feels tokenizing, which goes against the intention of the work. This is your first time hearing about this concern. In addition to feeling surprised, you're not convinced.

Sometimes, we receive feedback where the presenting issue seems relatively minor, but it's attached to bigger, multilayered, and complex problems, usually related to issues like power, equity, inclusion, or belonging.

The layers include:

- **The presenting conflict:** The field organizer doesn't believe the goals are achievable.

- **Underlying issue:** She sees the goal as tokenizing, which goes against the intention of the work. As the only Latine person on staff, she's worried about risking her relationships with community members.

- **Relational issue:** She's hoping you'll trust her and engage with her on this.

- **Structural:** In this organization, field organizers are the lowest paid, are rarely asked for input on big decisions, and have the highest turnover.

- **Systemic:** There's a broad progressive movement pattern of BIPOC field organizers being the least likely to advance into leadership positions within campaigns.

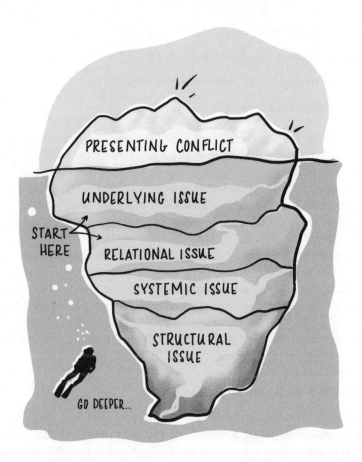

This type of feedback isn't easy to hear, but it's important to engage with it and get past the surface. And *how* you engage can have significant impacts. It can be tempting to focus only on the presenting conflict, but if you don't dig for underlying and relational issues, you might miss what's happening, causing long-term damage. You might not be able to address all the layers, but you'll at least get a deeper understanding of the dynamics at play to better *conspire and align* around solving the issue. And finally, even if there is no iceberg, digging for it won't cause damage—if anything, it communicates your openness to feedback and multiple perspectives.

To dig deeper, ask yourself:

- Has this issue come up before (either with this person or someone else)?

- What could be at stake for the person sharing this feedback?

- What are the lines of difference, privilege, and/or power between us?

- You can also ask the other person questions to probe further:

  - What else should I know about this feedback?

  - Is this connected to any patterns you've noticed?

  - What context am I missing?

Once you're aligned about the substance of the input, approach it as a problem to solve together. First, share what you're thinking and feeling, especially if you're facing pressures or have information they might not (e.g., "The truth is, I feel like I can't/must do X because. . ."). Then, tie together what's true for both of you. For example, you could say, "I love what you said about X; I think we both want Y." Use a pros/cons/mitigations chart (see Chapter 5) to look for solutions that go beyond either/or thinking and address the concerns raised.

In the Lobby Day scenario, you might engage by asking probing questions to better understand the layers of the iceberg. After, you thank her for the feedback and do a repeat-back to check for understanding. Then, you restate your shared values, share your concerns and feelings, and partner to find a solution. Ultimately, you agree to keep the Lobby Day goal but commit to recruiting and developing volunteer leaders who identify as Latine. You also plan to have bilingual training and interpretation so all attendees can fully participate.

PERFORMANCE EVALUATIONS

Performance evaluations are a critical tool for sharing and systematizing feedback. If performance evaluations make you nervous, you're not alone. Of all the things we're responsible for, evaluations are one of the highest-stakes parts of management for several reasons:

- Because they can be tied to promotions and raises, they impact people's livelihoods.

- Managers must be vigilant about their *choice points*, biases, and *PTR* to do them effectively.

- They take a lot of time and energy to do well.

On the other hand, performance evaluations help you align, share feedback, and in many cases, celebrate and appreciate your staff. They let you step back from the day-to-day, summarize feedback from the year, and reflect on the big picture. They allow you and your staff to conspire about developing their skills, reflect on overall progress, and discuss their trajectory at your organization.

How to Conduct Performance Evaluations

Your evaluation (and the staff person's self-evaluation) should assess the following questions:

- How did the staff person do at meeting their goals?[4]

- How well have they demonstrated the required competencies and values? What areas need improvement?

- Overall, what's your headline assessment of their performance?

Summarize, Don't Surprise

There should be no surprises in performance evaluations! By the time of the evaluation conversation, you should have given consistent and clear feedback in check-ins and 2x2s.

That said, because evaluations provide time to think more deeply about a staff member's performance, you might have new insights. If that's the case, pause and reflect. If it's your first time raising an issue, consider saving it for a check-in. If the issue seems important enough to mention in the formal evaluation, acknowledge that you should have shared it sooner.

Use a Rubric

Use an evaluation form with clearly defined ratings, like "Meets expectations," "Partially meets expectations," and "Does not meet expectations," or a numerical scale. Your staff person will fill out a form with the same rubric to evaluate their performance. Ideally, all managers in your organization should align on assessing performance so that one person's "Partially meets" isn't someone else's "Meets."

Remember that the evaluation form isn't a report card showing whether the person "passed" or "failed" the year. Instead, it's a tool for having a structured conversation about where they succeeded and what they could improve. To prepare for your conversation, think about specific examples to explain your assessment.

Steps for Conducting an Evaluation

Here are the steps for conducting an evaluation:

1. **Review the process.** Go over the process and timeline at a check-in. Share the goal of performance evaluations, review the form, and invite questions. Schedule the conversation and agree on deadlines for sharing your forms.

---

[4] If it's a mid-year, you're assessing whether they're on track to meet their goals.

2. **Seek perspective from other people.** Get input from others (including your manager) to balance your perspectives. Try to hear from a mix of people, including their direct reports (if they're a manager), colleagues from other teams, and even people outside the organization, if their work involves external stakeholders. Let your staff know that you're seeking feedback from others. You might even ask, "Who do you think I should reach out to for additional input?"

3. **Fill out the form.** Look at the "what" and the "how" of their work and consider their progress since their last evaluation. Draw on concrete examples, observations, and work products to inform your ratings. And remember to take stock of the entire evaluation period—not just how they performed recently. This isn't a competitive baking show, where your performance last week doesn't impact whether you're eliminated during Bread Week! Finally, reflect on how you did as a manager—what you did well in your management and what you could do better. See Tool 7.2 at the end of this chapter for a sample evaluation form.

4. **Review the staff member's self-evaluation.** If there are marked discrepancies, consider why. Did the person have different ideas about expectations and success? Are there factors they've considered that you haven't? Note where there's misalignment for your evaluation meeting, and reflect on where you could have clarified expectations. Or, if they wrote something that changed your mind, edit your evaluation.

CONTEXT MATTERS

If the events of 2020 taught us anything, it's that context matters. Don't get us wrong—results and outcomes are crucial factors in evaluations. But it can be important to weigh circumstances because being committed to equity means paying attention to factors that might create disparities in staff outcomes and experiences. Was there a dip in someone's performance? Get beneath the surface and understand why. If there were extenuating circumstances, it's especially important to consider the "how." For example, suppose your staff person didn't meet their goals because they had to take an extended medical leave. You might consider how well they reprioritized, communicated with the team about it, or handed off their projects.

Or, perhaps you had a staff member who did exceptionally well *in spite of* extenuating circumstances. Did it come at a cost to their health and well-being? Did they feel pressured to push their limits to deliver? If so, reinforce the importance of sustainability, re-align on expectations of success, and work with them to reprioritize if needed.

In some cases, understanding what was happening in the background might lead you to change your ratings. And even if it doesn't, it will help you reflect on how you can manage and support them moving forward.

5. **Send the completed evaluation form to the staff member.** Aim to give them at least 24 hours to review before you meet. (Pro-tip: combine your forms to see your comments and ratings side-by-side.)

6. **Hold the evaluation meeting.** The purpose of the meeting is to summarize and discuss. Start with the headline. You could say, "Overall, you're doing a great job. There are two things I think you could improve, but you're on track to be successful this year." Or, "Overall, you've had some bright spots, but I have a few concerns about your performance.

   Instead of going line by line, focus on key takeaways and dig deeper where needed. You can ask, "Was there anything I wrote that surprised you? Anything that's unclear?" If you need to, realign on expectations. If there are specific areas of improvement, make a plan and agree on how you'll assess progress.

   This is also an opportunity for them to share feedback about your management. You can start with a self-reflection and invite their thoughts to make it easier. For example, you could say, "One thing I could have done better was check in more during busy periods. I wanted to give you space to do the work, but I could have been more present. What would have made you feel supported?"

7. **Finalize the evaluation.** If the discussion changed your assessment, revise the form before filing it away (or sending it off to HR).

KEY POINTS OF GIVING FEEDBACK

Here are the takeaways from the chapter:

- Feedback is a gift. It helps us grow. It also helps us *conspire and align* with our team members and invest in our relationships. As managers, we should focus on how well we give feedback *and* how well we receive it.

- How we feel about feedback is connected to our upbringings, cultural norms, and past experiences. Differences in power, position, identity, and background can make feedback in the workplace even trickier.

- Develop a culture of feedback where it's normalized to give feedback routinely, early, and often.

- Feedback can be **positive** (praise—don't overlook this!); **developmental** (giving people suggestions for how to improve); or **corrective** (when something needs to change for them to meet expectations, or negative consequences will result).

- Always check for bias before giving feedback.

- To structure your feedback, use:

  - **CSAW**—Connect and ask for consent, Share observations and feedback, Ask questions, Wrap up with next steps.

  - **The 2x2 system**—The manager and staff each share two things that each person is doing well and two things they could do better, using concrete examples.

- To receive feedback well, take three steps:

  - **Listen** before reacting.

  - **Engage** with the feedback by pausing, acknowledging, asking probing questions, and doing a repeat-back to check for alignment.

  - **Decide what to do** about the feedback—either accept it and change your behavior, engage further, or take what serves you and leave the rest.

- Look for **icebergs,** where the presenting issue seems minor but is attached to multilayered or complex problems underneath the surface.

- **Performance evaluations** are critical for aligning with your staff about their performance and trajectory. They should be a summary of feedback your staff member will be familiar with—never a surprise.

APPENDIX TOOLS

TOOL 7.1

2X2 FEEDBACK FORM: MANAGER SAMPLE

Name: Colleen [Manager]

Date of 2x2 Meeting: 8/1

Instructions: Each person should fill out their own form completely.

	Competency or quality	Specific example or observation
Strengths for staff member	Persistence and problem-solving	You spent a lot of time on the grant proposal for funder X. The rejection was demoralizing, but it didn't stop you! You followed up and got us a meeting so that we could continue building a relationship with the program officer.
	Managing multiple work streams	You were great at juggling the demands of projects X and Y in our busy season. You communicated when you needed support and drove a strong planning process! And when there were hiccups, you navigated them beautifully.
Growth areas for staff member	Maintaining boundaries around capacity	Twice, I noticed you volunteering to help on a project that was outside your realm of work. I appreciate that you want to be helpful, but I wish you had checked in about your priorities first. Your workload was already full and it impacted other projects.
	Direct communication	On a few occasions, I've seen you couch constructive feedback and directions so much that your message got lost. It happened in our last check-in and I've observed it in meetings with others.
Strengths for manager	Direct feedback	I have shared direct feedback with you when I felt like things weren't totally on track—like with our donor engagement goals—and it gave us a chance to course-correct.
	Team connection	I've created lots of opportunities for team connection, even during such a busy season. One example: planning a team huddle right before our project launch. I think it helped us to feel grounded in our shared purpose.

	Competency or quality	Specific example or observation
Growth areas for manager	Giving clear guidance	I should have been clearer about the time constraints around getting board materials out—I could have prevented that last-minute crunch.
	Proactive coaching and support	Sometimes I don't realize that you need support until it's too late. I could do a better job of checking in earlier to help with troubleshooting.

TOOL 7.2

PERFORMANCE EVALUATION FORM

This is a performance evaluation form template, with some sample language for a strong assessment.

Employee Name, Position			
Manager Name, Position			
Review Period		Review Date	
Reviewed by		☐ Self ☐ Manager	

1. Getting Results

Goal *Put each goal in a separate row, adding more rows as needed. If you'd like, you can mark the most important goals in bold.*	Result	Rating E: *exceeds expectations* M: *meets expectations* P: *partially meets expectations* D: *does not meet expectations*
Increase number of individual giving at least $5–150K, with 40% of individual donors identifying as BIPOC	*170*	*E*

Staff Comments: To what extent did you achieve your goals this past period?

Manager Comments: To what extent did the staff member achieve their goals this past period?
Your results were spectacular. Even in a year when the economy was only so-so, we're on track to exceed our goal by $300K. You drove this by maximizing contributions from numerous national funders and getting more federal funding.
Going forward, in addition to keeping up the great work, the main area I think you should focus on is proactively engaging with the regional directors.

2. Demonstrating Competencies		
Core Values *Add more rows as needed*	**Description of Value**	**Rating (E, M, P, D, N/A)**
Tenacity in Pursuit of Results	We are determined to achieve ambitious results. We pursue our end goals despite constraints or obstacles we encounter.	E

Core Competencies *Add more rows as needed*	**Description of Competency**	**Rating (E, M, P, D, N/A)**
Problem-solving and resourcefulness	Identify issues, analyzes data to produce insights, and generates wise recommendations.	E

Staff Comments: To what degree did you demonstrate the preceding core values and competencies? In what values and competencies did you excel? In what areas is improvement needed?

Manager Comments: To what degree did the staff member demonstrate the preceding core values and competencies? In what values and competencies did they excel? In what areas is improvement needed?

As your exemplary ratings indicate, you embody our core values. A couple of particularly noteworthy areas:

- Tenacity in Pursuit of Results. You continued pursuing every channel and turned around applications for funds at the last minute.
- You're also operating at an exceptionally high level when it comes to skills:
  - Problem-solving and resourcefulness—It's hard to overstate your strengths as a thinker. On so many occasions, you've exercised great judgment about which opportunities to pursue. One great example is the last funding memo you wrote, which outlined our opportunities and constraints.

3. Summary Assessment, Next Steps, and Trajectory at Organization

Overall performance rating:
☐ Exceeds Expectations ☐ Meets Expectations
☐ Partially Meets Expectations ☐ Does Not Meet Expectations

Staff Member self-assessment of performance:

1. What are 1–3 notable areas of strength?
2. What are 1–3 areas of growth or improvement?
3. What do you see as your trajectory in the organization? What are the next steps?

Manager assessment of staff performance:

1. What are 1–3 notable areas of strength?
You're great at getting results while building strong relationships with your teammates. This is no small feat when you're managing a diverse team with ambitious goals. I could tell from my conversations with your direct reports that they see you not just as a manager, but as a leader.
2. What are 1–3 areas of growth or improvement?
As I mentioned in the goals section: engaging with RDs. This will be essential for us to continue meeting our funding needs.
3. What do you see as the staff member's trajectory in the organization? What are the next steps?
Will you commit to another 5 years? Seriously, I know we'll be having lots of discussions re: your future plans as part of our long-term plan, and I'm assuming we'll talk about this then.

4. Staff Feedback for Manager/Manager Self-Reflection

Staff Comments:

- What has your manager done well or effectively to support you?
- What might your manager have done differently?
- What support do you need from your manager moving forward?

Manager Self-Reflection:

- What have you done well or effectively to support the staff member?
- What might you have done differently?
- What support is needed from you moving forward?

I was able to be a thought partner when you were dealing with tricky decisions, and I balanced that with giving you the autonomy to make decisions and lead your team.
There were times when I wasn't as available as I could have been, which meant you had to chase me down for answers. I can't avoid the busy seasons in my work, but I want to be more mindful about making a plan for those times.

CHAPTER

8

INVESTING IN PEOPLE

"I tell my students, 'When you get these jobs that you have been so brilliantly trained for, just remember that your real job is that if you are free, you need to free somebody else. If you have some power, then your job is to empower somebody else. This is not just a grab-bag candy game.'"

—*Toni Morrison, American novelist*

"Danny took me from someone with a job to someone with a career. Before Danny, I had managers who saw I was good at what I did, but they didn't push for more. They didn't ask me what else I wanted to do or learn; they didn't talk about my potential or encourage me to grow. I never got feedback beyond 'keep doing what you're doing!' I spent a lot of time working and not knowing where I was going next. I didn't even know what else there was to grow toward. Then, I met Danny."

We heard this reflection from Kayla, a staff member at a client organization. Kayla and Danny met on a campaign—Kayla was a program assistant, and Danny was a volunteer member of the leadership team. A year into the campaign, Danny took a job as the campaign director. Kayla shared, "Even though my role was to provide administrative support, Danny always asked for my thoughts on strategy. So when he took the job, I became his right-hand person. And when he started managing me, I noticed a shift—in how I was treated, how I felt about the work, and how I felt about myself."

At the beginning of this book, we discussed the value of management—the incredible power and responsibility of managers to get great results *and* support the people we manage to accomplish great things. If you've ever had a Danny, you know what it means to have someone see your potential and invest in you.

When we asked Danny for his side of the story, he told us, "When I first met Kayla, I could tell she was great at her job. She was competent, creative, and thoughtful. But she was completely overlooked by her manager. She was in a support role on the campaign, but she always had ideas about strategy. Often, her ideas made me stop and think, 'Hm, that's interesting. I hadn't considered that.' So as soon as I took the job, I knew I wanted Kayla to be on my team. I had a feeling that we'd accomplish big things together, and I could help her grow in the direction she wanted."

Experiences like this might be our favorite part of management—identifying potential in people, offering them our guidance and mentorship, and watching them do amazing things. It's incredibly gratifying to see the "aha!" moments.

Ask any manager what they like most about management, and they're likely to say something like, "I like helping my staff grow and take their work to the next level," or "I love watching awesome people shine and knowing that I had a role in helping them" (these are actual answers we got from our colleagues!).

All three of us have benefited from the investment of mentors, and we've paid it forward. Bex's early investment in Monna at The Task Force helped launch her career and, more importantly, brought her into the LGBTQ movement. She then went on to work with and support people like Lily, whom we mention in Chapter 6. For Jakada, the investment and mentorship of Zef J. Aman, Elisha Miranda, and Hugh Vasquez helped him grow from a young, undisciplined activist in Oakland to a confident, principled leader. Later on, we'll share a story about someone Jakada invested in.

In this chapter, we cover the main principles of investing in your people and explain what to develop and how to do it.

WHY INVEST?

Investing in people doesn't just *feel* good—it makes us, our teams, and our work better. It's vital to the *conspire-and-align* approach because you're aligning on a vision for your staff's growth and your work together. Investing in our co-conspirators is also an investment in our collective whole. As Mississauga Nishnaabeg writer, musician, and academic Leanne Betasamosake Simpson wrote, "Strong communities are born out of individuals being their best selves."

Here are other reasons why we love investing in people:

- It improves *retention*—not just within our organizations, but also for our movements and sectors. Many of us know someone (or have been someone) who started out excited to do important, world-changing work, only to become disillusioned and leave because they felt undervalued and burned out. When people are the lifeblood of our movements, it's a shame when we bleed out.

- It builds someone's *power,* so it's a *choice point.* When we invest in marginalized staff who've had limited access to resources, mentors, and growth opportunities, it's one of the best strategies for equitable management.

- It creates *impact.* When we help our folks level up, that gives us the space we need to level up, too. When we all get better, we all get better results. Let's say you lead a development team, and one of your staff drastically improves their grant writing skills. This could mean you'll spend less time reviewing grant proposals, allowing you to build out the major donor program you've set aside for months. Or maybe it means the staff person can write (and get!) more grants over time because each proposal will take them 10 hours instead of 20.

Note that when we talk about "staff development," we're talking about investing in people's ability to excel *in their roles.*[1] Staff development is a core management responsibility that requires time and energy (it's not just a budget line item!).

PRINCIPLES FOR INVESTING IN PEOPLE

There's a reason we call it *investing*—you have to put something in to get results, whether it's your time, energy, or money. And because you're likely juggling many responsibilities, you need to be strategic and proactive about how and when you spend your resources on developing staff.

Consider these principles as you figure out what to prioritize as you develop your staff:

- Adopt an investment mindset.
- Know what you (and they!) can change.
- Focus on impact.
- Distinguish between development areas and performance issues.

Adopt an Investment Mindset

Remember the "Green Lens" we discussed in Chapter 2? The Green Lens is about seeing someone's inherent value and their full humanity, including their hopes, dreams, and potential. When we adopt an "investment mindset," we embrace our role in supporting them to tap into their potential. An investment mindset leads you to:

- **Be a hype person.** You're the one hyping them up before their big presentation (or their turn at karaoke!). You help them build and access power even when they're not around; you sing their praises to your colleagues and manager, spotlighting their skills and accomplishments.

---

[1] Supporting staff to pursue learning opportunities beyond the scope of their work can be a great retention strategy and support personal growth, but this chapter is about supporting staff to do their jobs well on a day-to-day basis.

- **Assume the best (even when others don't).** You don't let other people's biases or assumptions diminish your belief in them. For example, Danny saw that Kayla's skills went beyond the logistical. Where others saw her as "just" an admin person, he saw her aptitude for strategy.

- **Give them honest feedback.** You're willing to say the thing that others might not, giving them the feedback they need to grow and get better.

- **Open doors to growth opportunities.** You offer stretch assignments (more on this later) that provide new challenges, greater responsibility, and more authority. You also nominate them for opportunities to showcase their talents, leading to more recognition.

- **Get "in it" with them.** You offer support, so they don't struggle alone. When it makes sense, you roll up your sleeves and do the work together, giving clear guidance, feedback, and encouragement along the way.

Know What You Can Change

What can you reasonably expect to change based on the time and resources you can invest? Everyone can learn and grow, but it's usually not worth it to develop a competency at all costs.

Focus on the things that will help the person go from good to great. It's much easier to help someone build on their talents and expand their skill sets than to undo a "weakness" or change a deeply rooted characteristic. Remember that "strengths" is part of comparative advantage. For example, if you manage a strong writer who has never written press releases, it likely won't take long for them to learn. However, if this person is terrified of public speaking, it'll be tough for them to start representing your organization at press conferences. It wouldn't be impossible—and you might even decide it's worth it—but it'll require more resources.

Focus on Impact

One of the first things Bex taught Monna about supporting and coaching volunteers was to "find the difference that makes the difference"—that is, figure out the one improvement that would have the greatest impact on results.

In Kayla's case, that difference that made the difference was her confidence and feelings of legitimacy. Kayla often couched her suggestions, so others left meetings thinking her ideas were theirs. One time, Danny pointed this out to her: "Kayla, you just helped those people get to that idea. But it was yours first. You should own it. Next time you share an idea, start your sentence with, 'I think we should. . .'" Once she implemented his feedback, people listened—and she got credit for her ideas.

Danny also coached her to be more direct to get what she needed from colleagues. For example, he suggested that she say, "I need X by Y date. If I can't get it by then, here's what's going to happen. . ." instead of "How's that thing going?" When she did that, she spent less time chasing down people for things they owed her.

Danny could have (and eventually did) work with Kayla on other skills, like making a campaign plan or facilitating a stakeholder meeting. But he believed that helping her build her confidence and legitimacy would make the most difference—and it did. The confidence enabled her to take on bigger responsibilities. The legitimacy among her peers meant her (often excellent) ideas were taken seriously, which ultimately improved their outcomes.

Think about your staff person's role expectations (the "what" *and* the "how")— what's the one competency that, if strengthened, would lead to the greatest impact?

Distinguish between Development Areas and Performance Issues

In Chapter 7, we talk about the difference between "developmental" and "corrective" feedback. This is similar.

Let's go back to our previous example about the staff person who is a strong writer but a nervous public speaker:

- It would be a *development area* if public speaking were just a nice-to-have for their role. You might want to develop their public speaking skills so that more people on your team can represent your organization at events. Plus, doing so might open up more opportunities for the staff person to advance within your organization.

- It would be a *performance problem* if speaking at events is part of their role expectations—it's a requirement. Their job will be at risk if they don't improve this skill within a reasonable timeframe. You'll need to go through a separate process to address this issue (though you might use some of the tools and advice we share here!). (See Chapter 9 for more on how to address performance problems.)

If there's a performance problem, your investment efforts should be focused on addressing the problem, not developing other areas.

HOW TO DEVELOP PEOPLE

Whether it's your idea or your staff person's, once you know there's a competency to develop, there are three simple steps to get started:

1. Get aligned with your staff person.

2. *Make the implicit explicit*; name the skill and break it down.

3. Make a plan of action.

Get Aligned with Your Staff Person

You can't develop someone against their will. You also can't support someone if you're unclear about what they want to develop. If it's your idea, get the staff person's buy-in by sharing why you think the competency is important. You can lean on the three "why" questions from the five Ws in Chapter 4: *why this, why you, why now.*

In Kayla's case, Danny told Kayla what he observed about her strengths and growth areas. Then he said, "I want to help you build your confidence because I think it'll affect how people work with you and how you show up. You have the skills to be a great project manager—you just need the confidence and communication to back it up. I'm excited to work with you and want to help you get great at this."

This is also a chance to *seek perspective.* Ask them questions like:

- How does developing this competency fit into your long-term plans?

- Have you tried to work on this before? If so, what worked? What didn't?

- What support will you need from me?

Name the Skill and Break It Down

Naming what you want to develop helps clarify what the person should change or aspire to. It's part of defining success. Once you've named the skill, break it down into component parts.

When Jakada was at the EBC, he had to hire a campaign director for their Green Collar Jobs work. The obvious choice to him was to promote the campaign manager, Ian, who had been around from the beginning. Ian was great at bringing different groups together and building trust among them. This was a valuable skill given the contentious space they worked in, where labor unions, environmental justice groups, community members, and "big green" organizations frequently mistrusted each other or had competing interests.

However, when Jakada asked the other members of the management team why Ian hadn't already been promoted to campaign director, they said, "Ian's not decisive enough." When Jakada probed more, he learned that Ian had never gotten this feedback.

Jakada set out to talk with Ian about the role and the skill he'd need to demonstrate to get a promotion. He said, "Ian, you've done a fantastic job building this diverse coalition. I'd really like to have you lead the campaign strategy, but we need you to get better at driving decision-making."

Here's how he broke down the competency of "drive decision-making":

- **Inclusive leadership:** Leading decision-making processes with multiple stakeholders where people contribute meaningfully and feel heard

- **Discernment about decision-making modes:** Knowing when to focus on building consensus and gathering input versus when to make a call and bring people along

- **Ownership and integrity:** Not being afraid to make and be responsible for a decision

- **Communication:** Being able to clearly and persuasively explain a decision

Sometimes, you're working to develop a mindset[2]—how someone approaches their work—rather than a skill. For Kayla, Danny worked on building and communicating confidence. Her knowledge and ideas were already there—it was about how she expressed them.

Make a Plan of Action

Once you've agreed on the "what," make it real with a plan. Again, you can refer back to the five Ws. By when would you like the person to develop the competency? Where might they go for support? Who else can support them? And, of course, dig into how you will support them. Will you send them to a training, model the skill, or give stretch assignments (more on these later)? Your plan should include scaffolding, which means breaking the learning into chunks so they can learn progressively.

At EBC, Jakada and Ian's plan involved mapping key decision points over the next few months. First, Jakada would observe and coach Ian and share feedback, and then they would debrief the outcomes of the decisions.

HOW TO PUSH PEOPLE TOWARD EXCELLENCE (WITH HEART)

Developing people doesn't have to be overcomplicated. Supporting someone to grow can be as simple as encouraging them to stretch just a little bit beyond what they already do.

When we say "push," we don't mean shoving someone into the deep end without a life raft. We mean starting with connection and curiosity to get your staff person interested in diving in with you.

Here's some language you can use:

- **On quality:** "How would you get this from 'good enough' to 'gold star' if you had more time?"

- **On racial equity and inclusion outcomes:** "What are some choice points you anticipate for this project? How will you decide?"

- **On the logic or feasibility of an idea:** "I can imagine someone hearing this and being concerned about X—what would you say to that?"

- **On sustainability and pacing the work:** "Imagine you could take X weeks off with no big consequences for the work. What's in the way of making that happen? Talk me through what would need to change."

---

[2] Other times, you might actually be working to *undo* a mindset. Perfectionism, for instance, is one that we often encounter in our work. To tackle it, naming and specificity are your friends. You can break down the big mountain of "Be Less Perfectionistic" into little clumps of dirt like, "Set a time limit for your edits and stick to it," or "Celebrate one failure or mistake each week."

TOOLS AND PRACTICES

Some of our favorite tools and practices for developing people are stretch assignments, "I do, we do, you do," and feedback and debriefs.

Stretch Assignments

A stretch assignment allows someone to practice new skills by dialing up the stakes, volume, or complexity of a project or responsibility. Like stretch goals (see Chapter 4), they can help drive progress and growth. Stretch assignments are part of scaffolding.

When you give a stretch assignment, name the skills or mindsets it's intended to help the person grow or practice. Then, offer support and ask what they need to be successful. For example, you can say, "I know this might be a challenge, but I believe you can do this. I'm asking you to do this because I think it'll help you get better at X. What do you think? What support would you need from me?"

When you offer a stretch assignment, expect to be more "in the mix" (see Chapter 3). You might take more slices, do side-by-side work, or model using "I do, we do, you do" (see the next section for more on this).

Remember that stretch assignments are a *choice point:* who gets the opportunity to do more challenging assignments, which kinds, and how often? Be mindful when you offer assignments that could fast-track someone to promotion. Ask yourself if other team members get similar opportunities to showcase or level up their skills.

I Do, We Do, You Do

In Chapter 3, we talk about using "I do, we do, you do" to stay engaged in the delegation cycle. We also use it to help people develop skills. Here's how Danny and Kayla applied this tool:

- **I do:** Danny and Kayla's team was responsible for leading quarterly membership meetings. When they started working together, he planned and facilitated the first one. After the meeting, Danny and Kayla debriefed. He asked, "What do you think worked? What would you have done differently?" Then, he explained his choices: "Some of our members interact with each other pretty regularly between meetings. I like to mix up the breakout groups so people can connect with members they don't get to work with much."

- **We do:** At the second meeting, Danny took the lead with Kayla as a helper. She helped design the agenda and facilitated parts of it.

- **You do:** At the third meeting, Kayla and Danny reversed their roles. Kayla led, and Danny helped.

Feedback and Debriefs

As we discussed in Chapter 7, giving regular feedback is a core tool for building your relationship. It also helps you invest in people. The same is true of debriefs, which help people learn directly from recent experience.

Part of Jakada's plan was to shadow Ian as he led coalition meetings and debrief after each one. In the first week of shadowing, Ian led a meeting that went well—except for the part where the coalition had to decide their next steps. After the meeting, Jakada gave feedback. He told Ian that this was an example of how Ian needed to take more ownership of making decisions. A lightbulb went off, and Ian got it. After that, Ian started implementing the decision-making processes the campaign needed.

Overall, do as much as you can within your sphere of control to foster a culture of feedback. It's easiest to invest in people in workplaces where it's normal to talk openly about what's going well and what could be better (in the spirit of generosity and collaboration). See Chapter 7 for more on feedback and Chapter 11 for broader culture-building tips.

HOW TO RETAIN STAFF

Our best advice for retention can be summarized in four words: "Make it worth it." Create a staff experience that makes it hard for them to imagine working anywhere else. Think about factors like roles, goals, culture, and relationships as part of that experience. And make sure the pay, benefits, and hours are good enough that people don't *have* to work elsewhere if they don't want to.

Why do people decide to stay at an organization? There are many reasons, but it usually boils down to people feeling valued and supported, and believing they have room to grow.

Remember that retention, like staff experience, is usually not about a single factor—it's a cumulation of things. Monna had a friend who left her job despite being offered a promotion with a sizable pay bump and exciting growth opportunities. Why did she leave? It was too little too late. She'd been at the organization for three years, often doing multiple people's jobs with little support from her manager. When the promotion finally came, she was already in the final stages of interviewing at other organizations.

Here are more tips for retaining great staff:

Be Proactive

Staff development isn't just about giving guidance and coaching on the work you're doing now; it's also about taking a holistic view of the road ahead. This means discussing your staff member's goals, work, and ambitions—even when things are going well.

When a staff member already meets expectations, it can be easy (and necessary) to divert your energy toward those urgent *and* important things in the matrix, like the four-alarm fire blazing in another area. But don't miss opportunities to develop and retain high-performing staff because you weren't paying attention.

When it comes time for performance evaluations, summarize your past feedback *and* set your sights on the future. If someone is doing exceptionally well, use the evaluation to formally recognize their work. When noting "areas of improvement," frame your feedback in terms of how they could go from good to great (or great to greater!). Talk about what their next steps in the organization might be. What might the "next level" look like for them? What would it take for them to stay for another two years?

Offer Great Compensation and Benefits

Do everything you can within your sphere of control to make your organization a stellar place to work, from culture to compensation.

While most individual managers don't have the authority to change compensation policies, you likely *can* support your staff to access other material benefits. Study your employee benefits package, which might include things like professional development funds, home office stipends, or wellness programs. If you can, suggest other attractive benefits or policies to your leadership that might be worth considering.

As much as you can, be generous with paid time off—not just when it comes to vacation days, but also with sick time and bereavement leave. Supporting staff to exercise agency in how they spend their time builds trust and sustainability—two things that are key for retention.

Invest in Intangible Benefits

If nothing else, you can always invest in the intangible benefits of working at your organization. These things include the sense of belonging, camaraderie, and purpose that comes from getting lasting results with a great team. Find out what motivates your staff to stay and build on it. Is it:

- Being able to contribute and take on more responsibility?

- Deepening relationships and networks?

- Feeling validated by teammates?

- Rising to meet an ambitious challenge or trying new things?

- Having steady and predictable work and expectations?

- Being recognized for achievements?

- Having autonomy or flexibility?

- Some combination of the preceding, or something else?

Whatever it is, figure out the most important thing to each of your staff members.

Have a "Stay Interview"

"You are truly an asset to our team, and I wonder about your future plans. What can I do to support your growth with us?"

"What would it take for you to still be here in 5 years? Or 10?"

These are the kinds of questions you can ask at a "stay interview," where you talk about a staff member's future at your organization. A stay interview can be a scheduled meeting with a stated purpose that you share in advance. It can also be a more informal conversation over coffee or in a check-in. However you go about it, make sure that you:

- Express appreciation for them and their contributions.

- Learn more about what would get them excited to stay.

- Get feedback about ways you could better support them.

Don't Try to Retain Everyone at All Costs

Staff turnover can be good and healthy—and even necessary. When organizations grow and change, some people leave. Of course, you don't want people going because they're burned out or embittered. But if someone's no longer aligned with the organization's direction or the path to get there, or if they're just ready for something new, it might be good to part ways.

When staff express a desire to leave, it's completely fair to express how much you'd love for them to stay (if it's true!). However, persuading someone to stay against their own interests rarely results in long-term retention. It's tempting to ask a staff member to stick it out "just one more school year" (or campaign, or funding cycle. . .) by appealing to the organization's mission or their relationships. More often than not, however, this strategy delays the inevitable and creates undue pressure on the staff member (especially BIPOC or more junior staff) to sacrifice their interests and well-being for the sake of the organization.

KEY POINTS OF INVESTING IN PEOPLE

Here are the takeaways from the chapter:

- Investing in people, or staff development, involves identifying potential in people, and offering guidance and mentorship to help them excel in their roles.

- Investing in people doesn't just *feel* good—it makes us, our teams, and our work better. It's vital to the *conspire-and-align* approach because you're aligning on a vision for your staff's growth and your work together.

- Investing improves retention, builds the staff person's power, and levels up our collective impact.

- Taking an "**investment mindset**" about someone involves being their hype person, assuming the best about them, and offering growth opportunities, guidance, and feedback.

- Focus on impact and develop only what the person can reasonably change.

- To develop people, first, get aligned, then name and break down the skill or mindset, and finally, make a plan to help them develop it.

- Use **stretch assignments**, **I do/we do/you do,** and feedback and debriefs for development.

- Don't take **retention** for granted. Instead, proactively identify people to retain and learn what will make them most likely to stay—but don't try to retain everyone at all costs!

CHAPTER

9

ADDRESSING PERFORMANCE PROBLEMS

If you flipped to this chapter first before reading anything else, we're not surprised. One of the biggest reasons managers come to us for help is because they have a performance problem and they don't know what to do next.[1]

Imagine this: You manage a staff person, Sam, who's been struggling in her role for months. You inherited the managerial relationship after a team restructure. You realize early on that you probably wouldn't have hired her, given her inconsistent demonstration of the must-haves. So you spend the first six months building your relationship and offering as much coaching and development as you can. But the role requires a high level of precision and organization, which Sam doesn't seem to have, despite each of your best efforts to develop her. Eventually, you wonder if you need to let her go. But before you do, Sam decides to leave on her own. You wish it could have turned out differently, but you did your best to support Sam and part ways gracefully. Months later, a co-worker tells you, "Sam told me you're the best manager she's ever had."

Huh?

---

[1] Note that when we talk about "performance problems," we don't mean clear grounds for dismissal like embezzlement or sexual misconduct; we're talking about a staff member failing to meet the expectations for success in their role.

You might be thinking to yourself—how could this be? Sam struggled for *months*. She was on the verge of being fired. So how did she leave that job with such a strong positive feeling about her manager?

To be clear, the point of this story isn't that you should strive to be everybody's best manager. It's also *not* a case study of perfect management. When we asked Penny, the manager in this story, what she'd have done differently, she rattled off a list of coulds, shoulds, and woulds. Here's the point: it's possible to address performance problems with integrity and accountability to our results while leaving our relationships and each person's dignity intact.

Dealing with performance problems is one of the most uncomfortable and challenging parts of management. But, unfortunately, it's also incredibly common—and that's all the more reason to do it well. Effective management isn't about avoiding mistakes or problems—we're all human. As managers, we make mistakes. We don't always make the best hiring decisions, set clear role expectations, or give helpful and timely feedback. What sets effective managers apart from ineffective managers is that when we make mistakes or encounter problems, we address them with competence and integrity.

The good news is that many performance problems can be corrected (or, better yet, prevented!). The bad news is that not all of them can, despite everyone's best efforts. Effective management is about knowing when this is the case—and doing what's necessary to resolve performance issues, even if it's uncomfortable. And with a *conspire-and-align* approach, when we *do* encounter a performance problem, we partner with our teammate to address it without treating *them* as the problem.

This chapter explains how to evaluate, communicate about, and decide how to handle performance problems. We talk through your options for resolution: investing in the staff member's improvement, "coaching out" the staff member with a mutual agreement to part ways, or letting them go.

THINGS TO KEEP IN MIND

Before we get into the details, here are things to keep in mind when dealing with performance problems:

- **Own your part.** Whatever the origin of the problem, it's your duty as a manager to own the solution. Consider where you might have contributed to the problem because of implicit biases or management missteps. You're responsible for dealing with performance problems even (or especially!) when:

  - You haven't been an effective manager.

  - The problem is a result of a hiring mistake.

  - The problem started before you got there.

  - It seems like just a personality clash between two team members.

  - You think (or hope) the staff member might decide to leave.

  - You have too much else on your plate.

- **Be curious, kind, and compassionate.** Approach your staff person with respect and humanity, understanding that you might not know why your staff member is struggling.

- **Focus on what is *really* needed from this role.** Imagine that your staff person is a candidate you're considering hiring for the position. Do they meet the must-haves, and if not, can they develop the needed skills?

- **Be clear and decisive.** In our experience, this is where managers have the most trouble—and it's arguably the most critical part. You can't expect people to improve their performance if you haven't explicitly stated the problem or outlined the consequences if it continues. And once you've identified a problem, you can't just ignore it; you must take decisive action.

FOUR STEPS TO ADDRESS PERFORMANCE PROBLEMS

As a manager, you're responsible for spotting and addressing performance problems. Chapter 7 explains the difference between developmental feedback (giving suggestions on getting from good to great) and corrective feedback (identifying behavior that *must* change). Ideally, you'd provide corrective feedback early and often at regular check-ins, giving the person a chance to improve before it becomes a serious problem. But sometimes, that course correction doesn't happen or isn't enough to fix the issue.

In this chapter, we outline four actions to take to address a performance problem (reflect, check in, assess, and decide) and three possible decisions (invest, coach out, or let go). See the flow chart in Figure 9.1. Depending on your context, you might need to repeat some steps—such as reflecting and checking in a few times. Note that these steps outline actions you can take but don't represent an organizational disciplinary *process*. Tailor your approach to your organization's policies and employee agreements, and consult your lawyer as necessary.

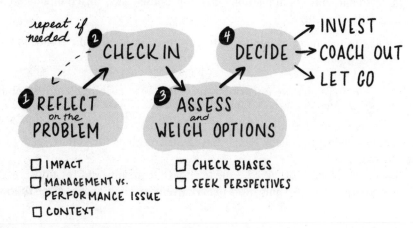

FIGURE 9.1 *A flowchart for the steps you might take to address performance problems.*

Step 1: Reflect on the Problem

To reflect on the problem, ask yourself these questions:

1. What's the problem and its impact (on people, relationships, culture, and/or results)?

2. How much of this is a management issue? How much of it is a performance issue?

3. What about the broader context should I consider?

The first question helps you make sure the problem is really a problem. Start by naming it and identifying what's at stake if it remains unaddressed. It's also a *PTR* and bias check: Is the person failing to meet *requirements* that are must-have skills or approaches, or is this just a conflict of *preferences* or *traditions*? Do you have biases leading you to judge them unfairly or harshly? If there's a significant impact on results or people, chances are it's a genuine performance problem.

The second set of questions helps you identify what's in your *sphere of control* and what's in the staff person's. The purpose of this exercise isn't to assign blame— it's to get specific about where you each have the power and responsibility to resolve the problem. Look at your staff person's role and goals (see Chapter 4). What expectations about must-have skills or approaches have you already aligned on? What other expectations—such as team culture, values, and norms—are relevant here? Have you communicated them? Where are they not delivering, despite clear expectations and agreements? What feedback have you given?

The third question encourages you to step back and consider the context—things out of everybody's control. The following are a few things that fall into this category:

- Extenuating circumstances, like a recent disaster or the death of a loved one.

- Organizational shifts or transitions creating bottlenecks, miscommunication, or sustainability challenges.

- Dynamics around margins and mainstreams, bias, or lines of difference that complicate the situation.

Often, these don't absolve either of you of your responsibility, but it's helpful to understand the conditions you're working with.

At this stage, consider consulting with your manager or a trusted peer who can (confidentially) help you check your biases, ask probing questions, and provide another perspective.

In Sam's case, Penny observed a clear impact on results and relationships. Sam and Penny worked at an organization that ran several civic engagement fellowship programs for public service leaders. Part of Sam's job was owning logistics for these six-month fellowships, which served hundreds of participants each year. She was also responsible for coordinating with the fellowship managers to meet participants' access needs.

Unfortunately, colleagues complained about balls getting dropped, like Sam forgetting to order lunch for participants for a daylong training session (being hangry impedes learning!). One time, Sam sent the wrong session date to participants. When she finally caught her mistake, some participants already had conflicting plans, so they couldn't attend. In addition, there was often miscommunication between Sam and her colleagues—and even participants—that resulted in bad feelings and damaged relationships.

When Penny reflected on her *sphere of control*, she realized she'd been using a "one-size-fits-all" approach with everyone she managed. Because her other staff didn't

LOOK BACK AT YOUR CHOICE POINTS

When you reflect on your staff person's performance problem, reflect on your past choice points that could have contributed to it. Use these questions to reflect on your management decisions:

Roles, Goals, and Delegation:

- Have you been clear about role expectations, including the *what* (specific areas of responsibility) and the *how* (values, mindsets, and approaches that are key to success in the role)?
- Have you and your staff routinely aligned on what success looks like, both in the role and for specific projects and assignments?

Relationship-building:

- Have you incorporated the four elements of relationship-building (space for authenticity, building trust, navigating difference and power, and aligning on shared purpose) in your interactions with your staff member? (For more self-reflection questions about relationship-building, see Chapter 2's "Relationship-Building Checklist for Managers" section.)

Check-ins, feedback, and development:

- How regularly did you check in, both generally and about specific assignments?
- Have you given clear and direct feedback about the problem?
- What have you done to support your staff person to develop the related competencies needed to address the problem?

struggle as Sam did, she expected Sam to "get it." However, when she realized Sam (reasonably) needed more support from her, Penny became more "in the mix."

A note about their context: Penny noticed some things about margins and mainstreams that influenced Sam's performance. Sam was newer to professional nonprofit work and had bad experiences with past managers, leading her to mistrust Penny at first. As a queer person in a fairly conservative town, she struggled with being out to colleagues and participants, which affected her mental health. Even though they had similar racial backgrounds, Sam didn't share these struggles openly because she didn't think Penny, a straight woman, would understand. Sam also lived with depression and anxiety, which sometimes made it hard to be fully present. With these considerations, Penny couldn't tell if Sam's performance problems were a matter of needing accommodations or if she didn't meet the must-haves (or some combination of both). Still, Penny committed to learning more about being an ally to LGBTQ staff and supporting people living with depression and anxiety.

STEP 2: CHECK IN WITH THE STAFF PERSON

After reflecting, check in with your staff person and have an honest conversation to share your feedback (using CSAW from Chapter 7) and seek their perspective. This conversation is your chance to be explicit about your respective spheres of control. Own your part and be clear about theirs.

If you've discussed the issue multiple times, skip to the next step (assess). If you're raising it for the first time, your goal is to sound an alarm and start a conversation—*not* to make or communicate decisions. Until the performance problem is resolved, you'll likely have to reflect and check in multiple times.

When Penny noticed a pattern of dropped balls, she brought it up at a check-in. She shared her observations about delayed work products and colleagues' concerns about follow-through and responsiveness. Penny outlined the impacts of these issues. Then she asked Sam, "What's been your experience? What am I missing?"

Sam shared that she had recently gone through a depressive episode—everything was overwhelming. On some of the recent communication snafus with fellows, Sam admitted that her anxiety made even minor social interactions hard, so she avoided them. She also expressed frustration that some colleagues complained to Penny instead of sharing feedback with her directly.

In their check-in, Penny asked questions to understand Sam's needs. She asked, "How would you describe your work when you're not feeling acutely depressed or anxious? Are there times or conditions when you feel most focused and present at work?"

At the end of the conversation, Penny better understood what support Sam needed. She recommended alternate work hours so Sam could work when she felt most focused. In addition, she reminded Sam that mental health was health, and she could take sick days when needed.

She also restated the impact of Sam's performance issues. Penny reminded Sam that she was responsible for communicating when she couldn't deliver on work that people depended on her for. They aligned on expectations about what Sam would do if she was behind on her work again. Penny and Sam also decided on process tweaks (like adding checklists and scheduling more slices and stepbacks) to help her stay on top of her tasks. They agreed to revisit the conversation in subsequent check-ins.

STEP 3: ASSESS THE PROBLEM

With the new information you've gained from your check-in, it's time to assess.

Go back to the three questions you asked yourself in Step 1 and see if anything has changed. Next, consider any impacts or context that surfaced since you last reflected. Then, seek perspective from others (such as your manager or peers—discreetly!).

Finally, ask yourself two other important questions:

- **Can the problem be improved through coaching, guidance, or training?** Consider the staff's ability (remember the context chart in Chapter 3) to own their part of the solution. Also, consider *your* capacity, skill, and will to support them.

- **If it improves, how likely is it that it'll be sustained and consistent?** Consider their overall track record of success in their role, including previous course corrections and development efforts. (See Chapter 8 for more on staff development.)

Penny's check-in with Sam helped her do better *perspective-taking* (see Chapter 2). Sam had raised issues that weren't on Penny's radar because she'd never personally experienced them (like depression, anxiety, and being out as queer at work). And as a manager, it was her responsibility to offer accommodations (to the best of her ability) and adapt her management to better support Sam.

She still had concerns, though. Some of the issues with Sam's performance persisted even when she was in a healthier mental state. She had given feedback to Sam before about follow-through and missed deadlines, and the improvements were inconsistent.

Penny was at a crossroads. She'd offered everything she could, within reason—accommodations to support Sam's health needs, timely feedback, professional development support, and investment through side-by-side work, modeling, and coaching. She'd checked her biases, examined her choice points, spent months learning about sexual orientation issues, and sought perspective from others. If Sam's performance was going to improve, it'd have to be through her efforts and willingness.

STEP 4: DECIDE

As a manager, you typically have three options for moving forward: investing, coaching out, or letting go.

> Before deciding what to do, *always* check your organizational policies and consult your HR or legal advisors. Some organizations have policies or collective bargaining agreements that commit the organization to follow specific disciplinary actions. With any employment issue where legal issues may arise, consider speaking with a lawyer.

Option 1: Invest

If you believe the staff person can meet expectations and you're able to help them do it, invest. Investing includes offering ongoing, specific feedback, coaching and training opportunities, and side-by-side work. You might do all these things as part of a (formal or informal) performance improvement plan.

LEGAL PITFALLS TO AVOID

We're not lawyers! You should talk to one if you have concerns about firing an employee. But, in general, make sure you're not leaving yourself open to accusations of discrimination. (We hope it should go without saying that none of the following behaviors are acceptable, but let's make the implicit explicit.)

Avoid:

- **Direct comments related to a protected class.** Don't make discriminatory comments (including "jokes") based on age, disability, gender reassignment, marriage and civil partnership, pregnancy and maternity, race, religion or belief, sex, and sexual orientation.

- **Disparate treatment.** Give equitable treatment (including compensation, feedback, development opportunities, etc.) to employees of comparable tenure, seniority, and performance level.

- **Pretext.** Don't lie about the real reasons you're firing someone; a jury might reasonably infer that you're covering for discrimination.

- **Retaliation.** Don't fire or discipline someone for exercising their rights related to employment discrimination, whether that's filing a harassment claim, inquiring about salary information, or requesting accommodations.

The following are a few common reasons for choosing this route:

- The problem is primarily a management problem, which means that the solution is in your sphere of control—you need to improve your management practices and systems to offer more clarity, support, and/or structure.

- Extenuating circumstances beyond the person's control have impacted their otherwise solid performance.

- The problem is coachable and the staff person is willing to learn.

- The problem is due to growing pains (the role has changed or the organization is growing). You and the staff person need additional time and/or support to get settled in.

The steps you take to invest in your staff person at this point will be similar to what we discuss in Chapter 8. But, of course, the stakes are different, and staff development is not optional.

When we're trying to get better at something, we're much more likely to do it when there's someone in our corner. One TMC colleague shared that he struggled to perform in one of his first jobs. His manager gave him feedback and said, "Listen, you're struggling right now, but I *know* you can do this." To him, both her faith in him and her honesty were critical for his improvement. He shared, "I felt like she respected me enough not to downplay or avoid the problem. She wanted me to persevere because she knew I could succeed."

In Chapter 2, we talk about Libby, our colleague's former manager, who kicked off a manager/staff relationship by talking about power. That TMC colleague shared another story about a time when he struggled to hit his targets for a project. Libby said, "These results aren't what we'd expected. What do you think is going on? I don't think this is an issue of competence, and I know you want to do a good job. Let's find the right levers to pull for you to be successful."

These two stories show the power of *conspiring and aligning* with a staff person to address a potential performance problem. For Libby, the problem was about strategy and support, not our colleague's competence. In both cases, the managers truly believed their staff could be successful—they adopted an investment mindset. Contrast this with Breanna's story in Chapter 7, about a manager who brought a deficiency mindset, often approaching her with the sentiment of "Here's everything you're doing wrong."

Make a plan to improve the staff person's performance, outlining expectations for success, a timeline for improvement, and the support you'll provide. (Whether or not you go the route of a formal Performance Improvement Plan [PIP]), see the self-reflection questions in the next section).

Penny had chosen the "invest" option for Sam's situation when she first noticed a problem. Her final attempt to invest in Sam was to put her on a PIP, which formalized the feedback she'd given previously. With the PIP, there was a strict timeline and an explicit understanding that Sam's job was at stake—Sam had two months to show consistent improvement. In Penny's words, "Sam knew that if her performance didn't improve, at the end of the PIP, it wouldn't be a question of *whether* she left—it'd be a matter of *who decided*. Either she'd choose to leave, or I'd have to coach her out or eventually fire her."

PIPs

When Penny put Sam on a PIP, she believed Sam could be successful. Unless you're legally obligated to, don't use a PIP as a formality when you know you're going to fire somebody at the end of the process. It wastes everyone's time and gives the staff person false hope.

As you consider implementing a PIP, remember the following:

- Check in with your staff person and share direct feedback about their performance first. *A PIP should never be the first way your staff member hears your concerns!*

- Stay open to the possibility that your staff person can succeed, and think about ways to support them.

- Communicate the PIP verbally and in writing, and check for understanding. Explain that this is a formal, time-bound opportunity for development and coaching, and clearly state the expectations and potential consequences.

See Tool 9.1 at the end of this chapter for a template of a performance improvement plan.

Before you create your plan, answer these questions to help you prepare:

- What needs to be improved? Why is it a requirement? What is the impact of the problem?

- What have I done to support improvement? How well have I performed my role as a manager (checking biases, giving feedback, conducting check-ins, delegating, communicating expectations, etc.)? What else can I do to continue to support them?

- What would success look like in X weeks? How will I know improvement when I see it?

- How and when will I provide support, such as coaching, feedback, modeling, or training?

- What actions will I take if I see improvement? What if I see no, minor, or inconsistent improvement?

Other questions to consider:

- What factors do I need to consider (context, staff relationships, bias, etc.)?
- What additional input do I need to gather, and from whom?
- Who can I run my thinking past to check for bias?
- What of their strengths can we leverage or build on?

A SUCCESSFUL PIP

Thuto was the organizing director at a statewide civic engagement organization with a mission to educate and mobilize immigrants and refugees. She hired and managed Kendrick, an organizer responsible for engaging community members about the upcoming election and representing the organization at coalition meetings. After a few months, Thuto observed that Kendrick was excellent at the relational aspects of his job. He drew in community members, got along with his fellow organizers, and won over their coalition partners. But as he continued to settle into his role, she also noticed that Kendrick had issues with follow-through and accountability. He frequently showed up late to organizer meetings, and on several occasions, missed coalition calls entirely. One time, he procrastinated on a project until the last minute, creating a scramble close to the deadline—forcing his teammates (all women of color) to pick up the slack.

Thuto regularly shared feedback in their one-on-one check-ins after these incidents. However, while he was receptive and made some improvements, it never seemed to stick.

After a few months, Thuto put Kendrick on a PIP. In their PIP conversation, she restated the expectations for the role, reiterated her feedback, and laid out the consequences of not improving. She painted a picture of what was at stake—not just for him, but for the organization. She said, "Kendrick, it's amazing when you're on top of your game. But when you let things slide, it adds up. This is a critical election year. We can't afford to miss coalition meetings. We have to be in the arena with our partners working to change politics in our state. When you miss meetings or delay your projects, the people you've organized don't get a seat at the table."

Kendrick was grateful. Even though they'd been having regular CSAW conversations, this conversation helped him connect the dots between the piecemeal feedback he'd gotten before. It helped him see how his behavior impacted his colleagues, their work, and the organization's results. And finally, he left with a complete understanding of the consequences of not improving. He took the feedback from that conversation more seriously than he had in the past—it catalyzed him to fully commit to the role's requirements.

After the PIP conversation, Kendrick's performance turned around. He showed up to meetings, executed project plans promptly, and communicated with his teammates when he needed support.

Option 2: Coach Out

Sometimes after reflecting, checking in, and assessing your options, you might decide that the best option is for the person to leave the role. In a coaching out conversation, the manager offers options, shares their recommendation (that the staff person leave), and leaves it to the staff person to decide. This could sound like saying, "You have a few options for moving forward. You could stay in this role and commit to meeting expectations and improving. If so, we'll make a plan and check in after X weeks. Another option is for you to decide that this role isn't a great fit, and we'll make a transition plan. Given what I've seen, I'd recommend the second option, but if you want to stay, I'm committed to supporting you."

You might be on your way to coaching out if any of the following are true:

- You've already tried to invest through an informal performance improvement process and the person still isn't quite meeting expectations (or meets them inconsistently).

- The staff person is uninterested in changing or growing alongside the organization.

- The staff person has become bored, disengaged, or stagnant in their work.

- The staff person's capacity or circumstances have changed, impacting their ability to meet expectations.

Coaching out can sometimes mean moving someone into another role (more on this later). But we only recommend this if you believe that the staff person can competently help your team meet an unmet need. Don't move someone into a different role as a last-ditch attempt to avoid the discomfort of firing someone—that's prioritizing your needs over your team's results. If the staff person negatively impacts your team culture, moving them to another role will only exacerbate the problem.

The key to coaching out is offering real options so that the staff person has a choice. And if they choose to stay, be prepared to support them. When the options aren't real, coaching out conversations are disingenuous—they're letting go conversations in disguise.

In Sam's case, the PIP conversation could have also been a coaching out conversation. As we mentioned, Penny was at a crossroads. She'd done her best to support Sam—at that point, it was up to Sam to either give another good-faith effort to improve her performance or leave the job.

See Tool 9.2 at the end of this chapter for a sample coaching out script.

Option 3: Let Go

Your final option is to let go, or "fire"—terminating someone's employment at your organization due to performance problems.

Before you consider this option, check your biases (again). Make sure you've reflected, sought perspective from your manager or a colleague, and done everything

COACHING OUT TO A NEW ROLE

Giselle was the regional leader of an educational nonprofit. She managed Justin, the director of school partnerships, who was responsible for working with school leaders to hire teachers. Justin was an incredible strategist—he was sharp, motivated, and always a few steps ahead of everyone else. Unfortunately, he sometimes moved so quickly that he left his teammates behind. Justin would get frustrated by his colleagues when they didn't immediately get on board with his ideas. And while he had great ideas, he struggled with motivating and getting buy-in from others to implement them.

Giselle learned that Justin's communication style was also off-putting to the school leaders they worked with. This was a big problem, given that Justin's goal was to recruit and get teachers hired at their partner schools. When the school leaders didn't like working with Justin, his teacher recruits didn't get hired.

Giselle gave Justin feedback about his communication and leadership style. But he'd heard it all before, and despite his and others' best efforts, he had only made minor improvements. Giselle suspected that implicit bias was part of the problem. After all, Justin was a Black man on a team of mostly white women, interacting with mostly white school leaders. People were more likely to judge him as aggressive and outspoken. As a Black woman, Giselle was familiar with this type of bias. Still, she could see that Justin's behavior created problems. He spent more time defending his ideas than taking in other people's input. He didn't show that he valued what his colleagues brought to the table.

After a few months, Giselle faced a choice. She could either put Justin on a PIP (knowing he was unlikely to succeed) or have a coaching out conversation. Giselle reflected, checked in with Justin, and assessed the situation. Finally, she decided to move him to a different role. In this new role, he could apply his comparative advantage, and he wouldn't have to win over school leaders or manage collaborations. Before making the move official, Giselle tested her hunch that a role shift would address the performance problem and fill an unmet need on her team. She temporarily reduced Justin's partnership portfolio and assigned him a short-term stretch assignment of redesigning their teacher recruitment and hiring system.

After Justin successfully executed that project, Giselle formally offered him a new role as director of special projects—where he thrived for two years before being promoted.

reasonably in your control to support your staff to improve. Then, try the following thought experiments:

- Imagine yourself in six months and nothing has changed—you're still dealing with the same problem and impacts.

- Imagine that the staff person came to you today and told you they'd accepted a job offer. They're putting in their two weeks' notice.

How would you feel in either scenario? (Note: this isn't a "trust your gut" moment! These experiments allow you to tune in to your feelings, which are data.) If your answer for the first scenario was something like "dread" and your answer for the second was "relief," that's a sign that letting go might be a wise option.

For many of our clients, letting go is the last resort. We get it—firing someone is *hard*. After all, we want our movements to bring people *in*, not let them go. In the United States, where people rely on employers for health insurance and other necessities our government and society fail to provide, losing a job can be devastating. It can jeopardize someone's ability to survive. Any manager with a heart would feel this weight. Whew.

Humans are great at talking ourselves into—and out of—anything. With performance problems, we find lots of reasons why we shouldn't fire someone. We tell ourselves that the person's performance is "good enough" because we've come up with sufficient workarounds for whatever they're not delivering. We know they're going through so much—it's hard to imagine piling on to the stress. We feel guilty about our failures as a manager—it would be unfair to fire someone because of our shortcomings.

Sure, these are valid reasons to pause and assess. Sometimes, they *might* be reasons not to fire someone. But often, these are just things we tell ourselves to avoid the discomfort of a hard decision.

When someone isn't a good fit, you do no one any favors by avoiding the problem. Nobody likes being stuck in a position where they can't thrive. Performance issues usually have ripple effects that lower staff morale. And most importantly, you have a duty to manage toward strong, equitable results. Once, Jakada told a school leader, "Imagine yourself explaining to the families you serve that you chose to keep someone on staff at the expense of providing a quality education to their children. Could you do it?"

Ask yourself: What is at stake by having someone who isn't a good fit in this role? What could you gain from having someone who is excellent at it?

The indicators that it might be time to let someone go include all the indicators for coaching out, plus two others:

- The staff member is unwilling to grow or take feedback.

- The problem creates a significant burden or harm to others that can't be reasonably mitigated with the time and resources available.

See Tool 9.3 at the end of this chapter for a sample script for letting someone go. Take a deep breath—you can do it.

MAKE A DECISION!

Did you notice that none of the options we laid out include "do nothing," "get your boss to deal with it," or "wait for the person to quit?" That's because whatever you do, *you need to decide*. You have options, but you must be deliberate and proactive about pursuing them. The longer you delay, the more the problem will grow—impacting others and your results. So, again, test your thinking with your manager or a trusted colleague to check for biases. Then, communicate promptly with your staff person. Schedule a time to talk to them, prepare a script, and practice with someone if necessary.

Note that investing, coaching out, and letting go are *not* mutually exclusive options; they're steps on a path. Depending on the problem, circumstances, and organizational norms and policies, you may choose to invest first, and only progress to coaching out or letting go if the problem persists. In other cases, you might go directly to coaching out or letting go.

No Surprises

Getting fired should never come as a shock. Follow your organization's process and consult with a lawyer before letting someone go. If you don't have a formal process, be explicit about expectations—and the consequences for not meeting them—at every step.

Your organization's process might look like or include the following:

- **Informal Warning.** This is a verbal discussion in which you bring the problem to the employee's attention. If you follow the four steps we laid out, an informal warning might happen during the second step—check-in. Be clear that it's not a typical feedback conversation, and there might be severe consequences if they don't improve their performance. You could say explicitly, "This is an informal warning. The next step is X if we don't see improvement by Y." You can use CSAW for this discussion.

- **Formal Warning and PIP.** If the staff member's performance doesn't improve after the informal warning, you might escalate to a formal written warning. Formal warnings are often shared along with PIPs.

- **Letting go.** If you haven't seen improvement from the PIP (or if you don't believe it can be sustained and consistent), it's probably time to let go. (In rare cases, you might coach the person into a different role.)

HOW LONG SHOULD IT TAKE TO RESOLVE A PERFORMANCE PROBLEM?

Many HR policies and all union agreements outline a process to follow that might include specific timelines for disciplinary actions. If this isn't available, your timeframe for resolving a performance problem will depend on your context. Factors like your capacity for providing coaching and support, the urgency and impact of the issue, and your staff person's capacity and willingness all influence your timeline. In general, we'd want to see significant improvement within three months from when you share explicit feedback about a performance problem. If the issue can't be resolved through investing in the person within that time, it's probably time to consider moving that person out of the role (whether through coaching out or letting go). Still, we share this advice tentatively, knowing that there are a lot of factors to consider.

Other Considerations after Coaching Out or Letting Go

Penny's work didn't end when Sam decided to leave. Once Sam chose to go, they talked through her exit plan. This plan included closing out and passing off her responsibilities, communicating with the team about her departure, and negotiating severance.

Severance Package

Your HR department may have guidance or protocols for severance packages. You might have a union agreement that lays it out. In general, we recommend being as generous as possible to ease the transition. When you inform your staffer of your decision, be prepared to discuss severance, COBRA or other healthcare options, and other logistics.

In Sam's case, the organization didn't have a formal severance policy. Still, Penny was able to offer a severance package that allowed Sam to exit sooner and have enough financial stability to meet her material needs like rent and healthcare.

Logistics

Logistics will vary depending on your organization's policies and practices. For example, some organizations expect employees to leave immediately; others allow more time. If you've coached someone out, they might stay for a few extra weeks or months, depending on your agreement. Consider logistics like cleaning up their workspace, closing accounts, removing access to tech, and returning items that belong to the organization

Sharing the News with Staff

In most cases, you'll make a plan with your staff person to share the news with the rest of the team. At TMC, most departures are announced by the staff person, followed by an email from their manager to appreciate the person's work and contributions and outline the next steps. Depending on the circumstances, you might build in time for the staff person to have one-on-one conversations with colleagues before making an announcement to the broader group.

Dealing with the Aftereffects

You might be (understandably) concerned about the adverse ripple effects of a staff person leaving. Every transition—even the good kind, like when someone decides to leave on their own accord—comes with uncertainty, change, and grief. A staff person leaving the organization could mean shuffling responsibilities or delaying work until you hire a replacement. It could also mean a shift in culture or a morale dip, especially if they were close with their colleagues.

Here are tips for navigating the aftereffects:

- **Give people space to react.** In a one-on-one check-in, you could ask, "I know that you might have some reactions to the news about X leaving. Is there anything you want to share with me? Is there anything you feel concerned about or want me to know?"

- **Name the impact and offer support if you can.** In one-on-one check-ins or a team meeting, acknowledge what it will mean for the remaining staff. You could say:
  - "I know X leaving means you'll have to field media requests until we hire someone new. Let's make a plan so that it doesn't become too overwhelming."
  - "I know you and X were close, so it might be weird to not have them on the team anymore."

- **Respect the person's privacy.** When you make a plan to announce the news, check with the staff person about what they're comfortable with others knowing about the circumstances of their departure.

- **Don't over-explain.**[2] If someone left because of performance problems, talking about those problems makes you look unkind and untrustworthy. And if the circumstances of their departure were controversial, you'll come across as defensive. You could say, "We respect everyone's privacy and won't share personal details. Everyone deserves confidentiality on sensitive matters."

- **Accept the discomfort.** Sometimes, you have to make a decision and let it stand the test of time. There's no pill you can swallow to make a decision less hard or uncomfortable to make—you just have to deal with it.

---

[2] Yes, this might be the only context in which we don't whole-heartedly encourage you to "share the why."

It's worth noting that it's not *always* doom and gloom when a staff member leaves. We sometimes find that letting go of someone who wasn't a good fit for the role can ultimately *improve* staff morale. After all, the person couldn't meet their role expectations, which tends to drag down their team members' work and have other negative impacts. If you've been fair and thoughtful with your process, your staff may feel relieved—or at least understand—even if they're disappointed to lose someone they care about.

KEY POINTS OF ADDRESSING PERFORMANCE PROBLEMS

Here are the takeaways from the chapter:

- When we use a *conspire-and-align* approach, we partner with our staff person to address the problem without treating *them* as the problem.

- Many performance problems can be corrected (or, better yet, prevented!). Others can't, despite our and our staff's best efforts.

- There are four main steps to addressing performance problems:
  - **Reflect** on the problem, including what's in your and your staff person's respective spheres of control. Also, consider the overall context.

  - **Check in** with the staff person. Share your honest take on the problem, its impacts, and (if applicable) the consequences if things don't improve. Seek their perspective to get a fuller understanding of the problem.

  - **Assess** the problem and your options. Consider how likely it is that they can improve in a sustained, consistent way.

  - **Decide** on how to move forward with one of three options:
    - **Invest** in helping the staff person improve (which can include putting them on a performance improvement plan).

    - **Coach out the person.** Let them choose between improving their performance or leaving the role, being clear about your recommendation. Be open and prepared to support them if they decide to stay.

    - **Let go** of the person if they are unwilling or unable to improve enough to meet expectations or if the negative impacts of their performance can't be reasonably mitigated.

- Getting fired for performance reasons should *never* come as a shock. It should be part of a transparent process of feedback and efforts to help the person improve.

- When you fire someone, plan for the logistics of their departure and how you'll communicate about it with other staff.

APPENDIX TOOLS

TOOL 9.1

PERFORMANCE IMPROVEMENT PLAN TEMPLATES

The following are two tools for managers to use as you're preparing a PIP. The first is a reflection worksheet to help you think through what you need to communicate in the PIP. The second is the actual Performance Improvement Plan, which outlines the goals of the performance improvement period.

Manager Prep Worksheet	
Staff Name: **Manager Name:**	**Today's Date:** **Timeframe: [from start date] to [end date]**
1. What do I need to see improved and why is it important? What is the impact of the problem?	* What must-have expectations for the role aren't being met, and what specific example(s) will I give?
2. What have I done or can I do to support improvement?	* How well have I performed my role as a manager (bias check, feedback, check-ins, delegation, communication about role/expectations, etc.)? What will I need to do better or differently?
3. What would success look like in [x]* weeks?	* How will I know improvement when I see it?
4. How and when will I provide support, such as coaching, feedback, modeling, or training?	
5. What actions will I take as a result?	* If I see improvement: * If I see no or little improvement: * Do those possible actions tell me anything I need to make explicit or do differently now?

*Use your best judgment to decide the timeframe (usually weeks, not months, but consider your context). Very serious problems may warrant immediate action.

Other questions to consider:
- What factors do I need to consider (context, staff relationships, potential bias, etc.)?
- What additional input do I need to gather and from whom?
- Whom can I run my thinking past to check for any unintended bias?
- What staff member strengths can we leverage or build on?

Performance Improvement Plan			
Staff Name: **Manager Name:**	**Date Shared/Discussed:** **Timeframe: [from start date] to [end date]**		
What needs to improve to meet performance standards (must-haves)?	**Goal(s) for the improvement period**	**Actions to be taken by staff member**	**Support from manager or organization**
Attention to detail and deadlines *Advance communication when support is needed*	*Submission-ready grant reports complete three days before deadline for manager review*	• Create proof-reading and report requirements checklist • Update calendar with due dates and alerts	• Review/approve checklist and calendar • Weekly check-ins, with one hour week for support requests
Schedule for Checking In/Reporting Back:		**What may happen if expectations aren't met?**	

TOOL 9.2

COACHING OUT [SAMPLE SCRIPT]

In this sample, the staff member (a director of technology) has been a loyal employee whose skills no longer are a match for the evolved position. The manager would prefer for the staff member to leave the role, but they're open to investing through a PIP and believe the staff member could be successful.

Therefore, the core of the manager's message is:

- The demands of the role have changed and your skills may not be a good fit for it.
- I'm willing to pursue the performance improvement plan route.
- I think that your transitioning out might make the most sense.

As I mentioned to you, I'd like to talk about concerns I have about your fit for the director of technology role as it has evolved. **I want to share my thinking, get your perspective, and offer two ways to move forward.**

Let me start by saying that I know how much work you've put into this job over the past two years. On a number of occasions, you've gone above and beyond. You're been great at paying attention to details and fixing problems. In our early days, you built strong relationships with vendors.

> Acknowledge the employee's strengths. Don't do this to soften the tough parts of the conversation; offer it to show you see the whole person and their inherent value beyond the specific problem area you'll discuss.

As you know, as our organization has grown, what we needed in our director of technology role has evolved. We used to be a small, single-site shop, and now we have multiple locations. As we've added new programs, our database development needs have increased.

When I realized three months ago that the role was changing, I came to talk with you. We discussed what we needed and why, and I asked whether you felt like this role was something you could (and wanted to) level up to. **Before I share my take, I'd like to hear from you. How have you been feeling?**

> Tell the story of how and why the role has evolved, and what the new bar is.

Thanks for sharing your thoughts. **I was excited that you were up for the challenge.** Over the last three months, I've observed you putting effort into growing your skills by attending a database management training and jumping into projects to get hands-on experience. Anything else I'm missing?

> Recognize the efforts this person has made to meet the bar.

Unfortunately, I'm still not seeing significant demonstration of the requirements for the role—things like big-picture conceptualization, ongoing communication with the program staff about their needs, and project management. For example, let's talk about our meeting with the digital organizing team about their plan. We need

> Share specific examples. Be clear about the areas that need improvement and define the bar you need them to meet.

someone who can sit in that meeting, gauge what the team is trying to accomplish, translate it into a set of technological solutions, and then explain the options in plain terms so they can choose. Once they've decided, we need someone who can manage the project and deliver a product that meets everyone's needs.

Unfortunately, I don't think those are your core strengths. For instance, when we tried to develop the new subscriber database, there were quite a few issues, including missing the final deadline. Even when the other team isn't performing perfectly, I need someone who will communicate the issues, help them understand what they need to do, and manage them to their deadlines. It's critical because our team and projects are rapidly growing. As I mentioned already, I definitely see your efforts and strengths in other areas; my concern is about your fit for this specific role.

How is all of this landing for you? Do you feel like I'm capturing our past conversations?

So where does this leave us? I want to discuss two paths we could explore. As you know, we have a formal process for staff members who aren't meeting expectations, and that would be our **first option.** I want to be clear that this is a real option—if you choose to go this route, I'll work with you to set clear expectations and support you to develop your skills. **I think you could meet the bar for performance if you work really hard.**

> If you are willing to develop a formal improvement plan and really believe it could work, note that.

This meeting would be the first step in that process—this would be the **informal performance warning**, and we'd talk about how we'd know over the next three weeks if your performance had improved. After that, if your performance doesn't improve, there would be a **written warning** and a **performance improvement plan**, which would last another four weeks. At the end of that, if your performance doesn't meet expectations, I'd have to let you go. If it does improve, then we'd move ahead with you in this role.

> Lay out the next steps according to your organization's policy (remember: this is just a sample!)

The second option is this: if the role isn't what you want, then we'd make a plan that lets you do a job search and gives me time to hire someone new.

In this option, we'd agree now that you'll leave the role in three months. In the meantime, you'd continue ensuring our tech needs are met, but we wouldn't expect you to take on new projects. We'd continue to pay you through your last day. (If you found a job sooner, then you could leave before that, but we'd stop paying you.) All of this would be contingent on your continuing to perform as you have been.

> Offer a win-win path that could work for both of you. Preemptively address the preconditions of the offer and check with your lawyer or HR in advance about what this agreement should look like.

I prefer this option because I'm genuinely not sure that the evolved role is a great fit. But the decision is yours to make, and I will support you either way.

> Be honest about any preference you have and why, while being clear that the decision is theirs to make. Include a clear deadline, but don't force them to make a decision on the spot.

We can talk more about this now, or I can give you some time to think about it and then we can talk in the next day or two about which way you'd like to go.

I do feel urgency around figuring this out, so I'd like to meet no later than Thursday to hear your decision. **Do you want to talk now, or would you rather wait?**

TOOL 9.3

FIRING [SAMPLE SCRIPT]

In this sample, an administrative assistant has been given feedback and received coaching and training as part of a formal four-week performance improvement plan. At the end of this period, they have not shown the agreed progress. The written plan specified that they would be dismissed if performance did not improve by the end of the PIP.

As I told you yesterday, I wanted to use our meeting today to reflect on your progress toward the improvement plan. I know you've tried hard, particularly with creating a welcoming environment in the front office. When I asked the rest of the team (as we discussed that I would), I received several positive comments about your improvement. But on the other two dimensions we've spoken about—handling the daily flow of work and returning calls within one business day—your performance isn't where we need it. There are at least three items that I asked you to handle more than two days ago that are still not complete: scheduling the meeting with Melissa, printing background materials for my meeting next Thursday, and completing my expense report.

> Refer back to the earlier agreements you made and be upfront about what is happening.

> Acknowledge improvement that's been made, but be clear that it hasn't been sufficient. Give specific examples of what areas have not been met.

We talked two weeks ago about the fact that if you couldn't meet the expectations of the job, I would have to let you go. We're now at that point.

I want to reiterate how much I appreciate you and I'm sorry we've reached this point. Before we talk through logistics, do you have any questions?

> Give the employee a chance to digest the news and react if they want to.

You can use the next week to clean out your desk, say goodbye to people, and wrap up loose ends. I would really appreciate it if you would go through your emails and send me an update on where each item stands—whether you haven't gotten to it yet, if it's partly or fully done, and anything else I should know. This afternoon, you should talk to Erica in HR about exit procedures and severance. She'll give you a list of other things (like returning keys) to take care of.

I know that this has been a challenging experience and that, particularly over these last few weeks, you have been trying hard. On a personal level, I've enjoyed working with you, and I really do hope you find a job that is a better fit. Is there anything else you want to know or discuss?

CHAPTER

10

MANAGING
UP AND SIDEWAYS

For most of this book, we've focused on how to manage the people who report directly to you—in other words, how to manage with *formal authority*. Formal authority might include the power to hire or fire someone, evaluate their performance, or determine or influence their compensation and benefits.

But often, you'll find yourself managing *without* formal authority—such as in external partnerships and collaborative projects. Or, you might be at a workplace with a nonhierarchical or matrixed structure. And middle managers, you're managing in all directions simultaneously! For all of these reasons, managing without formal authority is an important skill—and the *conspire-and-align* approach is especially helpful for this kind of management. Managing without formal authority can look like:

- **Managing up**: Using management skills with your boss (or boss's boss, or the board, if you're an ED).

- **Managing sideways:** Managing work with a peer, either within your organization or outside it.

- **Managing diagonally:** Managing work with someone with a power differential (one person has more or less position power), but neither of you has formal authority over the other.[1]

If the phrase "managing up" makes you uneasy, we get it. After all, most traditional advice about managing up normalizes bad management behaviors. It sets up the expectation that staff people serve as their manager's assistants no matter their official titles—and the burdens fall hardest on staff with marginalized identities.

Managing up isn't about folding yourself in half to make your boss's job easier. It's about getting what *you* need to do your job effectively, which will create better results. The same goes for managing sideways or diagonally. While managing up, sideways, and diagonally requires work for the person with less power, it doesn't have to mean more stress. On the contrary, managing without formal authority effectively means you exercise agency, strengthen relationships, and tap into your wisdom—and your work will be better off as a result.

TOOLS FOR MANAGING UP AND SIDEWAYS

The following are some essential (and familiar!) tools for managing up and sideways:

- Reflecting on your sphere of control.

- Practicing perspective-taking.

- Engaging in relationship-building.

- Using the five Ws to get clarity.

- Offering slices.

- Making proposals.

- Making strong asks.

- Sharing and inviting feedback.

Reflecting on Your Sphere of Control

By now, you've seen *sphere of control* mentioned many times. And here it is again—because it might be the most essential tool in your "managing up and sideways" toolbox.

In Chapter 1, we compare sphere of control to a game of spades, where winning is possible even if you're dealt a bad hand. At its core, managing up and sideways is about understanding your circumstances and identifying what you need to succeed.

---

[1] For simplicity's sake, the rest of this chapter talks about managing up and sideways; our advice for managing diagonally will be similar to our guidance for managing sideways.

It's also about understanding where you can influence others to help you get what you need. And, unlike spades, where table talk might get you kicked out of the game, clear communication about strategy is highly encouraged. Even when we have limited positional power or social influence, we have agency. We can decide how we communicate with others, spend our time, and build relationships.

Note that your sphere of control isn't static; it can expand or contract. You may never have direct control over some things, but you can grow your sphere of control by thinking about these questions:

- What relationships or skills could you build?

- How might you shape your trajectory (within your organization or beyond)?

Managers, consider how your actions could impact your staff's sphere of control. What might you do to help your staff recognize their choices and agency?

Practicing Perspective-Taking

In Chapter 2, we discuss the importance of perspective-taking, the practice of putting yourself in someone else's shoes. Ask yourself, "What demands, pressures, or challenges is the other person dealing with?"

Perspective-taking won't change the *impact* of someone's behavior, but it can help you manage your response and avoid climbing the ladder of assumptions. Perspective-taking enables you to see where it's not you; it's them—and it's a reminder that they're human, too.

Here's an example of how it can work: Mario had a colleague, Manoj, whom he found difficult to work with. Whenever Mario shared an idea or suggestion for a process tweak or improvement, Manoj resisted, saying, "That's not what my manager said to do." Mario, a fast-moving go-getter, felt frustrated by what he perceived as Manoj's inflexibility and lack of initiative. Then, before climbing the ladder of assumptions, Mario paused to reflect on his assumptions and biases. He realized that Manoj, a new immigrant working in the United States for the first time, came from an entirely different context and culture. The ways he had learned to relate to colleagues in India, his home country, didn't apply in their workplace. As a fellow immigrant, Mario could empathize—he knew intimately the pressures of acclimating (and assimilating) to new cultural norms. Ultimately, it didn't remove all of his frustration about Manoj's resistance, but it helped him take it less personally. And knowing that he and Manoj shared an identity as immigrants, Mario found different ways to relate to him.

See the "Perspective-Taking" section in Chapter 2 for more on perspective-taking and the ladder of assumptions.

Engaging in Relationship-Building

When you don't have authority, you must rely on influence. One way to build influence is by building relationships.

Have you ever gladly done something you'd typically avoid because you cared about the person who asked you to do it? It's human nature to feel more willing to stretch for people we have stronger relationships with. This happens socially, like planning a friend's baby shower, and professionally, like making time to share feedback on a colleague's presentation.

To be clear, it's not about being *well-liked* (though that could be part of it)—it's about trust and care. One TMC colleague shared this reflection about our operations director: "When Addae asks me to do something, I prioritize it. I trust they wouldn't ask me to do something if it weren't important because they always consider the requirements and potential burdens. They've also taken the time to get to know me, so I believe they care about me. At my old job, the operations person didn't do any of that, so when they asked me to do something new or different, I always wanted to know why. I couldn't be sure that it was a thoughtful request."

A stronger relationship makes it easier to ask for things, share and receive feedback, and hold each other accountable. In addition, the time you spend building a relationship saves you time later—from explaining, defending, and persuading.

The core principles of relationship-building that should guide managers—authenticity, trust, navigating power and difference, and shared purpose—can also guide you when managing up or sideways. Even when you don't have positional power, you can do these things to build your relationships (for more, see Chapter 2):

- Check in with the people in your MOCHA (ideally before the work gets underway or early in the process). Get to know them, learn about their work and communication styles, and share and invite feedback.

- Appreciate your teammates for their contributions.

- Acknowledge your mistakes.

- Celebrate wins and milestones with your team.

Using the Five Ws to Get Clarity

Whether you're managing up or sideways, aligning your expectations is essential. Use what you've learned about delegation, roles, and goals to manage up and sideways (see Chapters 3 and 4).

Use the five Ws (and an H) to ask your manager or team members about their expectations. If you're the project manager, be prepared to communicate your answers and seek input.

Ask:

- **What** will success look like? What outcomes are expected?

- **Why** is this task important? Why now? How big of a priority is this relative to other work? What background and context do you need about the goals/project?

- **When** does it need to be completed? What are benchmarks along the way?

- **Where** can you find resources, examples, or other guidance?

- **Who** else is involved? (Use MOCHA to decide who is doing what!)

- **How** will you check progress and ensure alignment?

You can turn this into an alignment activity with your manager or colleague at your next check-in. First, have each person fill out the five Ws for an assignment. Then, compare them. When managing sideways, pay special attention to:

- The "who": It's easy to inadvertently miscommunicate about roles and decision-making power when delegating to a peer.

- The "why": Getting consent and buy-in is especially important when you lack formal authority.

Offering Slices

As we shared in Chapter 3, slices are a great way to get aligned on the work during the "staying engaged" part of the delegation cycle. Slices are a chance to get the guidance and feedback you need (and deserve!). Here are a few tips for using slices to manage up:

- Once you're aligned on the 5Ws, decide when you'll share slices. For example, if you're writing an annual report, you could say, "Here are the slices I think I should share with you: an outline, the first few paragraphs, and the first draft. What do you think?" Then, once you agree on the slices, map out the deadlines (and make sure your manager sets aside time to review!).

- Use your standing check-in time to share slices along the way to keep your manager up-to-date and avoid surprises at the end.

- Offer slices of things your manager is most likely to care about—the new, tricky, or high-stakes stuff.

- In addition to getting general reactions, prepare specific questions to ask to get feedback. For example, you could say, "I'm still not sure where to put this—do you think it works better here, or should I incorporate it there?"

Making Proposals

It's sometimes not enough to ask questions. Sometimes, you need to make proposals. Proposing solutions to problems helps move the work forward and gives you greater influence over the outcome. Sometimes it's more work to come up with a solution, but it also creates space for more of your agency, wisdom, and perspective.

Asking your manager to choose between three options will get you a faster reply than making a general complaint. See Table 10.1 for examples of complaints versus proposals.

Table 10.1 Complaints versus Proposals.

	Complaint	Proposal
Problem 1	"There's no way to meet this deadline—we have so little time to prep for the team meeting!"	"I know we have a firm deadline on the data request, but if the team meeting is flexible, I'd propose we move that back a week."
Problem 2	"It's going to be hard for me to make progress when you're out next week and can't respond to my questions."	"I'd love to make sure we can move the project forward while you're busy at the meeting next week. I can give you some options for check-in times to make sure I'll have what I need."

You might be thinking, "But some problems shouldn't be on me to solve!" You're right. Some things sit squarely in your manager's realm of responsibility and *sphere of control*. And other problems might be outside both of your spheres of control—issues that need to be addressed at the organizational level. We're not suggesting you do someone else's job or take on structural problems. (In those cases, you might name the issue and ask your manager to raise it with people who *can* address it.) Making proposals is best when you're on the hook for the final outcome, such as if you have to make a decision or drive work forward on a tight timeline, or you've hit a stumbling block in your project and have to reprioritize tasks.

The One-Minute Email

The one-minute email is a simple tool for getting a prompt reply. It can also be a helpful way to make a proposal.

Have you ever glanced at an email on your phone, seen that you wouldn't be able to respond before your next meeting, and set it aside for later—only to never reply? We've all done it. So how can we prevent it from happening to us?

You have a much better chance of getting responses to your emails if you make them easy to respond to in one minute or less. Avoid asking open-ended questions like, "What should I do about X?" that burden your recipient with thinking of an answer—unless you're okay with waiting a while to get one. Instead, here's how to write an email that passes the one-minute test:

- **Use a clear subject line.** We once heard about a manager who used the subject line "Hi" for every email she sent. Don't be that person! Use a descriptive subject line that indicates whether there's an ask or a deadline. For example, "(Reply by 9/17) Should we hire a facilitator?" is more helpful than "Question about meeting logistics."

- **Ask a "yes"/"no" or multiple choice question.** For instance, you might say, "I believe we should spend the money—do you (A) agree; (B) think we should tell them "thanks" but "no"; or (C) want to discuss more before deciding?"

- **Make a recommendation.** Give them something they can easily say "yes" (or "no") to. For example, "Here's the deal with X. I've thought about A, B, and C, and I think we should do C because. . .Does that sound okay to you?"

- **Put the reply options at the top.** Open with what you're looking for. For example, "I need your quick sign-off on the plan below."

- **Suggest a default plan.** Try, "Here's the draft. If I don't hear from you by the end of Tuesday, I'll assume you have no feedback and send it out." When taking this route, give the person reasonable time to respond (not, say, two hours in a non-urgent situation).

- **Provide background information.** Include a brief reminder of context or past decisions. For example, you might say, "Remember that we decided to skip X and focus on Y. We wanted to get this out by mid-June, which means we should finalize it by next week."

Making Strong Asks

If you need help, but don't have the authority to delegate, take a page from the canvasser's playbook and make a "strong ask"—which includes the "why," a specific request, and a deadline.

For example, if you need a draft report by March 15 so the final can go to print by March 25, don't say, "It'd be great to see a draft around mid-month." Instead, try, "The final needs to go to print by March 25, and we need 10 days for editing and layout. Can you get it to me by the 15th?" Your colleague might negotiate, and that's okay—just state what you need upfront so you can talk about it.

MANAGING SIDEWAYS: HOW DO I SAY IT?

The following are some sample lines you can use throughout the delegation cycle when managing sideways. Always be clear, direct, and considerate.

Assigning Work

- "I'm on the hook for getting XYZ done by the end of the month. I'm hoping for your help with. . ."

- "Given your work with X, I would love your help with. . ."

Arranging a Check-In on the Work

- "I'd love to stay in the loop to keep a birds-eye view of the work. Can we check in biweekly? How does Friday work for you?"

- "We've learned that X has impacted people, so we want to be careful with our message and timing. Can we touch base on your draft before we send it?"

Inviting Feedback

- "What can I do to better support you?"

- "I'd love your perspective on what worked and what didn't. Here's what I think. What would you have done differently?"

(continued)

(continued)

Giving Feedback

- "I know figuring out how to deal with X has been tricky. Can I share some feedback?"
- "I had some thoughts on X. Can I share them with you?"

Debriefing

- "I'd like to debrief how X went so we can capture lessons while they're fresh. Does that sound good to you?"
- "I know X was a challenge. Did you have any takeaways for next time?"

Sharing and Inviting Feedback

Feedback is the breakfast of champions. Just like we all deserve access to nutrient-dense and delicious food, we deserve rich, meaningful feedback. Great feedback does the following:

- It helps us feel seen and invested in.

- It gives us specific, concrete ideas for how to improve.

- It allows us to see our strengths and contributions.

- It helps us get aligned with our teammates.

In managing up and sideways, feedback serves multiple purposes. First, *inviting* feedback gets you the investment you need and deserve. And second, *sharing* feedback helps you communicate your needs and requests while building the relationship.

Here's an example of feedback Monna received from Justine, one of her direct reports, about clarifying expectations: "Hey, can I share feedback with you? When you delegate stuff to me where the five Ws aren't fully fleshed out, the expectations sometimes feel fuzzy or shift over time. I get a little confused about what the requirements are. For example, when you originally asked me to connect with our contact at XYZ organization, you gave me an end-of-year deadline. But in our check-in today, you told me to hold off until early next year. I couldn't tell if you were reprioritizing or if something had changed. It'd be helpful if you could be more explicit about why expectations change. This isn't a major deal to me, but I wanted to flag this, so you know."[2]

Before receiving this feedback, Monna had no idea she hadn't been clear. But when Justine pointed it out—with a specific example and an explicit request—Monna

---

[2] Note: this feedback was shared via chat. When you have a strong relationship where feedback is normalized, feedback really can be as simple as taking a few minutes to send a message. In this case, Justine decided to send her quick thoughts rather than waiting until their next check-in. Note that Justine still used most of the elements of CSAW. Monna responded via chat, and they revisited the conversation in a check-in to make sure nothing had been left unsaid.

realized that she'd forgotten to use the five Ws in that initial delegation. And, when it was time to reprioritize, she had left out the "why" (see, we make mistakes, too!). So, moving forward, she was much more diligent about using the delegation worksheet.

Strategies for Middle Managers

No matter what shows like *The Office* might tell you, middle managers—people who *have* managers and *are* managers (that's most of you reading this)—are critical. You see the pressures senior leaders contend with *and* the challenges your staff face on the ground. But middle managers often feel stuck in the middle of expectations from their manager and their team's realities. You're managing in *all* directions. Here are some strategies for managing in the middle.

Be a Bridge

As a middle manager, you're a bridge. You have information about your team and your manager that they don't have about each other. Your vantage point allows you to build trust, empathy, and awareness on both sides, supporting staff and senior leaders in perspective-taking.

You can bridge the two sides by sharing:

- **Struggles and challenges.** When you sense a gap in empathy on either side, be honest about what the other person or people are struggling with. For example, if you think your manager might be expecting too much from your team, you could say, "Right now, my team is trying to cram six days' worth of work into five." If your staff members are frustrated that an initiative is moving too slowly, you could tell the team, "It's budgeting season, so department heads are prioritizing planning for next year so that we can have the resources we need."

- **Information and input.** When decisions will impact your team, relay relevant information from senior leaders to staff and collect input from staff to share with leadership.

- **Bright spots and shout-outs.** In Chapter 8, we talk about the importance of being a hype person. It's a way to advocate for your team members when they're not in the room, and it's also part of being a bridge. For example, you could tell your boss, "Jamilah's been doing an awesome job connecting with fellows and getting them excited about the upcoming retreat. She's been so thoughtful about accommodating their needs." You can also help build trust in leadership by sharing things you think your boss or senior leaders are doing well. For instance, "I can tell that the leadership team is trying to approach goal-setting differently this year. I think they heard the feedback we shared about last year's process feeling too rushed."

Set Boundaries

You are human, too! Getting aligned with your manager, team, and colleagues (while getting all your other work done) is *a lot*. And most middle managers we know have individual contributor responsibilities on top of their management duties, making boundaries crucial.

For middle managers, setting boundaries with *your* manager isn't just about your time, energy, and priorities—it's often about protecting or advocating for your team and communicating tradeoffs. Try saying:

- "I hear that X is the new priority. To accomplish it, I'll need to delay Y. I'll also need to pull Ben off project A so we can focus on X. Are you okay with that?"

- "I want to highlight my staff's four big rocks for next week. This is different than we originally planned because. . .Do you have any concerns?"

- "My team is in a sprint, and there's a time crunch. Can you help me minimize requests for my staff until after our deadline?"

Setting boundaries with your staff can mean avoiding the delegation boomerang (see Chapter 3), managing your time and systems well, and maintaining healthy emotional limits (see Chapter 2).

KEY POINTS OF MANAGING UP AND SIDEWAYS

Here are the takeaways from the chapter:

- **Managing up** means using management skills to get what you need from your boss. **Managing sideways** means doing so with peers, partners, or others you lack formal authority over. In both cases, it's about *conspiring and aligning* to get what *you* need to do your job effectively, which will create better results.

- You can use some of our fundamental management tools and practices for managing up and sideways, like sphere of control, perspective-taking, relationship-building, feedback, and the five Ws.

- Other tools that are especially helpful for managing up and sideways are:

  - Offering **slices** of work to get feedback about high-stakes work earlier.

  - **Making proposals** and offering solutions to make it easier for someone to say "yes" to what you need.

  - The **one-minute email**—writing your email or text so that it's easy to read and respond to in one minute or less.

  - Making **strong asks**—asking for help in a way that's more likely to get you a "yes."

- **Middle managers** can see the pressures senior leaders contend with and the challenges their staff face. So **be a bridge** between the two spheres by sharing information both ways. Set **boundaries** around what you can (or can't) negotiate or change.

CHAPTER

11

BUILDING
A HEALTHY CULTURE

When a workplace has a great culture, you can *feel* it. Bex remembers visiting Monna's field office during the 2012 Mainers United for Marriage campaign—they felt transported. The camaraderie was palpable, the communication was easy and effective, and staff were hitting and exceeding their goals. This was a place that made people look forward to going to work. In fact, several college students joined the campaign for a summer internship, then got so invested that they took the fall semester off to see it through. (And the end was a victory for marriage equality!)

There's an old adage that if you ask a fish what water is, it won't know what you're talking about. It's so constantly surrounded by water that it can't imagine water as something separate. Culture can be a lot like that. We're so immersed in it that we don't always know what we're swimming in. But, unlike the fish, we can shape and co-create culture, which comprises the policies, practices, and little daily *actions* we take that manifest our core beliefs and values.

Every culture is different. Think about your favorite restaurant. Is it loud and bustling, or quiet and serene? Does it have white tablecloths or tabletop jukeboxes? These elements and more combine to create a unique experience for diners.

The same is true of workplace cultures; all kinds of cues can give you a sense of an organization's culture. For example, do people regularly drop by each other's desks and chat? Do colleagues socialize outside of work? Do most people keep their cameras on during virtual meetings? Are chat channels strictly business or peppered with jokes and anecdotes? Some of these differences flow from the type of work you're doing (campaigns are quite different from libraries!), and some are the quirks of a particular office.

Most differences aren't good or bad. But because culture is a core part of every staff member's experience, how you instill a sense of belonging (and for whom) is a *choice point*. And some differences can make or break someone's experience at work. For example, if the managers at Organization A treat mistakes like learning opportunities, Culture A likely fosters growth and exploration. On the other hand, if the managers at Organization B publicly berate staff for every failure, Culture B probably breeds fear and dread. Where would you rather work?

Culture might seem hard to describe and even harder to change. But building a healthy culture doesn't need to be a mystery. Your culture should be:

- Intentional, in that it's not left up to chance.

- Explicit, in that it's clear to everyone in your organization (and those who want to join it) what you value and what those values look like in daily practice.

- Strategic, in that it supports your team in achieving its goals.

Monna knew going into the campaign that she wanted her team's culture to be different than any other campaign she'd worked on. She wanted it to motivate people to do excellent, fulfilling work, stick around until the end, and bring other talented people in. So she and her team *conspired and aligned* on core values, which included honesty, interdependence, and fun. They talked through what each of these would look like—teammates routinely asking for and offering help, sharing feedback freely, and regular (sometimes over-the-top) displays of gratitude. As one of her former staff, Benn, shared, "I came because I cared about the issue; I stayed for the community."

While much about an organization's culture is often shaped by leadership, you don't have to be a CEO or an executive director to be a culture-maker or culture-keeper. Everyone on a team helps implement or co-create culture—and as a manager, you have an important role to play, whatever your position. In Maine, Benn was instrumental in co-creating that culture—first as a volunteer, then as an organizer in Monna's field office, and finally, as the lead organizer in another region of the campaign.

ELEMENTS OF A HEALTHY CULTURE

Culture isn't one-size-fits-all, but the healthiest cultures in the most successful organizations we've seen are grounded in three things: *collective purpose, care for people,* and *commitment to excellence.* We believe purposeful work and accomplishments can help people feel powerful and connected. We also believe there should be room for everyone's full humanity in our work, especially during times of crisis. And when we strive for excellence in our work together, we're more likely to create our desired impact.

Collective purpose, care for people, and a commitment to excellence help social justice organizations "walk the talk." Together, these three elements enable us to make an impact without sacrificing respect, kindness, and humanity.

Collective Purpose

The "conspire" part of *conspire and align* is rooting our work in collective purpose. This purpose can be our mission, vision, or just one sentence about why our work matters. Without a shared purpose, our teams are just a group of people with the same email domain. When we know what we're doing together and are fully aligned, we can move in formation to get the results we need. With collective purpose, we also get:

- **Shared accountability.** A sense of collective purpose inspires people to follow through on commitments—not just because they feel accountable to each other or their manager, but because they care about the overall vision. Each person sees how their role and goals connect to the purpose and feels responsible for doing their part.

- **Shared ownership and agency.** When people see themselves as key contributors to a collective purpose, they take more ownership of their work, exercise agency, and feel like they have a voice in the organization. Managers can help people see themselves this way by *treating them* this way—which often involves meaningfully sharing power. No matter our positions, the more power we feel we have, the better we engage, stay open to new ideas, and remain flexible. (The opposite is true, too—the more powerless people feel, the more likely they are to disengage or lash out.) In cultures where people routinely share power, people are more likely to incorporate others' perspectives, share credit, and share information freely.

At Mainers United, one former staff member shared that she felt her role was just as important as her teammates'. In contrast, there was an implicit hierarchy in other campaigns she'd worked on. "As a data and leadership development lead, I wasn't on the 'cool canvassing' side. But I still felt like part of the campaign," she said. "The canvass team often reminded us that they could do the work to win votes because of our confirmation calls, data entry, and volunteer leadership trainings. This affirmation helped our team feel connected and motivated, and we pushed even harder."

Care for People

We've mentioned that people are the lifeblood of our organizations and movements—which means our organizations and movements will suffer if we don't care for people. Monna's staff at Mainers United worked hard, but there was also a heavy emphasis on self-care to avoid burnout. They knew the big-picture goal of winning marriage equality nationwide would be a marathon and not a sprint.

In a caring culture, people respect each other's humanity and agency. People don't feel they have to hide parts of themselves to succeed, be accepted, or belong. With care for people, we expect the following:

- **Spirit of community and interdependence.** Some of the strongest organizations we've seen are ones where people don't just feel like a team; they feel like a *community*. They reject individualism and an "every person for themself" mentality and see themselves as part of a greater whole. This mindset is similar to concepts in several languages and cultures—*ubuntu* (Zulu), *kapwa* (Tagalog), *in* *lak'ech* (Mayan), and *gadugi* (Cherokee). These terms don't have the same definition, but they speak to a fundamental belief in the deep interconnectedness of humanity. They convey that we are not wholly separate from our fellow humans and must care for each other as we would ourselves. In an organizational culture that embodies these concepts, people see their wins, losses, celebrations, and struggles as tied to their teammates' (and vice versa). They honor each other's strengths and support each other.

- **Trust.** People trust leaders' intentions and judgment in making decisions in the organization's best interests (even if they may not necessarily agree). They trust their teammates to act with care and consideration. They believe the people they work with have their back, see them as people, and genuinely want the best for each other. (See the "Cultivating Trust" section in Chapter 2 for more on cultivating trust.)

Commitment to Excellence

In healthy cultures and organizations, everyone strives to deliver outstanding results. We hold ourselves to high standards and maintain integrity in our outcomes and relationships. Cultures that focus on excellence (not perfection!) care more about growth and progress than appearances, leading to better results, greater sustainability, and stronger relationships.

With a commitment to excellence, we expect the following:

- **Rigor.** Whatever their realm, people take ownership of their work and strive for rigor in the process. Everyone (including managers and leaders!) is willing to set aside their egos, preferences, and traditions to get great results. Ideas are given fair consideration *and* rigorous scrutiny to assess what works well in practice and what doesn't.

- **Commitment to ongoing growth and learning.** People see growth and learning as necessary parts of getting results. TMC coach Alyssa once had a manager at a new job who said, "When you make your first big mistake, I want you to come to me and tell me so I can take you out to celebrate! Those moments are the best for learning and growth. It's not a matter of 'if' you make a mistake; it's 'when.' So when it happens, I'll be here for you." In healthy cultures, if someone takes a risk and fails, they're supported to learn (and maybe even praised for taking risks!). And managers also hold themselves to this standard by acknowledging their own mistakes, admitting when they don't know something, and seeking perspectives and feedback.

Bex saw the culture at Monna's field office as a virtuous cycle of all three elements. Care for people was part of the purpose. They wanted not only to win, but to win sustainably—with marginalized people flexing their power and preserving their energy for the long haul. (Many of the organizers of that campaign continued onto other campaigns following that victory.) This was very different from the conventional wisdom of how to run campaigns (remember Bex's response to the yelling guys in Chapter 2?). Most of the people on the campaign were queer or loved someone who was. The strength of their shared purpose and deep care for each other motivated them to hold a high bar for excellence.

PRACTICES FOR CULTIVATING A HEALTHY CULTURE

We believe (and we've seen evidence in the results repeatedly) that consistently using the tools in this book will get you a long way toward building a healthy culture. So if some of our advice sounds familiar from other chapters, that's why!

Here are some essential practices for cultivating a healthy culture:

- Lean into conflict.

- Define and reinforce core values.

- Make culture a part of everyone's job.

- "Hold" your team.

- Share and solicit feedback regularly.

- Follow through and be true to your word.

- Establish meaningful traditions.

Lean into Conflict

Conflict is a natural and necessary part of human interactions and organizational evolutions. As is discussed in Chapter 2, conflict, reconciliation, and repair are essential for healthy relationships and teams. When handled effectively, conflict can lead to breakthroughs that shift how we work with others to get stronger relationships and better outcomes.

Too often, we fail to address conflict constructively—or avoid it altogether, so disagreements and conflicts simmer below a thin veneer of surface niceness. But agreeableness doesn't make a strong organization or community—realness does. And realness comes with open disagreement, naming tensions, and working through the discomfort.

Here are a few ways to build a culture that embraces conflict:

- **Seek out dissent, disagreement, and differences.** In Chapter 2, we talked about the dangers of minimizing difference. In Chapter 5, we talked about the value of seeking dissent in decision-making. The more we normalize and celebrate differences—of identities, opinions, and perspectives—the less scary it is to disagree. And the less scary it is to disagree, the less we take it personally, and the better we engage in constructive dialogue.

- **Practice listening and engaging.** In the "Strategies for Receiving Feedback Well" section of Chapter 7, we talk about listening and engaging as part of receiving feedback. To listen effectively, we must relax and remind ourselves that we're safe. To engage, we need to acknowledge the other person's perspective and get curious about it. Both of these skills help with working through conflict.

- **Incorporate conflict into your core values** (more on this in the next section).

Define and Reinforce Core Values

In Chapter 4, we talk about articulating the "how" of a role—the mindsets, values, and approaches someone should bring to their work. Core values help you articulate the "how" across the organization, regardless of role. Think about what qualities or behaviors are most important to your team or organization's success. Consider what values or qualities will enable someone to succeed and what's needed to get results. As part of setting your core values, you might want to identify the aspirational parts of your organizational culture—how you hope to be.

Like most decisions you'll make that broadly affect your team, you'll need to *seek perspective* and get input from your team on how you should define your core values. (Try using fair process, which we discuss in Chapter 5.) Then, reinforce the importance of core values by including them in job descriptions, role expectations, goals, and performance evaluations (including for leaders!).

Here are two of TMC's core values:

We value. . .	Which leads us to. . .
Focusing on impact	• Prioritize actions that we believe will lead us to better results. • Consider our impact on people with marginalized identities in our actions and decisions. • Invest deeply in clients who can benefit the most from our work.
Learning and growth	• Approach mistakes with honest acknowledgment and seek out opportunities to improve. • Strive to be accountable when we cause harm; acknowledge mistakes, solicit (and share) direct feedback, and repair relationships. • Welcome conflict and work to engage in ways that generate more possibilities and fuller expression.

Make Culture a Part of Everyone's Job

Over the years, we've heard countless variations of this conundrum: "I have a high performer who always delivers the results we need. The problem is, they're unpleasant to work with."

Here's the thing: someone who "gets the job done" but doesn't contribute positively to your culture is only getting part of their job done. Under a *conspire-and-align* approach, *how* we treat people matters.

You can be explicit about these expectations in the "how" part of your role expectations sheet (see Chapter 4). Here's some sample language for setting expectations for positive cultural contributions:

- **Relationship-building:** You value connecting with other people, including/especially those who are different from you. You're self-aware, open to feedback, and willing to own your mistakes. You bring a spirit of flexibility, openness, and collaboration to your interactions.

- **Organizational and cultural contributions:** You model our core values. You see your work as supporting the whole and as integral to our team's effectiveness. You exercise good judgment and good faith in your interactions with others.

"Hold" Your Team

Management scholars define "holding" as a leader's ability to 1) *contain,* or provide reassurance during times of crisis, and 2) *interpret,* or make meaning of what's going on.[1] Holding gives staff the *tools* to process what's happening and the *space* to exercise their autonomy. "Holding" is often a critical unnamed aspect of the "culture" part of a manager's job.

When a major funding source dries up, for instance, a manager might demonstrate holding by first reassuring staff that the organization has enough resources to pull through (only if it's true!), and then explaining what the plan is to secure new funding, including how staff will play a role in it.

Holding doesn't mean always having explanations or a plan—it can simply be about acknowledging what's happening and letting people be present with it together. For example, after the U.S. Supreme Court decided to overturn *Roe v. Wade* in June 2022, TMC had our regularly scheduled staff meeting. Here's how Jakada "held" the team with his opening words for that meeting:

I invite us to breathe together. Put your hand on your abdomen, right on your belly. Breathe in deeply through your nose. Exhale all the way out. In and out.

This moment is a study in contradiction. At this exact moment, I am safe in my home. I am safe in this room, with all of you.

---

[1] Gianpiero Petriglieri lays out the concept of "holding" in a management context in his article "The Psychology Behind Effective Crisis Leadership," *Harvard Business Review*, 2020, hbr. org/2020/04/the-psychology-behind-effective-crisis-leadership

And, more than ever before, I am at risk. You are at risk.

I'm often reminded that Breonna Taylor was safe in her home, behind a locked door, snuggled in bed, peacefully asleep. I'm aware that even in places we consider sanctuary, we are not always safe. In the churches, the synagogues, and the temples. In the schools and the grocery stores. In the streets and at Pride. And with last Friday's Supreme Court decision—even inside our own bodies, we are not always safe.

And yet and still, at this moment, as I take this breath, I am safe. Trying to hold both of these things can be exhausting. Trying to stay present with what is—the breath helps us do that sometimes. So I offer that to you, as a way to ground.

Holding doesn't have to look like leading a meditation or giving a speech—it can just be creating space at a team meeting or in a check-in for people to process and connect. It can also be a simple acknowledgment of what's hard and an offer of support and resources (like reminding staff that they can take sick time for mental health).

Share and Solicit Feedback Regularly

We've spent a lot of time in this book talking about the importance of feedback and how to give it effectively (see Chapter 7). The same principles apply to culture. Get (and share) feedback about your team's culture and what you could do (as the manager) to strengthen it. As you solicit feedback, watch out for patterns or disparities in identity, tenure, and position.

Questions you can ask:

- What's something you appreciate about our team culture? What's one thing you wish were different?

- What could I do differently to contribute to a healthier culture?

You can also use feedback to name what's working and what you want to change. When you spot something going well, celebrate it! For instance, if a colleague helped you work through a tricky problem, you could say, "I was having a tough time, and you pulled through with support and guidance. You really demonstrated our value of teamwork." And if you're seeing people behave in ways that detract from a healthy culture, say something. For instance, if you're in a meeting and people keep interrupting and talking over each other, you could say, "I'd like us to be a team that respects each other by listening and trying to understand each other's points of view, even when we disagree. Let's let people finish their sentences."

WHAT IF I'M THE PROBLEM?

When soliciting feedback on culture, be prepared for some of it to be tough (see the "Strategies for Receiving Feedback Well" section in Chapter 7). If there's a problem with your team culture, you're likely part of it—and it might be hard for your staff to tell you.

If you've gotten defensive about criticism or bristled at challenges to your ideas, you'll need to build trust so your team members can believe they will be taken seriously. Own up to your impact on the culture and plan to do better (see our advice in Chapter 2 about relationship repair).

You can also let your team share feedback anonymously, such as through a survey or by sharing feedback with a colleague who will summarize and report it to you. (And because these options make it easier to be candid, it might be a good idea to offer them even if you're not the problem!)

Follow Through and Be True to Your Word

Have you ever been inspired to make a dramatic change, created a 10-step plan to do it, and then. . .completely fallen off the wagon and back into old habits? That lack of follow-through might not be a big deal for your annual New Year's resolution, but it *is* a big deal for your staff and culture. An under-appreciated source of a strong culture is integrity: simple alignment between what you say and what you do, over and over.

Consistent follow-through by managers and leaders, on big things and small, can have a bigger impact on building trust than elaborate team outings. Most people prefer a manager who always shows up to check-ins prepared, to one who's hardly available but organizes epic game nights.

Say what you mean, mean what you say, and do what you say you will. All of us have probably experienced the frustration of feeling that the culture we are a part of (whether at work or elsewhere) doesn't live up to the values it claims to represent. Finding 100% alignment on values and practice is rarely possible, but it's always worth trying.

As a mentor of Jakada's once said, "There will always be a gap between our aspirations and our practice. That gap can't be tragic."

Establish Meaningful Traditions

Your workplace doesn't have to be a summer camp (well, unless it is). But having rituals, shared language, and other consistent cultural practices will help your team build shared identity and belonging. Belonging and shared traditions make us feel like the people we work with are "our people"—they help us feel that sense of interconnectedness (or kapwa, or ubuntu. . .).

As always, we must be mindful of "like me" and "I like you" biases regarding relationship- and community-building. Rituals from our personal and cultural practices can be great, but make sure they're inclusive and not alienating (especially if you're part of a mainstream group). For example, organizing a workplace "secret Santa" gift exchange might sound fun, but it could also marginalize people who don't celebrate Christmas.

Here are some examples of rituals:

- Hosting an annual event or celebration to mark a significant milestone (at TMC, our admin team throws an annual—virtual—audit completion party, including prizes and games about numbers).

- Creating a song or chant (the National Network of Abortion Funds has a call-and-response chant to get hyped up: "Fund Abortion! Build Power!").

- Saving time at the end of every meeting for appreciations.

- Planning a welcome lunch for new staff.

- Sending gifts to celebrate personal milestones and achievements or to offer sympathy during times of grief.

TRANSFORMING AN UNHEALTHY CULTURE

Do any of the following experiences resonate with you?

- "It was emotionally draining. All of our interactions were high stakes, like even the smallest decisions could have the biggest consequences. There were icebergs everywhere. One morning, I walked into the kitchen to get coffee. When I entered, two co-workers who'd been chatting immediately got quiet and watched me as I prepared my coffee. This totally innocuous thing—getting my caffeine fix—suddenly felt loaded."

- "It seemed like my boss was constantly watching and waiting for people to mess up. It was like anticipating a car accident every time I got behind the steering wheel. Any time I did something, I'd brace for impact."

- "It felt like another conversation was happening that I didn't understand—everyone was nice to each other, but there was always an underlying tension."

We got those quotes—and heard similar variations—from people across many identities, roles, and organizations. When a culture is unhealthy, *everyone* can feel it.

Beyond the personal discomfort we all experience in an unhealthy work environment, there's also the *impact* of an unhealthy culture on our results. One TMC coach worked with a newly elected official, Fiona, who inherited most of her staff and entered a 500-person office that was disconnected and fractured. People were unclear about what success looked like and how to approach their work. Bias ran rampant in decision-making, including about things with huge racial equity implications. Decisions included: which communities got funding for local projects, who got in-person meetings with the elected, and whose complaints about flooding or power outages were addressed (if at all). (We'll share what Fiona did later in the chapter.)

Over the years, we've seen organizations fold for various reasons—financial instability, failure to adapt, and more. But the most harrowing stories are about organizations that died because an unhealthy culture spiraled out of control and became toxic—the water was so polluted that it became inhabitable.

Identifying the specific causes of an unhealthy culture can feel like a chicken-or-egg situation. Is it a lack of unity that created it, or did the culture breed and perpetuate disunity? Is the lack of trust a root cause, or is it a symptom? What we know for certain is that regardless of its origins, an unhealthy culture is often a vicious cycle. And, just like dealing with performance problems, when your culture becomes a problem, managers and leaders must own the solution.

Thankfully, it's often possible to repair an unhealthy culture. Most advice in this section is for leaders with the power and responsibility to do so. However, for culture to transform, you also need broad buy-in from people at all levels who are committed to change. That's why many of our tips also apply to middle managers, team leaders, and individual contributors. Like many aspects of management, improving an organization's culture is not about a single monumental action. Shifting culture is a process that requires multiple tactics, time, and a team effort. As you read this section, think about what's in your *sphere of control*.

WHAT IF MY ORGANIZATIONAL CULTURE IS TOXIC?

Cultural health lies on a continuum, and a toxic culture is on the far end of it. We've found that toxic culture usually takes root because patterns of harm go unaddressed (or are addressed unskillfully). As a result, staff people feel powerless and frustrated, losing faith in leaders (if team members ever had it in the first place). When this happens, people talk, and factions form, creating an "us" versus "them" dynamic. Any pre-existing political and ideological misalignments become magnified. Add to this external pressure from stakeholders and community members, broader political tensions, widespread grief and trauma, and you have a pressure cooker environment that amplifies internal conflicts. People end up spending more time fighting *against* each other than fighting *alongside* each other. This dynamic usually results in high turnover, internal organizing,[2] or public callouts of leadership (or all three). We'll be honest—we haven't seen many examples of organizations coming back from these circumstances, and the advice in this chapter might not be enough in those situations.

---

[2] To be clear, internal organizing can be an important strategy for holding leaders accountable and pushing for much needed change. But when internal organizing and advocacy *becomes* and *remains* the primary work for some people, you're in trouble. When this happens, you're no longer conspiring and aligning toward your mission.

Tips for Transformation

Whether you've been around since the problems started or inherited them, you can take steps to improve your culture. It won't be easy and might not be cheap, but it's essential.

Here are five actions you can take to transform an unhealthy culture:

- Acknowledge and take accountability.

- Go on a listening tour.

- Go for "win-wins."

- Go back to the heart of the work.

- Do a reset.

Acknowledge and Take Accountability

When tensions and mistrust run high, there's no point in hiding or denying it. Instead, be honest with your team about what's happening, including mistakes you've made, what you think needs to change, and how you feel. If your actions have been out of alignment with your values, say it. People hate hypocrisy and dissonance, but they hate feeling gaslit even more.

One TMC colleague told us about a previous work experience where she received hard feedback in a 360 evaluation.[3] Some staff shared, "When things go wrong, she takes it out on us. When we make mistakes, it clearly upsets her." As you might imagine, this was hard to hear. She told us, "I didn't want to be *that* person. The way they described my behavior didn't reflect my values. I had to ask myself why there was such a disconnect. Why was it hard for me to self-regulate? Why did I take my stress out on my team?"

Our colleague set out to make amends, starting with one-on-one check-ins. She told her staff, "There was a trend in the feedback I got, and even if you didn't share it, I want you to know my takeaways. I need to manage my stress and respond better when mistakes happen. When there's a problem, I want you to feel like you can come to me to help you solve it." She shared what she planned to do differently (which included setting better boundaries so she wouldn't feel overworked). She also asked what else she could do to make things better.

Go on a Listening Tour

When people disengage, it's often because they don't trust that their concerns or ideas will be heard. Even when people *do* engage in an unhealthy environment, it's often not constructive. One tactic we recommend, especially to new leaders entering a bad

---

[3] A 360 evaluation is a process of evaluating performance that involves getting (usually anonymous) feedback from multiple people that an employee interacts with—including, but not limited to, their manager, peers, direct reports, and even external stakeholders (like members, donors, and staff at partner organizations).

situation, is to go on a listening tour.[4] Our colleague Stephen described what he did when he became the principal of an elementary school in Chicago: "In the first month, I held one-on-ones with every person in the building. I talked to teachers, custodians, food servers, and admin staff. I asked them about their experience—how they got there and what kept them there. My goal was to get to know people and better understand the context. I asked, 'If you could wave a magic wand, what would you change about this place? What would you keep the same?'"

TMC coach Avione shared something similar about leading a team that had been feeling neglected: "Going into my job, I knew that the people on my team knew much more than I did about the organization, their roles, and our overall context. I was a newcomer, and I had to be humble. I went into my one-on-ones with a facilitator's mindset—I wasn't trying to bring all the changes and solutions. I needed to surface all the problems first. In fact, I started writing down everyone's complaints on the wall behind my office door, which everyone could see. I used it as a parking lot for my team's grievances. Then, people started adding to it on their own. I think people felt validated when they saw their concerns were shared by others. They also believed I was really listening and taking in their feedback. They knew that when they left the room and closed the door, their problems would be staring me in the face—there was no ignoring them."

Go for "Win-Wins"

When our colleagues completed their listening tours, they didn't stop at listening—they tried to address the concerns.

Remember Fiona, the newly elected official previously mentioned? Her team didn't exactly embrace her with open arms. Some staff were excited for her to be there, many more were skeptical but open, and others were openly against having her in office. When Fiona and her senior leaders went on a listening tour, they surfaced many complaints, some more challenging to address than others. But they identified quick wins, like fixing broken watercoolers and rescheduling a team meeting from 8 a.m. to 9 a.m. These helped build trust among staff that Fiona was responsive and invested in improving things. The leadership team then tackled some of the more complicated challenges. For example, the team established communication and decision-making protocols so that people got input and approval faster. It also set monthly office hours so people could share ideas.

---

[4] A listening tour might be considered a series of "insight interviews," a concept we learned about from the Center for Black Educator Development. This is an open-ended conversation that digs into a staff person's experiences with workplace culture and their treatment at work, and explores how those experiences compared with expectations. These interviews make room for the likelihood that your staff person has had some negative experiences at work. For more information, check out Sharif El-Mekki, "Respecting Educator Activists of Color: The Anti-Racist Guide to Teacher Retention," Center for Black Educator Development, 2021, issuu.com/thecenterblacked/docs/anti-racist-guide-to-teacher-retention

In Avione's case, the visible nature of the complaints wall helped. As people added more items to the list, themes started to emerge. People began suggesting solutions. One person pointed to a section and said, "You know, this could all be addressed if we overhauled our hiring system." (He ended up leading that project!)

Finding win-wins—improvements that benefit everyone and are relatively uncontroversial—helps build momentum and excitement for bigger changes on the horizon. In addition, celebrating wins reinforces shared purpose and camaraderie in an environment where people might feel hopeless or angry.

Go Back to the Heart of the Work

Conflict is natural, but sometimes, it can get unwieldy—to the point where the conflict can feel like more of the focus of the work than the work itself. And when organizations don't have practices to deal with conflict constructively, it's easy for people to fall into harmful ways of relating. They lash out, gossip, or disengage, reinforcing destructive dynamics and creating disunity. When this happens, you're no longer *conspiring and aligning* toward your mission.

One antidote in these situations is to go back to the heart of your work—your mission and vision and the difference your organization is trying to make. This doesn't mean you minimize the conflict or push it aside—you work to resolve it *so that* you can fulfill your collective purpose. As a leader or manager, it can help to share your personal why: "I'm here because people are counting on us. I believe that our work is so important. Our community needs us to figure this out. It's our duty to do right by them." One leader shared, "When I came in, there was an intense 'us versus them' dynamic. As a senior leader of color, I was walking a tightrope. People were wondering if I'd side with our ED, a white woman, or if I'd side with the BIPOC staff organizing against her. But I allied with the mission instead. I wasn't there to take sides—I was there to understand what was going wrong and try to fix it so we could work together effectively."

Do a Reset

Sometimes, you can transform an unhealthy culture by making many small changes over time. But often, a reset is the best option when even getting a cup of coffee puts you on edge, like in the quote we shared earlier. A reset is also a good idea when you're new to the role and have inherited a problematic culture.

Here are some things to reset and realign on:

- Roles and goals.

- Expectations around communication.

- Decision-making procedures and norms.

- Feedback and evaluation practices.

- Management expectations.

If you do a reset, name it explicitly and engage staff. Stephen, who ran the elementary school we mentioned earlier, worked with his team to create a mission and vision for their school. They used those aspirations to set expectations for their work together. He asked them, "What will we need to do every day to live out this mission?"

You're also essentially drawing a line in the sand with your expectations when you do a reset. This clarity is necessary for moving forward—both to get aligned and to give people information so they can choose to stay or go. For example, one organization called a staff meeting in which the ED announced: "Clearly, things are broken. We're resetting the organization. Moving forward, we're going to invest deeply in our culture." They went on to share more details about the reset plan. They also said, "This is going to be a new chapter. Everyone here has to decide whether you want to be a part of it."

Once you've reset, remember to consistently enforce the new standards and expectations—especially for leaders. As one leader put it, "If you have people from 'before,' they'll hold on to the old way of doing things. Even if they didn't like it, they probably internalized it." Habits can be hard to break (and form!), so creating shared accountability is essential. For example, let's say people are used to talking behind each others' backs instead of sharing direct feedback. In your reset, you've agreed not to do that anymore. The next time a colleague comes to you to complain about someone, you could say, "I know it feels good to vent, but we agreed we'd work on direct communication. I think you should share this directly with Emma." It can be hard at first, but consistently reinforcing and modeling your new expectations—especially as managers and leaders—is the key to a successful reset.

HEALTHY CULTURES CAN EVOLVE, TOO!

Every workplace (we hope) aspires toward growth. Your culture can and should evolve as your organization grows. These changes might reflect the *preferences* of new team members, evolving team *traditions* or practices, or new *requirements* expected of your work from your community or your movement.

As of this writing, Bex has been leading one such transformation at the Rockwood Leadership Institute as its managing director. In its 20-plus years of existence, Rockwood has developed a strong culture of care, joy, and community. But as Rockwood started a new chapter with a new CEO, the vision for the work naturally evolved. Bex came on board to help the team apply that same clarity and alignment around their culture to their results. Bex helped lead the cultural and practical shifts required for the new, explicitly pro-Black and pro-Indigenous vision for Rockwood. Getting through the big changes required constant attention to the balance between pushing for more explicit rigor in defining roles and goals while doubling down on care for people. More than one person at Rockwood has said that Bex has given them a new and richer idea of what intentional management can do to shift and transform culture.

Whether managing a large organization or a small team, you should work to grow into the culture you want without getting stuck in how it is now. And at every step of your growth, continue to *make the implicit explicit* about your core values, aspirations, and practices.

KEY POINTS OF BUILDING A HEALTHY CULTURE

Here are the takeaways from the chapter:

- **Culture** at work comprises the policies, practices, and daily actions that manifest our core beliefs and values.

- Culture isn't a force of nature; it should be shaped and changed. You can better *conspire and align* with your team if you're **intentional, explicit,** and **strategic** about your culture.

- The healthiest cultures are grounded in **collective purpose, care for people,** and **commitment to excellence**.

- Leadership shapes culture, but anyone can and should be a culture-maker or culture-keeper. Everyone helps implement or co-create culture, and managers have an important role to play.

- Tools and practices for building a healthy culture include:

  - Leaning into conflict.

  - Defining and reinforcing core values.

  - Making culture a part of everyone's job.

  - "Holding" your team.

  - Sharing and soliciting feedback regularly.

  - Following through and being true to your word.

  - Establishing meaningful traditions.

- Unhealthy cultures are characterized by disunity, distrust, and inequity. It's possible to **transform** an unhealthy culture. Tips for transformation include:

  - Acknowledging and taking accountability.

  - Going on a listening tour.

- • Going for "win-wins."

- • Going back to the heart of the work.

- • Doing a reset.

- Your culture should evolve with your organization. These changes might reflect the *preferences* of new team members, evolving team *traditions* or practices, or new *requirements* expected of your work from your community or your movement.

CHAPTER

12

CONCLUSION

"All that you touch you change. All that you change changes you. The only lasting truth is change."

—Octavia Butler, American science fiction author

"Balance is not a passive resting place—it takes work, balancing the giving and the taking, the raking out and the putting in."

—Robin Wall Kimmerer, author of Braiding Sweetgrass: Indigenous Wisdom, Scientific Knowledge and the Teachings of Plants

In Chapter 1, we told you that management is a balance. At times, striking that balance is unimaginably stressful—like being on a high wire 50 feet off the ground with no net. In our rapidly changing world, this is more often the case than ever. But change helps us grow. The act of balancing strengthens our muscles and improves our coordination.

We also said that management is a duty. We have a duty to put in the work—to manage for greater equity, sustainability, and results. And sometimes this takes less work than we might think. When we talk to people about how they wish their managers would behave, those wishes are often heartbreakingly simple. They want clarity and consistency about expectations and clear communication. They want to have agency in their work and to understand how their efforts connect to a broader purpose.

They want to feel like they're part of a team and that their perspectives and experiences matter. They want to feel valued and respected.

We wrote this book because management is too rarely thought of as a skill that can be taught, practiced, and improved. We've seen too many managers with all the best intentions and dedication to their work who struggled because no one ever taught them how to be effective stewards of their power or their responsibility. They never experienced effective management from their own managers. If they did, they couldn't figure out how to embody it.

At the beginning of this book, we said that management is a practice, like dance, sports, or music. These disciplines require fundamentals, freestyle, and flow. So we've broken down management into its fundamentals. We've defined a fundamental approach—*conspire and align*—about coming together for a collective purpose and getting on the same page about realizing that purpose. We've talked about the three dimensions and mindsets of effective management. We've shared the fundamental tools and practices, like *making the implicit explicit*, recognizing your *choice points*, and reflecting on your *sphere of control*. And we've discussed the fundamental *actions* of management, like delegation, setting roles and goals, and conducting check-ins.

"Fundamentals" are the basics—but that doesn't mean they're easy! All the great athletes still do drills, and great musicians still practice scales. The fundamentals keep you grounded and give you something to build from.

Freestyle and flow are where you come in. When it's time to perform or compete, you won't just stand there and repeat a series of scales or drills. Instead, you'll combine the discrete skills into a cohesive whole, adding your unique flavor and style. You might even cast aside best practices to try something new.

Once you learn the fundamentals, *how* you apply them in your management will be unique to you and your team. Your style will emerge from your daily practice—and it will also shape it. You'll feed off and respond to your teammates' energy. As Monna once heard a dance teacher say, "I've given you the steps. Now, the music will tell you how to use them."

For managers, freestyling might look like helping your staff member prepare for an unexpected leave of absence. Being in flow can look like going through the five Ws in a delegation without struggling to remember each "W." It can also look like giving someone real-time constructive feedback without it being scary because you have faith in the sturdiness of your relationship. In times of chaos or uncertainty, it's helpful to go back to the basics. But be open to remixing them to match what's needed and meet people where they are.

We know we've thrown a lot of terms and concepts at you, but many of them boil down to something pretty simple. If you get overwhelmed and need to get centered, ask yourself:

• Which parts of this situation can I control or influence, and which are out of my hands?

- Have I shared what's in my head and asked others what's in theirs?

- Is this something we really need or just something I'm used to?

- Am I giving this person what they need to succeed? Am I giving them unfair advantages? Am I getting in the way of their success?

- Will this choice reinforce the status quo, or could it forge a new and better path?

We can't change the fact that management is hard work. But we've shared the tools and insights we use to make it smoother and more impactful—so that we can experience the joys of management even more than the challenges. After all, remember that effective management is hard work, but it's also a privilege, an honor, and a sacred responsibility.

This is where you take the approach, mindsets, and tools we've given you, adapt them to fit your context, and accomplish amazing things.

ABOUT THE AUTHORS

JAKADA IMANI

Jakada is a spiritually rooted coach with over 30 years of experience in social justice movements. His leadership perspective is steeped in the Black freedom struggle, and he has been blessed to learn from some of the best leaders in the country, such as Erica Huggins, Amaha Kassa, and Boots Riley. Before becoming the CEO, Jakada was a coach at The Management Center, supporting clients such as Stacey Abrams's Fair Fight and the California Immigrant Policy Center. He served for six years as executive director of the Ella Baker Center for Human Rights, taking over from the center's founder, Van Jones. During his tenure at EBC, he led the efforts to stop the construction of one of the nation's largest juvenile halls—a "Super Jail for Kids." He also led two successful statewide ballot measure campaigns, No on Prop 6 in 2008 and No on Prop 23 in 2010. In 2013, he received a ChangeMaker Fellowship from the Pacific School of Religion, where he led a center for spiritual and social transformation. He is blessed to share his life with his wife Laura, and their blended family of six powerful and creative children.

MONNA WONG

Monna is a network weaver, facilitator, organizer, and writer from Queens, New York. She was politicized in New York City's Chinatown through learning about solidarity struggles, Asian American activism, and social justice histories. She launched her career as an electoral organizer, leading teams in Ohio, Maryland, and Maine to win LGBTQ nondiscrimination and same-sex marriage. She formerly served as the executive director of Lavender Phoenix, revitalizing the organization to build transgender, nonbinary, and queer Asian Pacific Islander

(API) power. Monna also coached and supported leaders of several Asian American social justice organizations as the Asian Americans for Civil Rights and Equality network coordinator. She is currently the chief content officer of The Management Center and serves on the advisory council of the Asian Prisoner Support Committee. Monna loves dancing, metaphors, and talking about money. She lives in Berkeley, California, with her family.

BEX AHUJA

Bex has worn many hats over the last 20 years, but will always be an organizer at heart. As one of the only nonwhite kids in their Long Island neighborhood, a queer and trans kid in the 1980s, and within their own family as the only mixed-race person, they learned from a young age what it meant to be on the margins. Bex has carried these lessons into their work, which is grounded in the sacred responsibility of bringing people into movements filled with love, fun, rigor, and discipline. Bex has trained thousands of people on running campaigns, community organizing, field strategy, fundraising, and management, and has held leadership roles in over a dozen winning legislative and ballot measure campaigns around the United States. Bex helped grow The Management Center's training department from two trainers to a 25-person team serving over 15,000 leaders annually, and spearheaded the development of TMC's racial equity in management curriculum and knowledge base. Bex currently serves as the managing director at Rockwood Leadership Institute and is also a coach supporting people of color in nonprofits. Also, Bex loves their wife, Tasia. A lot.

INDEX